unHISTORY

ALSO BY KWAME DAWES & JOHN KINSELLA

*Speak from Here to There*
*A New Beginning*
*Tangling with the Epic*
*In the Name of Our Families*

# unHISTORY

## JOHN KINSELLA & KWAME DAWES

*being*

Codicil to History
Coda to History
Footnotes to History
Index to History

PEEPAL TREE

First published in Great Britain in 2022
Peepal Tree Press Ltd
17 King's Avenue
Leeds LS6 1QS
UK

© Kwame Dawes 2022
© John Kinsella 2022

All rights reserved
No part of this publication may be
reproduced or transmitted in any form
without permission

ISBN 13: 9781845235321

Printed in the United Kingdom by
Severn, Gloucester,
on responsibly sourced paper

## CONTENTS

Codicil to History     7

Coda to History     199

Footnotes to History     307

Index to History     405

I: CODICIL TO HISTORY

# INDEX OF FIRST LINES

All the odd-numbered poems are by John Kinsella (JK) and all the even-numbered poems are by Kwame Dawes (KD).

1. This is not my history, but people call it history — 11
2. I do not know how to mourn what I have only — 12
3. There's been a silent but total war against poets — 13
4. Here is a fine promise that begins with the most ordinary of sins — 14
5. What history is to be made — 15
6. No one wants to be Jonah, carrier of the flame — 18
7. The 'vision splendid' neo-romantic collapse is an unravelling — 19
8. Repent says the rain man on the moon — 21
9. Afraid of the history about me but full of the bluff and fear — 23
10. On mornings of a reggae, spongy as the body in repose — 24
11. Maybe planetary history isn't the occlusions or avoidances — 26
12. When I makes tea, I makes tea, and when I makes water — 29
13. Where things start, where they head, where they end up — 31
14. We are the ones who stumble into meaning every day — 34
15. It's more disturbing that it's not — 36
16. On the eve of it, which is the eve of nothing and everything — 38
17. Where will we meet outside — 40
18. We have talked about the taste of memory — 43
19. I still have in my head — 47
20. Who holds the keys? There is always a guardie at the gate — 50
21. Whose histories do we need to build a single-hulled history on? — 53
22. There is a knocking at the door — 54
23. The plagiarism of the dead by the living — 57
24. "Is the water getting hotter?" Says Citizen Crab — 58
25. To be heard through noise- — 60
26. The realization is not sudden, but the knowing feels — 66
27. Silence often wrecks me as I feel guilty if I am still — 69
28. After the news of violent death in another country — 71
29. I am lost in our all being lost, Kwame — 73
30. You ask me why we say African — 75
31. That I should 'smart' when I read the specific — 78

32. That week, as if on the edge of some cataclysm, 80
33. I realise I have other homes to go to as well 83
34. My repeated self on video and appearance 85
35. I am leaning on you in this, Kwame, this need for support 87
36. And at almost midnight, we said farewell, and embraced, 89
37. I am losing what language 93
38. The leaves are slow in changing, 97
39. There are always thankyous embedded in these lines, 99
40. "Ought". "You ought". "No more than you ought": 100
41. Cutting grass I switch tones as I think of legacy, 102
42. Every sentence torn open reveals enough 103
43. Birth can heal rifts of decades and a grand-daughter born 106
44. And so, twice a year, I test the perfume of poetry 107
45. 'History in the making'? Locally, it's hearing the hot winds 109
46. Consider the revolutionary, consider the monster. 110
47. Today hottest record November since weather began 113
48. I do not trust my poems, and this knowing 115
49. The deniers collect dates 119
50. There is an art of silence here, 121
51. Will I be able to find you, Kwame, 124
52. Dobet Gnahore sings with that warm 125
53. Should we escape the hooks and ropes of history? 127
54. And how are you? I ask, though his smile, 128
55. Noongar Elder Len Collard calls it 'receiving stolen goods' 130
56. Here then is the book of transgressions, the secret plots 133
57. Far from Jam Tree Gully we don't know if we will have a house 135
58. And these words, dreams, rounded and sleep, 136
59. Again, I've transplanted my head into the lantern of Fastnet 138
60. The undocumented fall into single file to thread 139
61. Between bays the narrow eye-lashed Cooltrain Lough 140
62. Nearing Christmas now, the televangelists 141
63. It's not as easy as saying that *I understand*, Kwame, but I want to 144
64. It is only in the dispassion of a photograph 145
65. A small Swiss town's suburbs near great mountains 147
66. I am chasing my language, 150
67. It's likely a mistake 152

68. And here on the west coast, weather batters the body 154
69. Mental travellers and those of us left with tribulation 156
70. I sift these shadows hoping to gather in small piles 157
71. I am saddened that the palindrome 158
72. It is only one part of our history that eventually we choose 159
73. I saturate myself in film and stick in its depths. 160
74. So, John, Kamau dead. There is something deeply silent 161
75. 'Consequence of fact' is an *impossible* dismissal 164
76. The camera follows the limping poet through the city 166
77. The photographer demanded removal of eye-glasses 168
78. This deep throbbing hunger is my belly's elegy, and history 169
79. Sometimes I attach myself to a musical phrase 171
80. She writes, "five generations, I come from five generations 172
81. 'What if?' cannot let be collapse 174
82. On the dreary trudge – the frontier begins. 178
83. History will give nothing back – it takes and takes 180
84. And what we have not said, John, is wider and broader 182
85. I am listening to Jimi Hendrix's set 189
86. On Sunday, I walk out of her many paragraphs – her versos 192

1.

This is not my history, but people call it history
as if it belongs to all of us, detracts from us, builds
us into what we are and what we're not. Those dates
that pin lies as truth, that make fact emanate over
fallout. Whose history is made in the telling?
Whose is morphed into the bubble of nitrogen
on the root of a legume in a field tilled down
to its relics, yielding wars and the charred offerings
of campfires? These stones that cut our feet, transport
us during a museum visit, behind their glass,
labels slipping, or the digital bands of now
breaking up. I am here at the end of one
possible scale, carbon dating my learning,
my teaching. Land, sea, land. Dilution of days.

JK

2.

*For Toni Morrison*

I do not know how to mourn what I have only
barely consumed, and by "consumed" I mean
the eating, the settled rest after chewing
and delighting in the sudden first sweetness,
the unfamiliar growing into greater sweetness
until I know before the first swallow that my body
will never be satisfied without this food, this food
set out before me. And I hoard that pleasure,
that knowing, kept it for the secret place
of empty roads, of unfurnished rooms, of lanes
with no names, of a world where the whisper
of electric sensors has overlooked. I do not know
how to mourn her language, her art, her music,
her wizened beauty; but this hunger, this deep
throbbing hunger is my belly's elegy, and history
is the persistence of tyrants while the poets die.

KD

3.

There's been a silent but total war against poets for millennia,
unless they are poets who herald or track or celebrate
war itself, and even in such cases the eyes are picked from paradox
to display labelled (mace, spear, gun) in the trophy-cases of language.

When the cries of the dying are separated from the battlefield, when heroics
lift torn bodies to sites of epithets, to virtual shields of Achilles,
the tellers of wartales sigh, and let their violent hosts rouse
themselves to glorious deaths of the future, hooking on harsh

sounds murmuring into the blood of vowels and tones,
from the goat-grass-mountain message of life even warpoets
are telling. And the lifepoets who weave their way through
destruction and injustice, who link maps to trauma,

are left to speak among themselves, an 'effete'
or 'specialised coterie' of practitioners. Naturalists. Community
watchers. Psalmists. Preservers and resisters. Celebrators.
But sometimes a poet steps across the wastelands and lets voices

rise for themselves and those they love out of conflict.
They will be warred against by the violent, but they will bring peace
to the souls of the violated. Voice-writing, following the lost so they are found,
providing cover for the wanderer seeking shelter, for a family in need.

JK

4.

Here is a fine promise that begins with the most ordinary of sins –
sorrow; or better, a resignation to the march of mundane living:
you who wake each day and wonder what is the point,
but worse, you who upbraid yourself not for asking, but for chuckling
at the silliness of such a question – we die; eat drink and be merry.
That, or this: make the pact with two thousand years of waiting,
do not be alarmed – he's risen, it was all a practical joke.
Look at your face. See, see: gotcha! A heavenly April fool's season!
Is that you Edna? Is that you, Edna?
And so, the faithful call this remaking of hope "history",
though we who are forced to feel the scrutiny of history on our skin
each day, despite our rituals of forgetting – how nightmares come and go –
we call such stories "faith", and yesterday's complaints offer more satisfaction.
You see, how does one avoid what happens to the body when each morning
the news arrives of the tyrant's obscene genius? Remember, if you will,
that the monster always begins as a great jokester, a buffoon, a gentle
bully, a creature we all dismiss for his stupidity, but soon we grow
numb to the fresh outrage of his ways – do you see how used to it
we've become; how our bodies have grown used to outrage
and how outrage must be fed and then guarded for it to remain potent?
Eventually, we who live inside history go blind to its machinations
and this is the use of poetry – even the blind, sorrowful poet is written
by his own hand, and he does not know what he makes,
what he will leave behind, some say it's just a part of it.

KD

5.

What history is to be made
out of biography? What time
and place is conjured from
another's becoming in their
time, their zones, brushing
shoulders with proximity?
In and out of fashion,
barely dressed or dressed
to kill, hanging on till
the next meal, trying to
forget how they got there,
or crowing it like a self-help
manual – each caught or
adorned in their web
of history vicariously illustrating
our own possibilities?
This quoting of epiphanies
against the loss inside as
opposed to the loss without.
Sometimes the latter is so
overwhelming we hope
for the next chapter: how
to paint by numbers empathy,
our own place in the mosaic
or beyond the frame? How
easy to damn the wrong
choices, the clearcut
excesses, the out-of-character
strayings. No gate is straight.
How can I separate Lee Krasner
from the intermittent bursts
of rain and the annihilation
of the Amazon by the fires
of modernity? How can I

paint a biography from letters
I can't turn into words
though love to look at also,
when they are not part
of my formation? How can I
separate Elizabeth Barrett
Browning's high-tensile
anti-slavery poetry from
the slavery that cushioned
or created her ill health,
the made Hope End
the end of hope for many?
The meltdown of biography
in the selective apportioning
of history. She loved her
brothers, some more than
others, and some kept up
what they could of the old
imperial ways at Cinnamon Hill
plantation, Jamaica. Whose
legal records entails lines
of liberty? Whose chains?
Whose lines of liberation
against the violent flow?
Poems that break-
down control mechanisms
that arise from the forge?
The reader has a choice
to dip in, skip passages
be selective, read the whole
in one addictive trek
through widows and peaks.
Always on the verge of passing,
the thirst for life is intense
during the hotter months
of Florence? Of the poles?

The glowing searing white
stone of such sculptures
doesn't let anyone escape
that easily. And now I reach
Thoreau again, and pencil in
a time to start, and an imagined
point of completion. Allotted
to fit a life, a context of history
swallowing us whole.
Spitting us out.
The waste of footnotes.
Bibliography of triumph.
The lost names staying lost.
Mercator projection
of lives played
against each other,

JK

6.

No one wants to be Jonah, carrier of the flame of God's wrath,
but more than that, something righteous – the one who first
demurred, said, *No, don't send me*, and then after the machinations
of storms, and near-death encounters, of treacherous sailors,
and the entrails of sea creatures, finally came to see the light,
came to that wonderful place of peace and obedience,
only then to be told, "It's okay, let's not do that again" –
this to a man whose gut has grown stronger, whose body
has prepared itself to witness the destruction of buildings,
the crushing of bones, the blood, the stench of rotting flesh,
the guilt of it, the regret of it, the horror of not being able
to un-see what has been seen, the swarm of armies like cicadas
that spent the night on cool walls, pulsing there, to rest
in preparation for the slaughter to come – and then to be told,
"Its fine, let's not do that again. I am merciful
today." Every assassin's nightmare is to be halted before
the trigger pulled, the thrust of the knife, the button pressed,
to be pulled back from all that preparation – for a true killer
will kill a thousand times before each kill and will learn
to carry regret by carrying regret, just as a lover learns to love
by the imagination of love to come. We all, if we understood
our deeper self, long to be the harbingers of destruction;
the chosen prophets of doom and destruction striding the blast,
those remembered by history as the ones who saw and spoke;
to feel that righteous sense of being the saved remnant,
the one able to say, "I told you so." But we must deny this,
so as to hold it inside us like a cancer growing, and growing.
And we, the Jonah's of the gospel of peace, carry that secret
envy – no, more than that, resentment – for Nahum,
the one who stood on the high mountain and watched,
with satisfaction, the destruction of Nineveh; and this is how
we know that in us is seeded the destruction of all worlds.

KD

7.

The 'vision splendid' neo-romantic collapse is an unravelling
from high places and low, the Biblical maps I obsessed over
in my King James version confirmation gift from my mother,
which I still have, and which I have been recently re-immersing
myself in. I am trying to extract history, and leave vision
to the printing machines, the sources of ink, the concordance
of hierarchies and release, of miracles and tribulations,
and wondering how these are very different from the 'facts',
the clay tablets with inventory, the weapons recovered
from warriors' tombs. History for me is not a pattern of war,
and 'human advancement' contraindicates in the triggers
of mobilisation, of all hands on deck. It's hard for me now
in my decades of peace activism, to come to grips with my
boyhood obsession with war as history — the maps
with crossed-swords on the walls, the atlases of battles,
the interculturality that made we wondrous and invigorated
by the range of difference, which I celebrated, but then
reconciled in conflict. Not that I wanted deaths or maimings
or conquest; no, none of that, I just wanted the details
of patterns of engagement, of strategy and tactics —
the unreal, the 'history'. And the Bible gave me that, too.
At school, I was the history student par excellence,
the one who could tell you every detail of Nazism's rise
& fall while coming in from the far left, already having
read the economics of *Das Kapital*. So Hitler was a definition
of evil, and something to validate versions of history
in which conflict made the big decisions, the necessary
response. But in time as the histories of communities
and individuals came to my attention, as I began to personalise
each loss, each consequence, all of this shifted — one person
as evil did not answer for the untold numbers of people
who acquiesced, saw something in it together for themselves,
for their sense of history of their sector of existence. Understanding
that *Purnell's Second World War* issue on the Nazi death camps

ended the war gaming, the collation of data, the excusing,
say, Rommel ('Desert Fox'), because he opposed Hitler
and respected his enemy and fought as a 'professional'.
The excuses made to conjure a 'brilliant general' from
the murk of soldiering — that crappy *noblesse oblige* shit
that was ethics in the hardsell of human reality. No more. Vision
would come back from the bird that literally transformed
into an angel when I was four, into the angel that was a bird.
It happened high up in a silky oak tree, and I was looking
too high, far up beyond where I would climb even
when the tree was grown taller and I had grown
taller as well. That tree planted behind the house,
fast growing, refuge of cockatoos and angels and me.
Life. Life is history. Conflict is not life is not history.
Desolation and annihilation of habitat is no gods' desire,
it's the conflict-take on historicising metaphors
into excuse for weapons, 'defence'. and heroics.
I want none of it, but I still want the vision — the raw vision
shared with prophets and people just going about their
acts of living, feeding others, keeping the great trees
supporting the roof of the world, letting their own
family histories feed into others' histories, finding
common ground where none are driven out,
where all can tell stories of helping others
      live their own lives.

JK

8.

Repent says the rain man on the moon, repent says the cricket on the moon. Trelawny – a stretch of green bushes, the olive rustiness of a landscape that carries the sideways history of rebellions, of plantations, far enough from the main barracks, that a rallying of troops, after the runner arrives breathless, his sorrel horse sweating and bloody with the rush through narrow passages, bramble thickets and the rocky beach head; the officers know there will have been blood – you plan for that; it is the way of judgment, the price of colonization. A hundred and fifty years later, the school bus, cranky and rickety, making its way towards the sugar factory, red dirt and the neat order of cane fields, with their well-manicured cricket ground, the pitch quick as clay burnished to cire singing in the sun, and you think, bring them on, you think a slight slant of the bat off the pads, and red runs, red bloody runs into the cane groves – this is the history of an island's laws, the history of villages made from the barracks of old slave communities, the history of hunger, the history of black people huddling with machetes and sticks, plotting the path towards dignity and liberation; this is the site of the quick executions – no bullets wasted, no such dignity – but the hangman's noose, recycled for each rebel brought down, and a small squad of the compliant to gather the bodies and cart them to the open field long abandoned because of overuse, where the refuse of a city of mercantile order is disposed of, and there the bodies buried deep, the women and children singing their Sankies with politeness, and then at night, for nine nights, with the bitter lamentation of a people who will never learn the dialect of the pacified, this is the factory after the plantation, and here is the site of our unmaking, our legacy of blood. We arrive while the sun is still preparing for the day, and all in white, we roam the fields, skanking to the roots-man on the bus sound system, "Rocket on the moon", "Superman a-come". In the 1970s, I was a boy, learning the symbols of the easy spilling of blood, learning to place the language of history, the rebellion, the skirmish, the execution, the battles, while walking the places where these happenings would have taken place, and stepping into the terrible truth of it, how easily my face could be among the faces, my body among the bodies. One year, history is of wars with names of delicate alienation: "Roses", treaties of Antwerp and Versailles, battles on oceans, Waterloo, Trafalgar, nothing in this but smoke and maps, and the dates, the dates, the dates, and come the next, the books start to reek of the Kingston pyres where dead dogs roast and fill the air with that bitter acrid of bodies left to rot before the act of destruction, and in places I have planted my feet, on ground I understand, of bushes with names I know, and how quickly the drilling cadet marching around the school, saluting to commands, and watching the way that a crowd can turn into a quick and efficient mob, how war is as basic as the flash of blood and stone on my avenue; this is history, history in Burning Spear asking *Do you, do you, do you, remember*, "Kick the pope in his ass", "Babylon Mus fall", and this is war. I am padded up, tips on my hand, and openers, we stroll onto the green, the cane-workers grinning with glee, tossing the ball between them – I take my guard, survey the field, then tap, tap, waiting for the war to begin.

KD

9.

Afraid of the history about me but full of the bluff and fear
of youth, I needed to find an archaeological site on an island
in another sea that would fuse the real and imaginary –
I was barely aware of encroachment, of the literary

inoculation of 'dig', believing Homer was up for grabs,
was an answer in itself, was all of its time, and a universal
'he' that would allow me access, an 'in'. I was a kid
on a ferry searching for Pythagoras, for pillars

that were a gateway to the sun. I tried to learn
lines in ancient Greek to quote to the 'wine dark sea'.
But addiction already had hold of me, and I crossed
from zone to zone, lost in Ephesus, in remains.

Border crossings were submachine guns in the back,
and cavity searches. They found I was full of shit,
or empty from hunger. There was no feeding my
need for 'history' that made me a possessive

apostrophe along with everyone else. Back at home
the colonial chunking out of stone kept houses
cool, and the lessons of empires rising & falling
was taught along the river Capital was bending

to its shape. I thought of the shield of Achilles
and was lost in a realpolitik that would let me rot
in a prison cell or let me rise to the heavens
if I would play its game. History laughed at me
    and I hid in its cold stone folds.

JK

10.

*for Rainford Lee "Scratch" Perry*

On mornings of reggae, spongy as the body in repose,
the dreams of desire and the taste of curried goat two days old,
the rice grainy, softened by the coconut oil of sweetness,
I fail at language to describe this bass-line, for the spaces
it fills and the way the body softens to its graces.
And here I sit surrounded by the fat rhythm and melody
while a grainy-voiced upsetter, runs his eloquent
trap with the fully formed discourses of mystery and *livity* –
dipping and turning back – over the sallow earth of the boom
sound. To think of what history is lost in the silence of sounds
made only to vanish into the ether – as if the meaning of time
is the meaning of truest silence – what we record is the stain
of memory. Try, and all we have is language to construct
the vanishing of noise. The old reggae man has built a shelter
deep in the mountains of Switzerland, and there he steps
into the blue mornings, glowing with the inner light of snow,
and there he howls symphonies, the recollection of his being,
into the sky, and he does so in faith, though knowing
that every howl is an elegy for the dearly and un-dearly departed;
it is an elegy for the dubs he has constructed and discarded
in pyres, the tapes melting away, the skeletons of the reels
blackened and melted in a midden, the place where he has kept
the surplus toasters that kept arriving by morning mail,
long after he had completed the grand Rasta wall of toaster,
(not boasters). And on a night of sleeplessness, he opens
the sound system, and lets the tape roll, and in a trance
the riddim is made – he lays down his autobiography
against Babylon, his autobiography against silence –
first the stone, the boulder with eyes glaring out,
then the horses of white, and sorrel and red, stomping
in under the cypress trees; then the priest squatting in the temple's
backyard, waiting for the visitors to arrive with the news,

though they never arrive – where is the head corner stone:
*The Spiderman a-come*, he says, *the superman a-come,*
*sun is shining, the weather has changed, I rearrange, I rearrange.*

KD

11.

(i)

*'That though the earth may be wounded, it remains beautiful beyond measure, and that people will naturally incline to justice and goodness, given the chance. That the terrible noise is not to be mistaken for the sounds of a planet dying, but the just rage of life fighting for life and that one day, one day, things will be different. That is our conviction, our truth.'*

*Letter to friends and supporters from David Ritter of Greenpeace, Australia (28th August, 2019, as the Amazon forests burn beyond burning)*

Maybe planetary history isn't occlusions or avoidances, maybe it's
    increasingly the straining to tell
all stories when many stories resist telling, or their participants
    don't want them told, want to be left
to work outside history to make something that speaks better and
    safer and more justly than chronology?

Or am I simply rearranging as I search for another's bassline, taking
    the silhouettes and profiles of mountains
and sun low on the plain, cutting off the valley, to make sense of the
    silence I try to fill with recountings
and recollections and arrangements of voices I've searched out or
    encountered in lessons or chronicles.

I am not looking for an easy way out. I am my animal self. I am trying
    to say life into where it wants to be
without corrosion. When a destroyer of Indigenous cultures deploys
    'colonialism' as a personal insult, the codes
of ongoing existence outside the manifestations of prayer are
    scrambled into flame and ash and toxic wastes.

The horrors of history are expedient to such moments. Throw away
    lines that have a depth they've been severed

from. The back & forth of oneupmanship, the tetramorphs turned
 into idols of development, and the symbols
of so many belief-fields dragged into the trophy cabinet, kicking and
 screaming or dulled and confused, unable to breathe.

(ii)
I respond to lines you feed out from the visionary casualness of
 a waking day, Kwame. And I tell here
a little bit of 'hidden' or 'ignored' or maybe just known by few: Perth
 History. When we hear wonderful notes
of commitment and belief, I rekindle without damaging flames, but
 healing and phoenix-like growth

the Rasta gatherings at the Perth Town Hall in the 1980s some of us
 from outside that small
community gathered around, welcomed in, dreadlocked and
 undreadlocked alike, far from sources
but tapping in where it was okay to tap in, gathered in to hear the
 bass-story-song drive bands,

where permission was granted, the big boom across the dead
 business of the city, to bring life, rainbow
beanies and jackets and FREEDOM spiralling out and enravelling
 the colonial building, a statement of groove and other
empowerment and God and, yes, full tolerance for the decrepit and
 addicted like myself, who wanted to feel bass

notes through the body so life was restored, and songs of people and
 plants and animals wailed
and spat and smoothed into curves of rise & fall and lift and float –
 this truly happened, it was a small
group that gathered many to its fringes that made gravitational
 centres that rewrote and entwined

gender and fused oppositional beliefs into a planetary affirmation. I
 can name all the players

now, I can discuss details of access to plantings at full moons but
    won't reveal, and I can mention
a dedication to the tribes and the sharing of scriptures as a history
    so different from the town

hall's version, those ironies sweet as gunga wafts as the ironies of love
    and the anger, too.
There was that. Community that could not hold as the 'dance crowd'
    moved on, but the believers
stayed on and sometimes I see survivors of the original crew, old and
    few now, and we nod, apart

as histories diverged, though we peacefully raise a fist as we had done
    trying to stop
cricket being played by those who went on rebel tours of South Africa
    to support Apartheid
while saying they were supporting an a-politics of sport, when it was
    greed, pure sporting greed

with their notions of 'freedom' a canker on the freedoms non-whites
    were struggling for,
a play on suffering by clean-cut sportsmen who we resisted, if I can
    say 'we'. For the Rastas
of Perth sang it and pushed out the baselines, and we all remember
    in our fading,

and we remember and maybe recall together in our differences for
    the burning to be pulled back
to its safe and undamaging place where it nurtures soul instead –
    though all now
will be worried for the spirit of life, so threatened, no matter the
    paths to glory.

JK

12.

When I makes tea, I makes tea, and when I makes water, I makes water.
For first meal of the day, before the sun came through – though that day
the sun never came through but stayed consumed by clouds,
and the road looked soft and tender in the gloom, and the green
of the mountainside was dark and morose and constant,
gleaming with the dew and the light rain that dallied off the crest
of the mountain – we had dumplings from the night before,
fried in fat until the starchy slime was slightly crispy and the fish
stayed soggy as the evening meal, and the dumplings swam
in the coconut oil and over-abundant ackee – it was the season
of plenty, yellow ackee piled up, cooked tomatoes, onions
scallions and crushed scotch bonnet; and from an old cheese pan
we poured sweet chocolate with that oily skin over the top.

My family tells me I must write happy poems – every poem
I write is a failure, I know this now, and I wonder if my excuse
is the decay of all history. Who records the laughter? What tomes
carry the chronicles of laughter and joy, the teleology of gladness?
Though, once, while wallowing in my regrets and penitence, a shadowy
place from which I reached up as if out of a dream, for light,
there was this small news sandwiched by exile and assassination,
a jigging revolutionary, giddy with glass, "I saw, I saw! Did you see?"

*Jesus Christ rain, on the mawning train,*
*Haile Selassie rain, on the midnight train*

I rejoice in the breaking of the long fast of the night,
how the caramelized, sweet and savoury of a good meal,
laced with pepper, herbs, and more smoky herbs, makes me want
to do a quick step, a jig, to laugh. And we need not rehearse
the sources of our joy – the ackee, brought over in the bellies
of slave ships from Northern Ghana – imported for protein for slaves,
along with the Cook's breadfruits and the Newfoundland salted
cod – the food for the enslaved – such joy, such joy, such haute

cuisine for the hoi polloi. This, does not appear in our history,
for all joy is a prelude to history, a prelude to the recording
of consequence. Every day, Babylon sets the table for a feast,
and on the platter is my joy, my rejoicing, my lowered guard.

What time now? I don't keep time, brother. But you know the time.
Morning news come and gone. So, six-o-five. One gun, nine dead,
bought at a Walmart in Fort Lauderdale. That is Babylon. Ites.
Anymore ackee? Ackee fe stone dawg. Look inna the dutch pot.
Dumpling? Ah it dat, no more. But some dry bread deh behind the flour bag.

*I wish it would rain, rain, rain in my brain, Father, water, in altar*

Outside the rain arrives as a benediction, shimmering sounds
like light on the zinc roof, and the white rush of mist, of low
clouds hurtling past the open door, letting the peep of the mountain
peak come and go, come and go. Aieee, Babylon, Babylon, Babylon
your time has come, you better run Babylon, run, run Babylon run.

KD

13.

Where things start, where they head, where they end up.
I am trying to conjure joy as the soil won't work, as flowers
open and close too soon, and in the horrors of history
I also find signs of how things really could have been done
from 'inside' to lessen the harm. Increments of the local
to butterfly large incisions made by 'power'.
We eat our meals together, and we all
say thanks, and each meal had is a sign, too,
that our bodies are the history of us, and all
around us. I am thinking of how we make rapport
and fellowship across different branchings, those
dispersals and disruptions. We do. We can. These salient
moments stretched out across the spheres of soul.
That's it for me – the soul is round, like the earth (not
perfectly round), deeply affected and cajoled by gravity,
heavy as a boulder pushed up round in rearrangements
of erosion and earthquake, of revolutions and gentler moments,
and yes, like a balloon, but not one that rises and bursts
and is just a strip of material that chokes a passing animal.
The soul is the book that damages nothing – no paper mills,
no power drains on a grid that slices and dices all that is,
no toxic ink screening its own origins while teaching goodness –
no, it is the book written in air and on sand and in the texture
of bark and skin and feather, in the blade of grass striving
against the collapsed winter of here & now – yesterday, hottest
winter day on record, where winter doesn't map as cultural
understanding of long-range change, and rapid shifts
in policies of existence. I write to a publisher: 'could the journal
in the future be printed on either recycled paper or non-woodpulp paper?
Or, if woodpulp, then from organic plantations that have been grown
on recovered damaged ground (and not on spaces where forests
have been cleared to make way for them).' I have been involved
in alternative papers for decades and they are better
than running servers which are the energy suck of the planet.

My novel *Postcolonial* was printed on recycled paper and using soy inks, the first chapbook series I did in the early 1990s for 'folio/salt' was printed on wheat paper and I used an organic cotton paper for artwork in the 1980s. I do my little anti-capitalist *shed under the mountain* chapbooks on recycled paper (made, no money 'changes hands' – I cover costs of printing and then copies are given away). There are ways, and sometimes quite good ways – more trees planted than used, on recovered/repaired ground... produced without chlorine and other such chemicals... better than mining hardware for computers and that eternal energy suck. I've spent thirty-five years trying to work out best approaches, and this strikes me as a reasonable set of alternatives. As I fade from electronica again over coming years, and things here get slower and slower as the world hastens to an end it doesn't make, it doesn't envisage, it doesn't want – for it is the long-term repository of the dead as well as the living... yes, I will go back to making my own paper from the wild oat stalks... from grass cutting at Jam Tree Gully. I will make small books from that and they will get out and about by osmosis – person talking to person etc, hand to hand. A few years off yet, but I am setting things up. These things have to be holistic and contextual. These things are about our meals and our souls and our trying to find poems that show the relativity of soul to body, the spheres we converse between. I have researched the histories of paper-making, of book-making. Just now, and yesterday, because Tracy was discussing it, and because we share such things, I think of Wycliffe's Bible and the loops and jags of the English I misuse – I think of translation and death. I think of heretics and I think of the word and words. Unable to lift with eviscerated air, they fall down into ash. We need to give them lift without burdening them with consequences in someone else's post-historical recollection. We can use the word happiness, despite the weight, the heaviness of a planet we consign to a grammar of periods – a fullstop dead in the flow, an effusion of talk,

that gift we can make work across languages,
signing, but not signing off, no, not yet, not ever.
Where things start, where they head, where they end up.

JK

14.

*Poetry is a crematorium*
John Kinsella

We are the ones who stumble into meaning every day, never sure whether
poetry needs love, whether poetry is a pyre, a place where love burns,
a place where beauty is cremated. Mostly, what comes from the destruction
is not gold, not something burnished and shining, but something
that stinks, leaves a residue of glue on the ground, and turns
that which is elegantly unknown into what is crassly known.
Today, I skanked on knees that swell and hurt at the scent of water
to come. They say a storm, Dorian, is coming, but too far for my body
to record its arrival. Still, I am skanking to the Upsetter who calls me
a complainer, and upbraids me for complaining, though I think
of all this noise as radical protest; and I know that this too is a poor
simplification of his prophecy – for everyone, he says,
is complaining, the rich man and the bitch man, the bishop man
complaining, and cannibal complaining and Hannibal complaining,
though the animal is not complaining, the animal is not complaining
because it is not enough, it is not, it is not, it is not enough to be.
We are living in the House of Greedy, stained by the House of Greedy,
and those I envy are those who have found a way to live righteously
in the falling House of Greedy, in the House of Greedy that says
that the clothes I wear are the product of the House of Greedy
and the food I eat is in the House of Greedy, and outside
in the courtyard of the House of Greedy, the people are wailing,
the people are mourning, the island is lamenting – I have too much
irony to be complaining, and now I am complaining about not knowing
how to complain. Still, even he would know that all art is complaint,
and love is complaint, and memory is complaint – I am not just
saying this and hoping it will hold up; yes, memory is complaint,
it is the invention of meaning to soothe the disquiet or tedium
of the now. Before I was inducted into the House of Greedy, I lived
in the House of Angels, where history seemed full of discovery –
the excursion into the Cockpit Country, that dense world of thick

vegetation that is under threat by a bauxite lobby seeking to do
the practical thing of granting economic wealth to the nation,
ripping out ancient trees, plowing through the sod, promising
with the help of diviner geologists to avoid the underground
streams, yes that place. Well fifty years ago, as school children,
we entered the grotto of trees that opened into a sloping clearing,
a natural vantage point for the lookout spying for the line
of redcoats, probing, probing; and there drummers and fife players,
men with machetes and flintlock long guns, and a small trio
of abeng blowers; and there the word Maroon spoken
with reverence and meaning, and I imagine history to be as present
as the blood of sacrificed goats, the spray of rum from the diviner's
mouth, the metallic stench of sulphur after explosion
of the musket; and I knew my enemy to be the brutish
British, and my ancestor the bare-chested, cow-horn carrying
warrior, darting from cotton tree root to cotton tree root,

here in the House of Angels — and this was first history for me,
the first seeding of the desire for another life — nothing
deeply lustful, nothing to be fleshed, but enough to change
the colour of the day, enough to enliven each new page,
enough to turn my lessons into transportation. Every citizen
of the House of Greedy must have the gift of history.
I understand the conundrums set before us now — how paper
is the recording of memory, and how memory recorded
is translated into a kind of death, and how the dead
do not care for what happens to the paper, that is except
before they are dead, when they are already dead, like we all
are, dead, and caring, and seduced by the recording of paper,
or stone, or wood, or the hide of animals; and so we care
and do not care — only the almost dead understands vanity,
yet watch us, here in the House of Greedy shouting as we chase
after the wind screaming, "Bring me to the House of Angels!"

KD

15.

*'If, on the other hand, we are going to use history for our pleasure and amusement, for inflating our national ego, and giving us a false but pleasurable sense of accomplishment, then we must give up the idea of history as a science or as an art using the results of science, and admit frankly that we are using a version of historic fact in order to influence and educate the new generation along the way we wish.'*

"The Propaganda of History"
from W. E. B. DuBois's *Black Reconstruction in America* (1935)

It's more disturbing that it's not
uncanny to have just been writing
about 'pyres' before I read yours,
Kwame. It seems logical. As does
writing a history of greed, which
I have sketched in outline, calling
it *'Croesus' Translates as a Mass Noun*,
an uncountable poverty. Lately,
strands of conservative media,
and media which pretends not to be
conservative, have been lashing
us with 'The Richest of all Time'
lists, especially focused on gold,
retainers/slaves, and 'entertainers'
(to show the impoverished what
wealth is). Tech billionaires oscillate,
increase their storage capacity,
shrink down to increase (their) space.
Search the night skies for options,
concepts, possibilities, high-yield
dialectic investment opportunities.
Carbon-dating the chronology
of wealth, carbon-dated futures.

What Freud said re daydreamers
'forgetting' (or not telling) their
fantasies because of shame —
spaces for the commerce
of history. What we have overcome
of the ancient 'threats' and 'fears'?
Modernity given a grip to offset
the unconquerable. On top of the pile?
Richest of All Time. World's wealth
geography trade routes haulage
roads spice currents trade winds
market hunger meeting 'need'
accumulation texts of worship
okayed to maintain status quo
of greed as misinformation
to distract from the misinformation
of history that builds Trump Towers
that stacks benefits and make of the bull
an adjustable symbol in medias res
to combat its origins in flesh
and fertility and a fury the Big Boss
wants to apply like a coating of glamour
of generational ladder, the trickle
down effect of excess. Market bell,
first pitch of the season, gold reserves,
dollars floating in the Gulf
where oil and water are made
to mix. From the incident room
a call by the CEO to nuke hurricanes.
New markets, new demographics,
new death to sell on to the kids.

JK

16.

(i)
On the eve of it, which is the eve of nothing and everything,
I arrived at an understanding as one arrives at a dream's meaning –
that my days would be better were I to encounter history
always as a prelude to joy, meaning that were it possible
I would rewire my brain to believe in the relief of eternity –
the comic truth of things, that what I will cherish always
is the morning when one wakes with the bubble of delight
lurking in the brain, and the pleasure of sifting through
the morass of memory to find what is that thing that makes
the body reach for pleasure – hungering for pleasure.

(ii)
The next day the news that another has died. That is ordinary,
isn't it? But the strange thing is that I have not been able to say
what I have been thinking: "I do not want to die here in this city."
When what I should be saying is, *What delights await us tomorrow?*
I think that people like me leave people behind – which is what
we all think, even though we all think that we have been left behind,
and this is not the way that revelation should work, not at all.
I ask myself again and again, "Was he angry with me?" Which is
hubris, and not what I asked. I asked myself, "Where did we leave it?"
And we left it with politeness. And if not, I will still sleep fine tonight.

(iii)
Are you ready for the black magic? That is the question which, spoken
in a yardie accent, can sound like natural mysticism, or if we know
that the person who says again and again, and by that I mean
so many times until someone has to come to him and say gently,
"Enough, sir, enough. Let's go in now", and guide him from the verandah
where the moon is glowing silver over everything, "I think I want my mammy,
I think I want my daddy" is eighty-three years old, wears a denim jacket
and karate trousers of blue-bleached white cotton. Here is the way
the best news arrives – a mystic on a rock, her face without wrinkles

though she is not a child — though she has great grandchildren, and she says, "Get on board the African spaceship". It is all mind control, I like to think, but mostly I think it is having a heart. Which is why when I read these lines, "The local drunks came here to drown," I wince. I ask the Upsetter, I ask, "Did the men and women she is talking about, arrive on the African spaceship, and did they not have names, and if they came to drown, was it because they were drunk — and isn't drunk a verb word or an adjective and not so much a noun." And the Upsetter says back at me, "History is distortion, history is heavy distortion. And you know, crowd of people, you know I know a ting about distortion and musical contortion, and historical contrition."

(iv)
The scripture named for me, shall we say, The Book of Kwame, Chapter One, Verse one, should begin with a genealogy of begats, and this is how it ought to be. How casually so many understand the lineage of their being. I do not have the griot's burden of remembering. But it is not remembering, is it? It is knowing. Mine is shallow — what I know it is shallow, and what I envy is the choice of existentialist angst. My origin is a mess of ash and un-composted detritus in wasteland of the nineteenth century — the rest is myth, meaning kings and queens and princes, meaning the absence of meaning. And this is the intimate history of my people because history is not what has happened, but what is remembered, or retrieved. A week ago, I heard a word whispering in my mind, and I could not put music it to it, but I knew it was there, and then I found it somewhere at the feet of the Upsetter; it was midden.

KD

17.

*'psycho-analytical'*

Coleridge, *Notebooks* (1804-)

Where will we meet outside
the histories we refuse and
that refuse us, or don't let
us in enough to want to stay?
Or the histories we know
have spaces for us to slot
into but we can't get to
them, not as completely
as we might want? Possibly.

A going-back that can't
manifest on the voyage
against the winds, the fast
currents? Serpents and
leviathans. The bestiary
those empowered keep
under lock and key
to intimidate us with
when they're slowly
starving the creatures
to death. Wittgenstein's
lion – but he didn't get
that he would never
hear it speak. What did
he – with due respect –
know about how and why
a lion would speak? About
'us' not understanding?
About we and him, not us?

We work from proposition
to proposition, point to
point, axiom to axiom,
statement to statement,
working our way up
and down the ladder
of the fabulous, facts
curling around the rungs –
at someone's fingertips.
Lion's claws. Teeth. Argosy.
Slowed down by sea-anchors
just before hitting the reef.

What livestock was worth
hauling from famine-stricken
Ireland via Liverpool to the
Colony of Western Australia?
Ghosts of the Tain, the
cattle heroes, the skinned.
No, to be gathered from the folds
of agriculture elsewhere.
The passage to alternative
histories of fields and fodder.

And the winds tore at the sail,
and the planks creaked,
and the lions roared
from an interior they
barely guessed word
of mouth, Bible tales
most of what they had
to go on. In passing by.

The coinages, the first
usages show up in distress:
the bloody vision we all

have but can't read,
don't want to read,
are told we we must,
eventually. We were
never allowed on the ark,
we all thought up the
words psycho-analytic,
compounding from our
own languages, our
own journeys, the homes
we can't reach back to,
never completely.

JK

18.

> *I am tired of words,*
> *and literature is an old couch stuffed with fleas,*
> *of culture stuffed in the taxidermist's hides.*
> — Walcott, "North and South"

(i)
We have talked about the taste of memory,
the wooden house of elegant awnings,
the courtyard with trees without names,
or names I do not know, never knew,
but the fruit, poisonous, were green bulbs
and the leaves were tiny, and the branches
thin, and patchy like the skin of a child
burnt out of neglect, always in constant
renewal. The bats would swoop down
at dusk, and no one screamed;
the ornate carvings of the verandah's
poles, the delicate lime-green streaked
with the rust of age of the house,
and the shadows were a comfort:
this is the taste of a personal history,
a memory of those who are dead.
A man with cloudy eyes and a fist

full of bonbons and a mouth
of soft pronouncement names us
the gentle ones – to think that the languages
that carried across this city
were French, and Ewe, and the acacia
rattle of ancient people, and the stones
were a pale orange, the colour
of clay for the staining of the legs
of the penitents, for the mask,
for the ritual of our rite of passage.

It rained, for rain is the common
ledger of our time, and with
the democracy of its generous gifts
over the living and the dead,
over the wicked and the just,
no one can speak of what is
as if that's all there is, but of what has been
and what will be, and the sound
of the rain, falling through those trees
in the courtyard, is how the world
grows primordial in its darkness,
and how we sit as if we are in caves
and wait for the soft light of the all-clear,
and wait for the tall grasses near the fences
to offer up the snails, the creatures
of all first things. I say that this memory
is the taste of history, this and the knowing
that my grandfather, Felix, with the milky eyes,
carried in his head the history of the graces
in the dense back garden, and what we have lost,
what I have lost, is the legend of a beginning.

(ii)
We children bend over in a soft cabal,
to choose the blades of thick
edges, then consult, and then each
lift the blade of lime green
holding light and water,
and then blow.

The air is heavy with bated rain
and from here the anthills
are the tombstones of memory.

Ours, this whistling sound
is the magical delight of sound
made in the belly of memory.

(iii)
You must know that until there is an invasion,
all history is domestic, and it is fully messy,
for there are no easy lines, and how do I know
that the killing of a betrayer is never without
the resistance of a body that does not
understand the dignity of a resigned death,
and the blood, the blood. Remember the hog
that Christmas morning, how it squealed
and how the blood spattered on the lose bricks
of the unfinished quarters, and no one
thought to clean it off. And days later,
the base of the wall was black as tar,
though we knew it was blood, this ordinariness
of slaughter. I want to say I have seen
it all, but I have not. My body, though,
understands the panic of anger,
and I feel my bowels loosening;
this is why I fear going home,
for the constant sickness of this
anticipation — the nausea of history.

(iv)
They say you can tell your future by the lines drawn
by a dangling weight — a coin perhaps — on a sliver of cord.
Hold it, and let it sway — the magic is in the gravity,
and how to read the crisscrossing lines,
the pattern they leave in the air, the geometry
of divination — so they say, so they say —
which is its own cypher, and you will know
if today will bring laughter, or some disaster.

I was formed in a land where every delight
is a prelude to disaster. It is not so much the place,
it is more the grace I crave, the need for mercy,
the duplicity of orgasms. Why, I ask, could I not

have laughed in amazement, in sweet astonishment
at the first rush of blood through my body,
to see what I had wrought, what this lovely body
had wrought – instead, for my joys, for my impossible luck,
I could only conjure guilt, as if I had stolen something?

(v)
In the midst of a rainstorm deep in September,
on an island of flamboyant green and ochre-rich soil,
there is that moment when we forget that before
the skies opened up, the house was invaded
by drunken flying ants, alighting on every surface,
losing their wings and crawling about the place,
as ordinary a portend as the smug resolution of sums,
and then the rains came. Easy to forget that there is
what comes before and what silence follows;
that storms always move on. Yet, what I say now is,
always, as if to teach us how to live in the instant,
we forget that there will be no abating, that the storm
will soon pass – that, in cruder words and from
the apostate's pulpit, there is no future;
and in the resignation in the head's
thunder-lit storms, there is a kind of holiness.

KD

19.

*'the Blessed machinery of language...'*
— Coleridge

I still have in my head
the dry day that was Saturday
the York District Agricultural Show
and my annual crossing paths
with my cousin whose house
is made from the ground up
of mud and straw and beams
of home-grown wood raised
where salt had scourged and then
been sent back down with salt-
resistant re-plantings. He and I
hunted as kids before I turned
away from the gun, let the weapon
get eaten by salt and sun and dirt.
Broke it up and broke away from it.
But we have our moment together,
love as we always have, so different
in the paths crossing as region,
parallel lines that actually meet
and wreck the history we constructed
together in tents, out in the bush,
checking the cruel traps. War history.
Hunting history. All made to fit fantasies
that were locked and loaded
like myths of comradeship
and individual feats of bravery –
the one that fought the rear-
guard action so his mates
could make their escape.
The honourable enemy.
But we don't talk it over

now — rather, hockey
and tree-planting and land-
reclamation, leaving out all
reference to the history of damage,
our roles in a self-styled epoch.

It is the hottest beginning to spring
on record. Each record a mockery
of the previous record, of the next.
It's the only mantra for here
which is drier and drier,
and the farmers, set in ways
they don't seem aware were
constructed a mere forty or fifty
years ago by chemical companies,
rain down their sprays, the nozzles
of twittering machine cropdusters
scrawling Paul Klee Paul Klee
like a rebellious art act across
the skin — the raw hide — of the sky.

So, I keep records. Rainfall
and its lack. Daytime temperatures.
The higher highs, the odd lows.
I turn off as many machines
as I can and still try to send
messages out: observations,
maybe the vanity of calibrations.
I have made journals and newsletters
and magazines since I was a small child.
Family and the odd friend here
and there as subscribers.
And I think with irony of the irony-
less vision of Coleridge's 'Blessed
machinery of language', and stumble
over my words — all those family

gatherings on the farm
of childhood, the threads
that come together so far
down the tracks, the loose
threads in otherwise immaculate
tapestries on display at the York show,
the hooting and roaring of sideshow alley,
and the hope we speak less
loudly than we should — a show
of painted land-rights-flagged hands
reaching out of their school display,
saying who is here, who was always here,
who will be here, and whose can't be,
can't find sanctuary. A declaration
of land and people. Of knowledge.
That language I celebrate, if I might.

Yes, Kwame, domestic histories
exist before invasion. Here,
cross-referencing
weather observations
from all around the region,
I tilt the anguished raingauge,
tap the home weather station
on the wall; in the wake of arrogation,
offer psychological tours
of my footprints
crumbling into the dry;
or, looking out of the house
into a domicile
beyond my grasp,
my divination,
think of histories
of rain.

JK

20.

*The coinages, the first*
*usages show up in distress*
*the bloody vision we all*
*have but can't read,*
*don't want to read,*
*are told we must,*
*eventually.*
   — Kinsella

        *The dhow's silhouette*
*moved through the blinding coinage of the river*
*that, endlessly, until we pay one debt,*
*shrouds, every night, an ordinary secret.*
   — Walcott, "The Fortunate Traveller"

(i)
Who holds the keys? There is always a guardie at the gate,
but he never owns the mansion – the guard is an employee,
as loyal in the pragmatic sense of loyalty, as a house slave –
they are always taxed with sharpening the blades, and each
rub of the steel on leather is a chant deep in the head –
just think of such a one, staring out to the sea, bronze
at twilight, and with each sway of the blade on leather
is the contraction of the ocean, the waves pulsing
to the shore – only at the sea, its persistent movement,
do we truly understand that the earth will outlive our delusions
of uniqueness, our chosen-ness, we who imagine ourselves
to be special – the sea carries the coinage of our mortality,
the currency of the tribe, the sea reminds us that the earth
has deep lungs and some engine must pulse endlessly
beyond the rise and fall of sun and moon. But let us not
forget the guardie at the gate of the museum of our history,
asking for some coin of patronage, rattling his can, saying,
"You have to pay for the keeping of history, for the coin of the realm

Is what you use to preserve all memory." He stands
on the courtyard, points to the sky, its brass oppression.
Let us not forget the guardie at the gate, with no deadly
weapons, just the discretion of a coward, how to flee
and when to flee, how to discern the thief from the killer,
how to protect this open crypt curated by our creditors,
the ones we owe our names and language to,
though we have never enjoyed the things they have borrowed
us — you know that language, I will learn you this truth,
or with this language I gave you faith, you monster, ungrateful,
when all you know to do with beauty is to abuse it —
and let us not leave out the houseslave Philliss at the window,
rolling her blade over cured leather, counting out her iambs,
waiting for the moment when the fields are ablaze, to quietly,
and without gramercy, plant the blade deep into the sleeping —
the way we have always wished for our deaths, deep in sleep,
with just a hint of a dream of violence, followed by the orgasmic
letting of fluids, that emptying we call the violence of love.
I will bribe the guardie to let me have the key, and allow me
to walk through this museum of my memory on what is called
a dark day, the Monday of my reckoning, and here is how
I recover my history. We are walking through these corridors
where a voice — we call it disembodied for its hollow timbre
and the way it spreads throughout the showed halls — saying,
"Welcome to the Museum of Dreams and Stones and Bones Rattling."

(ii)
Bear with me, carry this word, grace;
it is the secret of our survival, the trace
of our bloodline's persistence beyond
the living now, the present firm ground

where our feet are planted. I will say
again and again, that we who parley
by the mawing pulsing of the sea
are begging for a kind of peace, for mercy.

In the land of dreams, the queen is dead;
the righteous wear this on their foreheads,
the glue of the prayerful perspiring,
for in the land of schemes the king is expiring.

KD

21.

Whose histories do we need to build a single-hulled history on?
The foundation stone of the house of sailing ahead,
the scaffolding for what rises, the ribs of the boats? We have
to go with the ash poured into sea-dust for images come to dissolve.

But then I am talking rural, I am talking of a group, a 'we'
of my astrolabed imagining – a gathering, a crew who
might say we know what we have comes from – the grinding down
of world of word of hull of walls of ship of house.

I reverse a current I reverse a wave I reverse the horizon
to unwreck the ship, to disembark at the port of origin.
The flux, the expansion and contraction that equates
to breathing, but is more like those sails edging the doldrums.

These correctives to histories that shift in the telling
though sediment and ash cling to the core
and are compelled by gravity, over which they
have little say. Rudderless. Weathervane. Who gets

to tell the histories to make histories better suited
to their ground plan? It's bothering to the group, to the little gathering,
to the crew around the poem, its windows its porthole less pristine
than it seems. Inland, I've had to make recourse

to turning this house built to best environmental standards
we could manage, could afford and imagine as adrift in the constellation
of the swan and landlocked beneath two black-tailed cockatoos
auguring over and older than me, as stretch-winged as little eagles

older than the vessel my body the house our boat whose places
of boarding are scattered, hard to find on the map we imposed.
Here, life-rafts lowered into the valley, the dry winter creek.
Here, erosions opening ways for history to back-flow. Flow back?

JK

22.

*And because I and I should not dead*
*I am not a vampire*
*I have become the children of the light*
      — Lee 'Scratch" Perry

(i)
There is a knocking at the door.
The dog barks and runs crazily about.
The Upsetter says it is the kete drum,
but the tone sounds like the funde drum,
and I say, what do I know about the drums
or the door-knockers? K-nock, k-nock, k-nock!

Knock, knock, knock! Who's there
in the name of Babylon?
This is a country of farmers
who are weaving ropes for the gallows.
Whose gallows? Their gallows.
But how is people starving, soh? Or is this not
the land of plenty – the land of green,
and the kind of green that after a storm,
the baldheaded mountainside
will dense up on you so fast
you won't know what hit you?

Bring nuff rag and towel, crowdapeople,
for the heat of Babylon's storm-broken docks
where the first ships are lining up.
Is pure rockstone and skull bone
stretched out like Beelzebub's playground.

Now, man cannot live on mannish water alone,
says the farmer, mawga like a stick.

Meeehh, meeehhh, meeehhh, meeehhh.
says the ram in the thicket,
Meeehh, meeehhh, meeehhh, meeehhh.

(ii)
*Let's just pretend that we are still in the high modernist moment and separate the person from the content.*
— As said by a 21st Century Provost to a Junior Scholar

I should add that the wittiness of this speaker
does not mask the fact that what is being deployed
is the language that protected racists, fascists,
Nazi-sympathizers of the modernist genius school,
in response to which, Achebe, despite all his equivocations,
despite his love for English, the Nigerian language,
could not restrain himself: "Conrad is a thorough-going racist!"
What Achebe did not say out loud was,
"I just can't keep this up, I can't continue this farce."
What Achebe did not say was that he knew
that coast at the mouth of the Congo,
he knew the bodies moving casually
across the dynamite blasted beachfront,
were African people, cousins, and lovers,
uncles and aunts and brothers and sisters,
were minding their own business. And he knew
the history of the apocalyptic docking of ships,
the first startlement of their very enormous size,
and our quick adjustment to their human scale,
their ordinary ways, their farting and shitting
and bleeding, so soon after their invasion,
so soon after their indiscriminate defecation
infested the beachfront and the gentle piedmont.

(iii)
*Soon we'll find out who is the real revolutionary*
      — Bob Marley

In his Autobiography, chanted over eternal dub loops,
this Upsetter steals the name "Upsetter" from the Upsetter
who lives in a cave of toasters in the mountains
of Switzerland. This act is a small defiance, and a wish,
as if to say, teach my body the equation of its mortality.
Today my wince and limp have grown pronounced – the pain
through my ankle has returned, and I envy the slivers
of bone and taut flesh of the sinewy old men
defying the body's decay. Such vain envy; it is nothing,
truly, and the Upsetter says the secret to peace
is the destruction of every ark we build on the surface
of the earth. Every cycle of revival is a pyre of flames
rising from the burning Ark. It was an accident, my love,
I left a candle burning and it taught me humility;
how to face the grey days before us. The truth,
crowdapeople, is that winter is coming, and the air
tells me that summer ends now, stooks and piles
of leaves, the darker mornings, the swoop down
of cold like a ghostly visitation there in the middle
of the brilliant day, and my skin prickles,
and I look up as if to say, "Who are you? What did you say?"

KD

23.

Plagiarism of the dead by the living
to inoculate themselves from a similar fate,
to take what they had and add the extras
of their 'modernity', that ruthless

insurance policy of the present, the ground
crumbling behind with each step taken,
and those movie choppers dollying in
to eat up staccato, eat up flash by flash

the set pieces, the crowds of extras, the scene
by scene edit of cultural strands into articles
of faith that will stand the test of the exchange
floor the bell the bull-at-the-gates' roar & lullaby

the scope of vision the proportions of screens
and misprision of senses we scry owl pellets for truths
of owl-presence, the melodies we fall to sleep by
inside music gathered and made and mixed

in exquisite darkness missed by the shoots,
missed in the audits of documentaries.

JK

24.

"Is the water getting hotter?" says Citizen Crab I to Citizen Crab II.
"Oh no, oh no, no, feels just fine, cause tepid is fine and perfect for us."
"Well don't you feel a slight chill, and then a tingling," says Citizen Crab I
to Citizen Crab II. "My claws are tingling with delight, and the water
is lovely, and perfectly right, for the scientists have studied our insides out,
and know just what we need – delight!" "Hmmm," sceptical Citizen Crab I
mutters, and crawls about the barrel of water, and thinks out loud
into the sky, "So, is the water getting hotter? You think? It feels hotter…"

We clown, we joke, we normalize buffoonery, and we feel so good
about our superior morality, while the Supreme Court, of vulture brains,
huddle and whisper the new laws of the brutish; and the alien is
      standing at the gate,
and the alien is bewildered at the gate, and the alien is asking is this
the place, the outer darkness – which is another delusion – the wall
is too high, and what is the glow lining its upper reaches? It is hope,
says the alien waiting at the gate with her petitions for clemency
and safety, with her satchel full of passwords and aliases, and the legend
of her secrets in her tiny box. Come see, come see, I am clean, you see,
a few indiscretions and once, I said the pope had lied, on Twitter
it was, on Instagram, but that shouldn't count, nor should my naked pics,
which are artistic and were gifts of love, and for eyes of pure
adoration only, not Hector for Homeland Security, who can't know
that I am not truly naked in them, not naked as my secrets, anyway.

There is no elegance in the elegiac, for where is the dignity
in the unexpected news? It travels as all gospels must – a way to comfort
the living through the betrayal of death. When a joke attaches
to a body it remains even when the body decays and this is a kind
of comfort. His wife says he reported seeing angels and then the Lord.
All that before he died there on a gurney behind a flimsy green sheet
in the cubicle of the A&E, this place of late nights and early mornings,
where I learned the unmaking of fatigue – in this place of slow disregard,
death can arrive as a reason to return home, to sleep, to think of the days

to come, and the sound of the dying is the sound of fatigue,
where pain screams, and the sound of resistance and survival softens
into a chant, please, please or help, help, or somebody, somebody come,
or I can't take it nuh more.
Today a new book of mine arrived, the cover
soft as animal fur stretched, and the words are neatly lined up – the designer
balancing with care the fonts, the weight of bold letters and the tight
lean of italics, and once again, I think that here is yet another testament,
the things I have left, what will remain of my time here: Nebraska, Nebraska.

*Tell your story from a story book,*
*tell your story from my morning glory.*
*Walking backward through the city,*
*walking backward through the city.*

I did not wake this morning with the whisper of death on my skin. I woke
and glanced at my profile, calculated the loss of pounds but feared the certainty
of the scale. I felt the softening of my navel, an insignificant oddity,
       and the moon
had filled the early morning with a precious light, before the sun's slow rise.
Outside the lawn glowed green and sparked with the early yellow leaves,
a kind of jewelled ease. I rose this morning to the psalm of our present
and our moment. Then the quick transformation of news – Andrew is dead,
and the mind seeks to organize the language of an elegy. Tonight, I binge
on impossible narratives shot through with history, Fidel, Cuba Libre,
       casinos,
and the bodies of the refugees of the revolution looking as un Caribbean
as Nebraska there on Miami's fantasy beach. I will wake's with his name
in my mind, but what I am doing is fingering the tomes I am leaving behind,
the notes I must erase from all records. I promise myself to learn a language
of delight, to live with joy in the moment; to know what the crucible
       of history is:
It is the bucket we crab our way through now. Is the water getting hotter?
Says Citizen Crab I to Citizen Crab II. Oh no, oh no, no, no, feels just fine,
because tepid is fine and perfect for us.

KD

25.

*'your last has many resonances... the joy and the complexities. the personal (and other) paradoxes of location and locale. the celebration and the echoes. actually, these might be lines in my next which are about so-called 'end of history' debate... positioning...'*
  — Message to Kwame

*'I am a parcel of vain strivings tied*
*By a chance bond together,*
*Dangling this way and that, their links*
*Were made so loose and wide,*
*Methinks,*
*For milder weather.'*
  — H.D. Thoreau, 'I am a Parcel of Vain Strivings'

*'Why was this such a discovery*
*to him? Why did history happen*
*only on the outside?*
  — Rita Dove, 'History'

To be heard through noise-
cancelling headphones. Limbering
birds whose beaks eat bothered air
and no sound emerges that rapid
travellers can detect. Shutters
making the sun more tolerable?

What sorts of history
began for me
out of Spenser and Milton,
scourges of my Irish
ancestors, apologists
for a tyranny
seen contrary

to actuality.
The sun set on them —
as I understood — but stayed
lensed on their lines,
their visual harmonics.
I hurt my eyes reading
Milton by torchlight
and the irony
didn't thread into my
own timeline till later,
eyesight breaking down.

Said before by the person in a position
best able to say it, to make the point,
or to be heard above others — the need
the compulsion, the corrective to resay
under the replanted tree, or, if still possible,
an ancient tree, maybe the last one
of a forest that has given so much,
and has had so much language
stolen from it?
                Bathetic machines
of making unmake themselves
to make way for new wording
beneath the sun that seems
to have got closer and larger —
our population one sun
we possess like body
& soul rolled into one,
plucking timbers, stripping
bark and ladder rungs.

A Cambridge academic
wants us to disconnect
from connecting the newest
politics of the far right

from the manifestations
the arisings of the 1930s.
He doesn't think it useful
to make comparison,
to see the hate-threnody
of now as 'fascism'. He
seems to think versions
of democracy will self-
correct. Or at least
his reviewers seem
to think he thinks this?
A big book the market-
place has conjured out of a person
in a position best to say his piece — part
of that chain of composition, replacement
parts to keep a status quo
whatever game theory
comes into play. He allows
himself levity to anchor his
professional seriousness.
I guess he used a thesaurus
for 'hate'. But then again,
I am sure his self-regard
is large enough to consume
all definitions, come up
with coinages.

Whose histories
are being told for all of us
with whispers of splintering
and diversion, of elision
and (re)connection,
of weaving as many new tales
as Netflix can manage? —
but few of those
retrieved from the gloss

and warehouses and prisons
and holding cells and graves-en-masse
of chosen narratives.
The spaces between palm trees.
Between farm houses.
Factories.

And the raw materials refined
to write down, collate,
make precedent
of the sun –
ownership of its fuel
quota, its remaining
five billion years?

So, the poor can make history
collectively but not
as single speakers
of what they see
are made to see
under the glare
of day that seeps
into night – reading
lights for a controlled
literacy?

In resetting the sun,
ground where the forest was
burns. This might seem
like a parody of burnings
that get away, are let go.
A clash of sustenance and extras,
of eating and stockpiling.
It has been said
under different conditions,
with voices coming through
at different volumes.

Sometimes it's hard
to put a name to them.
Sometimes the names
are erased. We are
post-nothing.

We are stuck
on a contents page
of a book we can't read,
curled by the sun,
its forest origins,
a pulp version.

What anyone is left with:
to remake the homes
some of us have occupied,
have looked out from
to shadows
with only people
to distort them, still
ignored, and the origins
of shadows
hidden through failure
to read.

I lapse into self
mythologies
to answer why I lift
myself back to an upright
on the incline of the hill,
why I remember the 'local history'
I read to make sense of this division
in a colonial absentee land grant,
of all the trails and stories
it attempted to rewrite.

Then I fall under a too-close-sun
because of its digitalised ink,
the body heat I exude.
That's what I record
for someone. Some.

JK

26.

*I lapse into self*
*mythologies*
*to answer why I lift*
*myself back to an upright*
  — Kinsella

*I caught Chris Blackwell in a sauce*
*Drinking chicken blood inna rum glass*
  — Lee "Scratch" Perry

The realization is not sudden, but the knowing feels momentous –
we have made the mistake of counting the dead, and because
we are all of a certain age, a certain myth-making self, the beginning
of our difference and our similarity – first form, 1973, Jamaica College,
all boys, and the number then was finite, and the decline was inevitable
even as we grew and grew. Now it is almost fifty years, and the bodies
are falling – we are creating lists of the causes: heart attack, stroke,
cancer in the blood, sudden dramatic crashes of airplanes and cars,
and the fit ones send admonitions to the rounding ones of what to eat,
of the poisons in our water, of the danger of red meat, of the gift
of lemon, moringa and herbs and spices and the choreography
of tai chi and karate. We are astonished at the parade of the dead,
and this is ordinary to all cohorts: as long as there is a beginning
there will be an end. Still we have lived through such things
as are now called history, and we imagined that soon the things
hidden would be revealed, the plots and the machinations,
the betrayals and the treachery, the heroes would have their heroism
tarnished, and the dead will leave secrets to be opened to the world.
It is the way we have expected history to restore in us the completion
of those unknown things, the broken narratives – the body and soul
now able to consume this. But according to Li Young Lee,
to a bearded poet from Omaha, the poet does not trade in words,
but in silences, though what he truly said was, I, the poet, meaning
this poet that I am, I do not trade in words, but in silences – and he

probably said I carve silence to make shapes, or that silence is my plaything, or that I am a sculptor of silences. And knowing me, I am misremembering what the bearded poet said, and "trade" is a crudity that neither he nor Lee would use; a better word might be "build" or "create" or something to do with the coinage of the craft — which is all very Zen, or close to the peculiar account of the freshly netted disciple asked to go to the lake, throw out a line, and open the mouth of the first caught fish, and there find a drachma, the coin of the realm, and pay unto Caesar what is his due, for peace's sake, or not to cause offence to the kings and the presidents, the rulers who forgo taxes from their people, but extract it from strangers — this odd transaction, the rendering in silence and not words. And who owns silence? Silence is shaped as a weapon when the blocking of ears is the act of oppression, and in the Deaf Republic, the tyrant is deaf and uses the coverage of silence to mute all conscience, and yet the poor are making music in their bodies, as Najlaa Osman Eltom says of the martyr before his martyrdom: "In his village,/ he was the sorghum field,/ brimming with heavily laden stalks./ The cotton field,/ blooming with luminous bolls." And as for Lee, he used to wear the peasant non la, balanced with grace on his head, and in the summer heat he wore loose calico trousers and leather sandals, and after every question, he would peer into the emptiness you imagined he saw before him, and wait, and wait until the wait became so pregnant with disquiet, and then he would say, "I am a sculptor of silence" or something such, and, indeed, the silence would take shape in the wake of such pained revelation. Of course, the cacophony continues, and the noise pollution is a function of geography — the loudest place in the natural world is the equator — the clamour of rain forests, the thundering, deafening rush of waterfalls. Silence is the luxury of nightfall in the Northern Territory, though once I walked out into the New Brunswick winter when the radios reported fifty degrees below, and I walked a mile to the St. John's River just where the Theatre New Brunswick's gothic facade rose from the white slope off the frozen river, and I stood there, and imagined silence — not a vehicle within earshot, not a body, just this bright cold. And then, for a moment I imagined the way of the deaf until the ice started its music, and

the wind started to shake the silvery branches, and the noise of the frozen
celestial air ticked and thrummed and tinkled and moaned.
All history begins in silence; and this is a kind of history, but it is
a lapse into my invented mythologies. The facts are certain;
the significance is a fiction that continues to be reinvented for every
new day of my living. The point is that history is also in the hearing
for there is always the noise. I am living on brawta time, and this is
why we are now making the deals of silence. Much of what counts
for peace is the absence of listening, and all of it is machinations.

KD

27.

Silence often wrecks me as I feel guilty if I am still
while others are falling, though I know it's a different
kind of silence we're talking about; I am stymied by categories
which don't have to link with errors but in me they often do.

What nature of burr am I inside the peace I seek, I crave?
News comes in of another killing, the police murdering
self-defence arguments as they mass around the 'perpetrator'
and shoot, pre-emptive preventative countering witness accounts.

Silence is what overwhelms with anger and grief when rights
to that anger and grief are distracted. But they are there. Must be.
It is that deep gulf of silence. That differing silence, that echoing
chasm of silence between communities pretended away.

But I don't understand what I am searching for in this cracking
springtime, this tediousness of collapse of record after record
being broken in the competition of endgame. That's why
I fill my head with the inside of the sun. It's so loud it's silent.

When we die, Kwame, will we keep swapping lines – rhizomes
that let us reach through the massiveness of day after day,
the massiveness we can't have the gall to call more than snippets,
nodules on the vaster root system, a trace of water in the freak dry?

Every link every fusion every entangling I make is flawed,
is ugly under the bare sunshine, out in the basking –
I mistake stillness for silence and I mistake silence for caution.
On Reunion, we ate the vegan mix-up mix-up in St Denis,

cooked in the Rasta kitchen, and language
lit up the room as it oscillated between Creole
and French and English, and I was silent when I half-
understood but too loud for the small room when I felt things fuse.

Silence often wrecks me as I feel guilty for keeping still,
but that doesn't account for the noise in my soul, the rubbing
of leaf on stem, the inside of the sun on the inside of my head.
The silence might flow out of its own accord, grow away the violence.

JK

28.

*The audience is a flower drowned in your silence…*
   — Najlaa Osman Eltom

After the news of violent death in another country – a Yamatji mother
buffeted by drink, drugs and the betrayals of her mind, wielding
a knife, so broken the neighbours who love her are in tears
when they call for help – or maybe, if this is my morning after,
it is her old neighbourhood, the place she returns to every time
her mind begins its slow elevation and she sees patterns in the trails
the words of people make from their mouths, how they intertwine
like a tangle of ribbons making a surreal design filled with messages
only she can read – things that say joy, in the end, is made by love
or faith, which each year, as the body ages becomes
acceptance, passion, hunger, the bubble of sweetness that arises
in the heart without explanation in the three minutes after waking up;
which is love – and faith being the angels we see waiting for us
in the valley of the shadows of death that we know will come
when our bodies finally succumb to the constant harassment:
"Can we die now? Please can we just die now?"
Perhaps, she says, that is everything about joy and it may well be
what she's contemplating while wielding the knife, and the neighbours say,
Call them people who can help – call the Authorities – and the news
is of the crackle of gunfire, but mostly of eight policemen surrounding
her twisted body, unmoving on the ground, their hearts thumping,
they petal like an audience, a flower drowned in her silence, her
silenced body. Their minds calculate the story – they never confer, never even
whisper, "This is what we will say…" For they have done this
before, they have always known the solidarity of their violence,
and without conference, they collude. They agree while breathing in
the metallic astringency of gunpowder: "We felt in danger for our lives,
we feared for our lives, we have seen what a knife can do,
and she was not responding, but was threatening." Somewhere at the back
of these things, a narrative of healing grows, the one that has made us accept
with some sadness, but so little fear, the dialect of veterinarians, "put down",

mercifully, "put down" mercifully, "put down". Which is what this becomes. For this is what we do to the alienated soul suffering in this world; and this is how in fifty years two billion birds have left North America – by which I mean they have been eradicated, or maybe I should say, slaughtered. The skies are barren; and this erasure, is quite like the history of Afric's wrongs and other wrongs, of a Yamatji woman – a bird of Australia. But, I must return to the body, for that is a shadow of my fears or the love of my own brother, for the knowing, that her body has stopped, that her voice has stopped, that her laughter has stopped, that her catalogue of language – every tenderness, every sharp blade of anger, every whisper of desire, every lament, the whole alphabet of her making – all stopped, all gone, all arrested in the body, curled as it is on the ground. I must, I mean, return to mourning, for it is mourning that is the counter-weight to the slaughter that continues the day after, and the day after. Someone says, "Avenger, rise!... Speak! From thy storm-black Heaven O speak aloud!" And the deaf Synod, the drowned audience, looks off.

KD

29.

*'The Great God Pan is dead.'*
         — Plutarch

I am lost in our all being lost, Kwame.
I have no ways of bundling and stringing
words into lines to follow or to act as trails
or to find my way back via. I read history
after history, I read the re-tellings and undoings,
I lift the flaps of picture books to find
what's inside the tableaux, see into the rooms
I would never be invited into, reconfigure
museum dioramas from childhood.

Milton seems, in his 'On the Morning
of Christ's Nativity', to make Pan the Christ
protector of shepherds and also the Devil
by whom shepherds were misled —
the ship's navigator overhearing the call
from an island sure that 'the Great God Pan
is dead' and the revisionism beginning
in conjunction with something brighter
than the sun, those folds in hills opened out.

Neither structuralism nor post-structuralism
can pin down or outrun meaning in a wild echo
out of the colonial European re-imagining
of its past — making Christ pristine white
in its mangers, bestowing appropriat(ive)
values taken up by good citizens and their
enforcers. But here and now, as Milton
made 'silver lining'-origins break into scaffoldings
of voice verse and line, all that learning

distilled to life and times and contradictions
that seemed a clear and logical path
to him, the commonwealth and the New Model
Army and his books burned by the executioner;
Milton, who did not love Ireland, who called Belfast
a 'barbarous nook', who laid out the ground rules
for heaven and hell in his times, here and now
it shakes the gouges that appear around here
as in cities the young march to call their elders

to awareness, to pull back from the brink,
and in Geraldton family and community
march to call for an end to the killing
of their people, and none of this parses
into the stories that tell of pasts because
past is the imprint of the police order
banning liquor sales to 'keep a lid on tensions'
which is brute racism which is the police God Pan
in all its variations imposing its missionary zeal,

covering the tracks of its own eschatologies.
And what right have I in its recounting, because life
that was is no more, and nothing said from outside
by me can repair and I am rubbish, I am shit
in the face of the failed religion, the failed hearing
of old messages from so far way, brought here
in wooden ships, in the holds along with farming
implements and items of 'culture' hidden behind
the flaps of picture books. Museums planned out
    before the settlement even began, set in.

JK

30.

You ask me why we say African,
or West Indian, or Black,
why we totalize ourselves,
we who are totalized by oppression,
and I say that we are constantly rebuilding villages,
remaking blood ties, reconstructing love,
or maybe something fleshlier:
we are cauterizing the separated flesh
with healing dialects, with family songs,
with the dregs of history,
the dregs of its memory – we are batiment,
we are mati, we are malongue,
we shipmates who crossed the alien waters,
who learned each other's rhythm,
who studied each other's breathing,
trying to calculate the moment
that air would leave the body
for the last, and the casement
emptied of the harbourless souls.

This is intimacy,
the last of the familiar thing,
not just our bodies naked,
vulnerable, not just the fluids
of bodies commingling,
not just the stripping of our dignity skin,
not just the inadequacy of language;
but the compromise of grunts
and gestures, the truth of our silencing,
and the tender acts of community
in the patois of our remaking.
And that patois is the prototype
for all acts of survival, for it mingles
the liberation of invention

with the tragedy of the things lost,
half-remembered, broken;
for the way civilizations
are invented by destruction.
But it is not just this,
it is something closer to the loss
of all security; to be replaced
by the synod of fear, of uncertainty,
of despair – it is in this invention,
this regathering of our broadcasted selves
that we understand the making
of our survival, our resistance.

Today, I read a truth I should have known,
a piece of historical fact,
a telling that is part of the inner lining
of my clichés of resistance
and survival; read how for the rest
of their lives those Africans
landed in Suriname, Trinidad,
Carolina, Haiti, Guyana, Jamaica,
not only remembered the name
of the vessel as others did the Mayflower
and other such fare barges,

but they formed tribes of shipmates,
and built secret shrines named for those
lost at sea, those last carriers of greetings
to the kraals left behind, to the spirits
hovering at the ocean's edge,
waiting in vain for the return.
And their origin stories begin
with the incantation of a ship's name:
*Guineamen, Hesketh, Parr, Diligent,*
*Clare, Venus, Gurbridge, Alarm, Rattler,*
Her Majesty's ships big and bloated

sailing the ocean full of commotion,
their landing dates being their new birth dates,
the singular date of arrival;
their history being myths and dreams
and the bitter loss of their person.

Who are we without a tribe,
who are we without the shrines of our becoming?
And all of them, these newly-named tribes,
scattered throughout these islands,
would find their way back to each other
each year to remember
their humanity, their tribe,
their only place of return,
for it is their only place of beginnings.
This is a requiem embodied in the rituals
of community – of the familiar:

"How are you, mati?"
"Still here, mati, still here. And you?"
"As you see me, mati, as you see me."

"How are you doing, Jahaji bhai?"
"Doing good, Jahaji behen, as you see me here,
as you see me here."

KD

31.
*holidays*

That I should 'smart' when I read the specific but distant
'you' of your utterance, Kwame, is a failure on my part to co-

ordinate histories — that 'you' is too often crouching behind
its white saviour narratives, its peeping out from foliage

draped across the corner of holidays snaps, whispering
'white fragility' outside hurricane season, when beaches

are at their best. Someone wrote to me the other day
'whining' (their disclaimer) about being 'irrelevant'

as a 'middle aged straight white male' and I — genuinely
surprised given the source of the words — replied:

'problem is that so many white middle-aged straight males
have long-term been criminal to others. i guess it's

just the fallout white middle-aged males have to cop
before things can get better for one and all'. This is

what happens behind certain half-closed curtains
while vacationers hunt out concord and unity with that wink

and nod of 'tolerance', that carbon paper emphasis of 'how
it was' — where 'tolerance' is implicated in contexts

as containment policy, as service, the boxes and albums
of photos pulled out from under the bed. And so,

some will plunge yet again into a 'history of ideas',
of 'we care for the environment' fresh linen,

from familiar foods on the exotic menu,
into a literary escapism of culpability (skin deep)?

To observe but not feel why a word a saying an incantation
is the camouflage ink in the sea is to write nothing down. Leap.

JK

32.

*Those stray trees untended
glower like wild planetariums,
a pleasure I'd neglect, brought
so close to you, here in the past.*
   — John Kinsella

*Love is over you my friend
What you give yuh gonna get*
   — Lee "Scratch" Perry

That week, as if on the edge of some cataclysm,
I woke each morning expecting to hear
the empire had collapsed and the emperor
with his flimsy hair was crouched catatonic
in the walk-in safe as large as a grand hall.
Each day, the wind turned violently cold
for just an hour – as if to say that winter
is the weapon of God, and his wrath
could tease us. Then, at midnight,
my bladder heavy, my body waiting
for the slow release, the tinkling of water,
the tender rain ticked against the window.
Of course, as with all encounters with history,
the trees are laughing, the breezes are laughing:
Ha ha – ha ha – haaaaa ha – ha ha!!!
By this I mean, none of it was funny, none
of the disappointment, none of the sermonizing,
or when the missionary to the East African villages
on furlough from the red earth and the heat,
pronounced conspiratorially to his home congregation:
"If the emperor loses his throne there will be civil war,"
before the exegesis on the camel and the needle,
before his literal soul became a shelter for metaphor.
"Love is over you, my friend," said the forgiving dub historian,

whose accounting is scattered across the prairie. "What
is the price of forgiveness, what is the cost of forgiveness?"
Where is the lineage of forgiveness? I ask.
Today, as if by providence,
someone asked, "That tree, what tree is it…?"
And, there, as if by design, was a plaque at the base
of the tree, among the pale orange berries
fallen around the edge, a tad too white on the underside
to be a fruit to be gobbled – Ginkgo Biloba.
And at last I stared into the dense layering of leaves,
and wondered where I read that the history of gingko
goes back two hundred and fifty million years, and this is just
one case of the absurdity of our heretical numbers.
In my head I call it an alien, brought here
to the bare and naked grasslands, an infestation
of beauty. So, do we preserve it, do we protect it?
How sacred is a body if it is a transplanted body?
I say, as it breathes; let us cherish its living breath,
its holy right to praise and clap its hands,
the dense curls of its dark leaves reaching upwards
into the bare blue stretch of the mid-western sky.
Remember, remember, the historical dub nurturer
says, remember that somewhere in another town
a genius is laid out flat and stiff as a slab of wood
on his bed, catatonic, where he has been for days
as if waiting for his friends to come and lift him
on his mattress, and carry him across the deep
valley of this green village, to the place where
a man has begun to break fried fish, over and over
again, his hands oily with the business. But no one
comes, and the poet understands the sadness
of his days, while a woman is screaming her laughter
at the YouTube channel, watching, she says,
the Iowa State Fair's "Man Calling Contest"; and when
there is a lull for ads, she sucks in her breath,
throws back her head and heehaws over heehaw

before the screeching bodily howl of his name
shattering the dead silence of his disappearing
self. And the sheer violence of this intrusion,
without guile, without tenderness, is the taste
of history in the moment.
                                    I wake up minutes later.
The cement in the back garden is dark with old rain.
The earth is the same, and yet so changed.
Lorna says, "Joy, joy, eat the carrot cake today!
The bride groom and parties won't last forever
and, you know, all that goodly theology.
For there will be no carrot cake in heaven.
All we are promised is milk and honey, which,
perhaps, is not so terrible, as long as it is frozen."
Forgive us our trespasses, oh do, sweet friends, please do.

KD

33.

I realise I have other homes to go to as well
as the home I rely on – in the spaces between
words and your life and your seeing, Kwame,
you have given me another home to be sad in

and to reflect over the best things, too.
So many of my 'colleague-friends' have remained
silent over my 'intervention' into yokings of 'defence'
of humanities, with only one sending support;

but I have found a new friend as well who says
he has nothing to lose, but he loses more by
speaking out. All are constrained by their jobs,
their needs. Some say it's a matter of understanding

the truths of what others do, really do, and I say
it's a historicism that teaches us its own wrongs,
that these wrongs replicate and mutate and leave
few if any standing, whatever the armour developed

on whichever side of semantics. I have swirled
in such violence so many many years ago and know
it can only undo all the glorious poems written
out of its refrains. I am made of violence

and do not want any of it because it gives
no home to anyone, past present or future –
see, even its clichés are like barbed wire – twisted
scare quotes – clinging to the paddocks and runs of here.

But I have homes I can go to in this, Kwame!
Sanctuary where I claim no innocence no aggrieved
party, and say, Yes, I stand by what I say, but never
mean any personal malice, nothing ad hominem,

but will resist the burrs and prickles and militarism
in all its theoretical camouflage in every way I can.
Okay, I agree not to use the university's mailing list
systems for future interventions, but will continue

to speak out as I have long spoken out in
'appropriate fora', because I am of the cocoon
of my own ejecta, my own body and spiritual waste.
Funny thing is that they wish to leave no room

outside 'self-mythologising', a licking
of wounds they might blame on their 'enemies',
of those who 'fail to understand', this inability
of people like me to understand who they are?

When, till now, what I do or say has never
been registered (who is this guy?), where fact
and metaphor are deployed as opposites,
blur to make each inadequate as basis

of the other,
the other,
the other?
Home now. Yes.

JK

34.

My repeated self on video and appearance
on the internet, these mirrors everywhere,
there is no silence, anymore; I long to disappear.
That is the appeal of history: to be the thing that has passed.

And the peace mornings come after nights
of listening for boots on the roof, boof, baff, boof,
boots on the roof. Yes, that may be in another country
where we knew that only two visitors came through the roof:

those carrying the sick and invalid to be healed,
and those pressing in to burgle our shelters, thieves
and murderers. And no one knocked in those days,
so the night was spent listening for the boots on the roof.

My daughter tells me that she is grateful for my art,
not for just its beauty, but for the evidence it leaves behind.
And she knows it is a morbid thought, though full of love,
to think of the silence after I am dead, and the whispers

of discovery in these lines, those that by now have grown
into mountains of evidence of a considered life. There is,
I confess, some mercy in that, a kind of embrace. So now
I think it prudent to say again, but more bluntly,

that I fear I live in a world of obscene pragmatism, such that
the stench and rot in the state, the corruption of money
and power in the presidency, is turning even the righteous
into pragmatists. Here is the logic, faulty as it is: God

raises tyrants over a people, and the ruler does not know
that he is a pawn of Providence, and this is the way things
end – the way that the last days will suggests themselves
upon us. How cynical a consideration – as if the besties

Herod and Pilate did not share notes on benevolent tyranny,
did not conclude that the dead will always be with us,
and the executed will come and go – sometimes as a head
on a platter, sometimes a hanged body, sometimes

the inconvenience of the crucified (just think of the stench
they leave at each road corner – yes, the people will live in fear,
but the tyrants can rely on the alabaster jars of purest nard
spilt into silken kerchiefs, for so long and no longer.) But they

did and the prophets said then that these are the last days,
that the world is coming to its fitting end – all our days are beautified
by the peculiar prophecies of the apocalyptic, and all is truth,
even if all timing is not predicated on truth – a truth.

And the days turned to weeks, and to months and to years,
and epochs followed, and reigns followed, and centuries followed,
and more centuries followed, and the pure truth of all prophecy
arrived in the theories of holy genius, the theology of atrophy.

So, each day, I find no mercies in "the End of Days", instead
I see the wounding of our better selves in the canker
inside the state, and this is the cause for lamentation, it's true;
the cause for prophets striding the blast, boldly speaking

as you do, John, with the screen at your back, a rapid epic
of evidence, the storms, the collapsing ice caps,
the consumed reefs, the slaughtered creatures, the starvation,
the exploitation, the stark abuse of power – every generation

must have its prophet and poets, and we are here, my friend,
making words arrest us, overwhelm us, guide us, while we lie
in our beds, listening for the boots on the roofs, the boof, baff,
boof of the boots on our roofs, of the boots on our roofs.

KD

35.

I am leaning on you in this, Kwame, this need for support
for solidarity for a way through the deployment of anti-
personnel mines of collegiality, of the sundering of all
words and sharing of knowledge for growth of the soul

into a policing of morals and viewpoints and 'the real
world' with a psychology of weapons-culture interface,
where humanity is undone by the strategies and tactics
of 'international relations' leaguing with 'defence'

and intelligence organisations, acting as authorities
on 'situations', delving into the covert, into the 'threat'
to their notions of 'democracy' and 'stability' which
are funding-compliant. The 'good people' will survive

if their advice is taken, the 'bad people' will be casualties
'there's no avoiding'… The semantics finds its home
in the university, and is protected by 'standards'
and 'integrity', and the 'values of the institution'

to keep the *peaceniks* muzzled. If 'we' actually
made the effort to understand what the 'just wars only'
people are doing with their conferences and papers,
with their arms industry 'stakeholders', with their

'national security' and 'saving lives' approach
to the grim realities of the world, we might come
across to their side? I fear they will never bother
to try and understand one word we ever utter,

but we are likely to at least to try and unpick
what they're up to. We need to watch so the fall
doesn't come from where we least expect it. The fall
is a grammatical anomaly, and a history lesson

at once. So, I say I will make an effort to be
neighbourly, but I still hold the absolute view
that all violence is wrong. I am told to 'extend
the olive branch' and then a 'best not' joke is made

because of Turkey's Operation Olive Branch military
foray into Syria two years ago. Brutal. That was explained
to me as if I'd have no idea of what was going
on 'in the world'. I said, I was '...thinking of a little

further back in terms of irony and olive branches
and the regionality...' But I said nothing further
because it is not gracious in such circumstances, is it?
What has Noah and the Ark and Mount Ararat

to do with 'tribalism' (whose word is this?) and other
sources of conflict? On the desk of the edgy young academic
is a defused or dummy grenade — dulled green
with pin in place — and a 7mm shiny machine gun round.

I am leaning on you in this, Kwame, this need for support
for solidarity for a way through the deployment of anti-
personnel mines of collegiality, of the sundering of all
words and sharing of knowledge for growth of the soul.


JK

36. For Alexis Levitin

*I am blackened by sorrow*
*My skin and my clothes*
    — Federico Garcia Lorca

And at almost midnight, we said farewell, and embraced,
then I walked him to the automatic doors, and we guffawed
and we guffawed, and then he climbed into his white sports car,
and drove into the night heavy with autumnal wet. Irmãos.

1
*Version: Post-Racial Style*

The photo is of a torso in white tunic and the gathering
of a white gown for fit, and her palm, open over her stomach
where the weight of its gathering of water is held, seems
to cradle the chiffon and her new substance, her evidence
of prophecy. The image travels into our bodies warmly and says,
"Here is surfeit, here is filling, where once there was
the emptiness of all beginnings." And this undulation
of drapery, stilled, like the topography of a fresh meringue,
or, perhaps, a snowfield after the sculpting of wind;
this is where all miracles reside, where the impression
of infilling, the promise of what might come
is the soft warmth of a question before it is answered,
before the yes, before the grace of Yes, I am. The poet says
she lives for days in this waiting, and the machinations
of duplicitous leaders, the surety of life, will not consume her,
which is, the poet says, what she calls "inspiration".
And there is another still, another caught moment
that she could not have invented except through
the observer's lens – the back of her body walking
into the unending light – into infinite shades of grey.

2
The translator tells me he hears my skin in my poems –
the ones that ride roughshod over iambics. And I can tell
he has forgotten that when we first met, a year ago,
after a reading in Newark, his statement then was that he liked
those poems – meaning my dialect verse. And I felt like Paul Dunbar
in a hall full of good-thinking Georgian poets,
there in the heart of swampy Washington DC, the few who turned down
Woodrow Wilson's invite to his viewing party in the White House,
where the gospel of the Birth of the Nation un-scrolled.
And they grew bored with Dunbar's elegant anapaests and guffawed
in delight at his Negro verse – "Sooo authentic," they thunder,
meaning, black as salvation, meaning, black as redemption.
Oh, the uses of Negro champions, oh the uses of Negro art!
So, a year later, he tells me he likes my native poems – how aphetic
my island syllables, how authentic my riddims;
but he did not say riddims, though he might as well have.
So, I told him of a night in Swansea with a gathering
of pensioners and lovers of poetry, when after the reading
over tea and biscuits, I glowed when a woman as kindly
as she was old, said, "Dylan would have loved you."
And I quoted my father who mapped out Jamaica
in the cadence of Thomas's art:

Have seen the summer convex of the wounded sky
want to catch it and clutch it and make it sing,...

And dah, da-da dah, da-da dah, da-da dah...
So up there near Canada in the village of red leaves,
I spent my night translating lines, first shaped in the flattened
lyric mode (I am making this up just for effect).

3
*Vershan: Yardman Style*

Inside the photo you have a woman body and she gathering

a thing like a white ballroom gown, but it pure-pure
and flowing, and she wearing behind it a ordinary frock,
so, the heap of fabric soft and chiffon, gather front of she,
with her right hand over where a belly would be to hold
up the fabric but it come in like she holding up she belly
and it seem like it full up with all kind of niceness and promise;
even though the fabric undulating like when you beat
the egg white until it fluffy and smooth like hill and gully,
or as them say a farrin, how groun' stay when time fresh snow
settle over everything. The poet say she live for days now,
just a wait and a wait, and not even all de madness
in fi her world, not even trouble and trouble cousin,
can mash up her sweetness and her ripeness for days
and days, true this thing what come only sometimes
is what she call inspiration. Is pregnant yuh pregnant
baby-love? And you see that in-between time before yes
or no, that, that thing name waiting, that hold breath, a-it
name sweetness; that is the niceness that touch the world.
So now, watch there, see a new photo, this time is her back,
straight up like a tree trunk, and she walking smooth and easy,
Everything a move like water over rockstone, and front of her,
is light cyan done, light pon top a light, pon top a light.

4
— *By the way, did you kill that Ulster man, what's his name?*
— *Campbell?*
— *Yes, Campbell.*
— *No, 'twas me aunt what did that.*
—*What interesting souls you gypsies are! Guffaw, guffaw, guffaw!*

5
My left foot has fallen asleep, the laces are so tight at the ankle,
it takes me a day to put on my accoutrements, the brace, the socks,
the insoles, the shoes, and the laces, looped and re-looped;
and contained like this, I walk as a pilgrim in the sun streets,
walk in anticipation of the jig and jag of a pensioner translator I will be —

the one who tells me he spends months on a line to capture
the rhythm of the thing or to crack the encoding of a language;
and he dreads, he says, the word "commitment" when women are the subject,
though we are discussing the making of poems, and the two things
he has not done – marry and make poems after, sixty years ago,
he wrote a perfectly scanned, wholly creditable thing at eighteen
with the cadence, he thought with shame at the time, of an eighty-year old,
which was bad, so bad, so he decided never to write again.
It was a moment as monumental as Walcott seeing Castries
for the first time, the tears, the gospeller's cadence, him saying,
Oh city, oh city of wooden spires, hand-crafted jealousies and French
arches, will you love me as I love you? – this before the fire razed her down,
this the beginning of his prodigious art. That he imagined it in water colours,
first and not terza rima is no matter – details, details.
The translator is a craftsman, a master of dalliance, the murderer with
an alibi, the counterfeiter of love – how gracefully his clothes fit
in a new country in a strange tongue. Though, he says, there is no
word in Portuguese for "take for granted" and in my head, I think there's
no word in English for "take for granted", just the loneliness of a man
with a houseful of paintings by famous men, living in a village where
the fascist has a campaign office and the ferry runs all through the night,
breaking the encroachment of river ice. We embrace – I call him
brother in the hotel lobby and a stranger says, "Forgive me for staring,
but I love to see two grown men say brother," though she means
a black man and a white man in this village of white roads, and don't
we all love this bas relief of contrasts, what is there not to love in this?

*And now for the kiss of the wind,*
*And the touch of the air's soft hands,*
*With the rest from strife and the heat of life,*
*With the freedom of lakes and lands.*
"In Summer" by Paul Laurence Dunbar

KD

37.

> '*beguiling as an elder
> brother's antic lore.*'
> — Robert Hayden, 'Paul Laurence Dunbar'

I am losing what language
I have in the disconnect
between mouth and words.

I search a small space
for the infinite but trip
over a thorny wave motion.

The expectation I will
come out with publicly-
acceptable well-rounded

syllables, sentences
full of content. But I know
I am always a semitone

out – a diminishing
circle, a collapsed echo.
The silvereye hung

on sideways in the nest
fallen from one anchor point
so the clock struck six.

If across the mirage
of distance, the heat haze
of water restrictions

imposed on ourselves
by ourselves to serve
ourselves so we can

hang on here a little
longer, if across
such a mirage that

mirage I see a 'neighbour'
walking I will yell a greeting,
hoping for something back,

hoping they're unarmed,
that they register in erosion
a vast knowledge they reject.

I am losing what language
I have in the disconnect
between mouth and words.

To quote to cite to riff
out of context is not
throwing in a lot,

not imagining myself
into another time and place
and the roles I might

slot into, or force
myself into, as if
imagination is choice:

consequences of hard-
ship and loss an array
of words shaped by

the mouth as you
imagine it, expostulating,
lull, speaking love –

an inheritance one
can afford to rearrange
to suit the phantasm,

the lexical expectation:
first readings I did in America
and 'audience' wanting

a wheat and sheep farmer
with an 'Aussie accent' as
fitted their historicism — travelogues —

but got something twisted
out of shape by pronunciation,
'attitude': Do you hate your nation?

I don't hate anything.
I once found a climbing rose
scaffolding a patch of bush

between The Hills
and an 'outer suburb' —
when I was a young father

wrecking my family
with my addictions — a rose that
was a beautiful soothsayer

of demise. I tried
to name it but no
words formed,

I was alone.
If I'd been with
others I might

have been able
to speak – lamenting
the rose as sign

of doom to banksia
woodland, an incursion.
But no words came.

I wanted brothers
and sisters and friends
whatever kinship.

None came and I left
those I had, who'd tried
to help me out of the malaise.

I sabotaged my mouth
my words and language.
I thought, This must be 'voice'.

Wasps seal my ears with mud
with their victims inside, red-
capped robins nest in crooks

of my arms, legs – 'strawman',
of course, easy as that, and fits
a pattern. My fingers are sun skinks

and my eyes are mouths
that take in more than they speak.
This desperate search for friendship?

I am losing what language
I have in the disconnect
between mouth and words.

JK

38.
*Such people should realise that what we are in our letters when we are absent, we will be in our actions when we are present.* 2 Cor 10

The leaves are slow in changing,
and the first snow, tendered as a whisper,

weighs them, so that near Andrews Hall,
a carpet of lemon green leaves on the concrete

is set off against the filtered chilled light
of the afternoon – it is winter, already.

I count my exile by the seasons,
and this is also a way to think of history.

John, I meant to say that we share the fears
and purposes of chroniclers, those who speak

with letters across time, preserving time,
our words come strong and forceful, though, sometimes,

searching for meaning. But always the arrival
of beauty is the music that settles on me,

that makes it worth the while. I meant to say
that I am listening to you, and waiting for you;

for your words to arrive with the regularity
of epistles carried by couriers across kingdoms,

dodging bandits and the distraction of wolves,
or the whispering of desires that shimmer golden

in the ginkgo trees, and of course, the buzzards,
white as cultic myths, with their flaming swords,

asking, "What are you carrying in that satchel?"
When they arrive, the words are warm,

thrumming with persistence, their hearts bent
on surviving the crossing, and this is great comfort.

KD

39.

*grass exiles,* for Kwame

There are always thankyous embedded in these lines,
words that can go either way, phrases that offer refuge.

It's grass-cutting-time here and each stalk or leaf that falls
is a page torn from the library replaced by waves

we can't see emanating from piercing silver towers
up on the high points of surveillance pretending witness

and conversation. I collect up a few cut blades and take them inside
to peruse under artificial light, to pick out cell by cell a translocated

history. A microscopy of origins and destinations,
the pasture that ate away the native grasses and 'blanketed'

the hills, the plains, framed by firebreaks sad
with presumption. The seeds seem so ready to fall

and be laid out as a contents page to hope, edited
by many species of bird as bonanza. Mutual aid?

Prelude to prevent a burning, prelude to prevent
a conflagration — but fire can run the seams

of grass laid down, and we have to be conscious
of that in the keeping of records, noting things down —

the printers' devils loose in the prospect of now
as its own future, a revelation for tomorrow.

JK

40.

"Ought". "You ought". "No more than you ought":
And this is a guard against hubris, though the complexity
of "ought" is not the language of the racist – it is dangled out to us –
as all morality – vague, uncertain and gut-ridden. "Ought not",
or "ought to", and there is in our world a notion of the norm,
Naipaul's ground rules of irony – elitism, and the vaunting of class,

and we share our sense of the norm, and the buffoons
who do not will not understand that we snigger at them,
or more, even more earnest than this, that we build ramparts
against their entry, against the barbarians at the gate.

And these days, age has made me a chosen – it is nothing
I have done, and something that as soon as a quick swell
of pain in my breasts, or a chaotic riot in my blood,
will make me as ordinary as dirt, and dirt, this dirt,
this grave we straddle, this shadow over all things,
is what the elite fight valiantly against, and perhaps
therein lies the calculus of "ought" the secret of "ought".
For what is enough, what is enough of vanity, what is enough
of confidence, what is enough of boasting, what is enough
of that man who says that the foreskin, trimmed and nailed
to the cross, is the sign of an elitist joy; and this is less
than an answer, less than the language of our history,
less than humility, less than the act of good Christian
translators, sitting in the cloister of their monasteries
overlooking the quays of Bristol, festooned with harboured
galleons: all that vomit and blood, all that shit and funk;
the boards marinated with lamentation.

And they translate "slave" for "worker", those unholy scribes
and this is what a destruction of a people is built upon,
this is what the assuaging of all conscience is built upon,
this is what centuries of reclamation is built upon.

One ought, one ought not, one ought not to think of oneself…
and how high is highly. And who sits below me now,
who sits beneath me, as I consider the dialectics of ought?

KD

41.
*voyager from interstellar space*

Cutting grass, I switch tones as I think of legacy,
of each cut of presence. It just doesn't go away,
introduced grass cut and dropped in swathes,
and my feet searching for holds on the rocky
hillside. Under the clutch of York gums
I disturb a fallen limb and a long-tailed
dunnart appears, tracks its marsupial way
to another hold-all, it's repository of safety;
cutting grass, I switch tones as I think of legacy.

Cutting grass, I switch tones as I think of legacy,
and question the claim that dunnarts – tail a store
of fat from nocturnal insectivorism – have in any
way benefited from clearing, 'favouring' their 'preference'
for 'grassland habitat', 'edges of paddocks', mixtures
of cover and openness. Where the feral cat roams.
And then the edges are erased as well. We see
very few. I am glad I didn't hurt it felling grass.
Cutting grass, I switch tones as I think of legacy.

Cutting grass, I switch tones as I think of legacy,
the trimmer line a line too many, the line I add
to the equation of here, the tangent that winds out
from the heliosphere, a deteriorating plutonium power-
source with eager listeners arguing 'the risk is worth it'.
It's not. The dunnart studied me while voyaging
briskly away. I am no sun. It can't know me as enemy,
surely? I move away, forget and remember its locality.
Cutting grass, I switch tones as I think of legacy.

JK

42.
*History is a nightmare from which I am trying to awake*
    — James Joyce, *Ulysses*

*Isn't he who is right here,*
*keeping both of us restlessly sleepless,*
*a drop after drop drawing us out of peaceful slumber,*
*the same one who is sound asleep down there?*
*Isn't he who is tonight pitting us against each other,*
*splitting us into two opposites,*
*the same one who will, tomorrow,*

*fuse us back as a perfect twin,*
*united by tormenting pain —*
*when the earth is shaken to her utmost convulsion,*
*and throws up her burdens from within,*
*and rage and storms through the morning veins —*
    — "Monologue" by Kamal Elgizouli

Every sentence torn open reveals enough
for me to sit outside the museum of modern art
in any city decent enough to commission someone
to draw the charts and the delicate lines,
to make the elegant blue prints on rice-thin
sheets of paper to be handed to the robust
team of makers, to build roughly and then with tender
smoothing and roughing, to plant cedars and crepe myrtles,
or perhaps olive groves scattered throughout the courtyard
with its marble benches, and its geometric paths, and its open sky,
and its walls of uneven finish now stained with the permanence
of murals, and me sitting here morose at the confluence
of meaning and unmeaning behind these sentences.

I am not tearing for our inadequate language, not for a city,
not for humanity, nor am I tearing because of my sins,
but because on days like this, dull with their grey persistence,

I think of my island, I think of its riotous green,
I think of the way the sun turns the hillside into sheer
plains of green, and I think of Aba dancing, turning, smiling,
as she did in a dream to her dear friend who mistook
it for a dream of resurrection, that she would rise from her bed,
fold her sheets and walk out of ICU – but her husband
the doctor and prophet wept and said, "She came to say
goodbye, she came to say goodbye." And the house grew heavy
with the tension of prophecies being tested, for soon we would know,
and it was all true, the dancing, the body renewed, the farewell;
and here, a year later, I am broken-hearted at the thought
that what I feel is not that I can't wait to see her, but that she is gone –
that what I am doing here is remembering the dead,
and this is why I sit outside the museum or the library,
or the cemetery, or the heavy stone intrusion of the ancient
parliament buildings, the wide courtyards of the legislators
of our small lives, why here in this place of grand edifices
of permanence, these custodians of history and culture,
of our human hubris, of our vain effort to remain here, I weep.

And at the edge of all sorrow is joy, whether joy lost
or joy to come, or joy hoped for. I do not allow myself the indulgence
of our rotting ecologies into a poem, my friend, and considering
its making – this seems like an intrusion of the crass and ungenerous sort,
but indulge me here, this once, as I say
that to come to this gathering of words, which is, really,
to come to this courtyard where you stand as audience to my words,
to my making of words, to my quest for words, for the language
to speak of the day, early in November, of ice storms and grey, grey roads,
of that woman in a red scarf scarring the day with her defiance of colour,
to be drawn here, to borrow from you, just for now, your ears,
though, I mean, too, your heart and mind, and something of your soul –
borrowing for this moment your ears; this is the comfort that stands guard
against the hollow avenues of history, how it makes itself without caring
who it controls, what enemies it arms against others, enemies, I mean,
whose single purpose is to separate us, to divide us and break us;

what wars history makes of us, and what monsters it shapes in us;
yes, the ears open to the sound of our art is the comfort that protects us.

KD

43.

Birth can heal rifts of decades and a grand-daughter born as far in Australia
       from here
as one can get is the retelling to make more of history than we had
       available to us —

no ultimate constant, no version to settle on, each story given
       time to run
in the omnibus of family. So, after decades, my son & I will talk in
       the same room,

talk when the weather should be getting cooler but shadows don't reach
from the low mountain in the same way. Next year. Father and offspring,
       antecedents

to the new baby's data: birth record, immunisation record, tax file number,
account passwords, even if gender and name shift across the barcodes
       of the circadian.

What to do with this, here, alone? — Tracy down in the city as her Mum
       is rushed
to another operation, so fragile and vulnerable, and the silvereyes with
       doubled nest-failures

and having just lost one of their small flock to a car-strike, ants eating out
       the yellow foliage
of its chest. And the photo of lineage — the vernix protection to answer
       all nurturing,

and the people we don't know but do know, and the genealogies that
       old poets
recite to ward off mortality, to announce a birth a rebirth a
       constancy of growth.

JK

44.

*I shall go back*
*before thieves turn my hair to ashes,*
*in my own, not God's time*
*to the immensity of love*
*and the perfume of poetry*
      — Neville Dawes, "Switch-back"

And so, twice a year, I test the perfume of poetry
and the ashes in my hair, letting things grow,
the clean baldness my imposition on self –
not to hide the balding (so far there is no balding,
I lack the virility of hairlessness) and not the ash,
for I relish the dignity and artistry of dark hair
accented by the wisdom of greyness. No, I shave
with daily ritual, to ward off the wars of roots,
the scalp-ache of a head of hair being combed –
the roots of my beginning, defiant as all strong roots –
there is a tender vulnerability and assurance
in the smooth topography of my bald pate;
in Jamaica they call us soft-headed people,
we who weep as we yank to order the knots and curls.
I read each indentation and gentle gully of my clean-shaven
head for my history – there is a name for that.
So, now is the season of my rebirth, the season
for my hair to grow, for my beard to grow,
for the marking of my days to be plain to the world,
and I am grateful for the short quick bow,
for "elder", for "oga" not with bombast but with grace.
My father, at twenty-seven, worried about thieves,
and they did come to break into his cabinet
of perfumes, and they stole much, but left him
that singular jar, poetry, that he cherished and rationed
until it, too, went dry, and all that remained
was the lingering musk, that thing that let him

look into the Blue Mountains on a deep bad-minded rain day,
and conjure in his head, the lasting nostalgia of home;
or the slopes of St Anne, where in that mountain village,
he arrived at the age I am now, to visit the dust roads
and the slave polished tombs, to then bend his greying
head and declare that history will continue its march,
and the thieves will not steal everything, not if we stand guard,
and make our bulwarks of language, the push against
all erasure. Still, I must say to him now, though I know
he knew after he had lived on, that God's time will overtake us –
our bones, our hair, our bodies; and that our last true defiance
is this music. If you see me coming towards you,
I tell my children, my head haloed with the ash of history,
look closely, and then embrace me, and you will,
with each breath, smell the lingering perfume of my making.

KD

45.

'History in the making'? Locally, it's hearing hot winds
rising around the house, hoping a spark doesn't manifest
and throw down its ground plan of furious consumption,
a lust for oxygen taking it faster and faster up steep gradients.

We hope for smokeless skies, for animals to cool in shade
to pant to make their saliva work coolness as body tricks.
No matter which way we look at it, we can't take on history
and want a lull in chronology's hotpoints, 'crucial

moments'. The Prime Minister is cool in Kirribilli House
and praying, and the militias are festering in 'Liberty State'
(across the other side of the world), maybe discussing the nature
of history as they revise and negate, footnoting assault rifles.

And in 'the West' of Australia — here — where we fear the worst,
we learn that 'the East' is already kindled, is already caught
in the burning. We are so on edge that we wake to forget
our dreams are so moved by hot winds behind our walls.

Flux. Fire. 'Heraclitus' — thanatology for satellites. Stateless.

JK

46.

*Mi verso es de un verde claro*
*Y de un carmín encendido:*
*Mi verso es un ciervo herido*
*Que busca en el monte amparo.*
— Jose Marti

1
Consider the revolutionary, consider the monster.
Consider the slaughter of the innocent, consider the slaughterer
of the guilty. Consider the decorations on the valiant whose hands
remember the last breaths. Consider our heroes, consider these
slave-polished graves. Consider the survivors, those stumbling out
of bombed-out buildings, or those sitting soaked in the anaesthetic
of liquor or the sweet amnesia of orgasms, the emptiness of that hunger.
Consider that deep into the night, the people, the people cannot sleep.
They say, "I see him, I see her, I see him coming over the hills."
Consider the martyr who is mad, who is so worn with this world
that she says, "It is me, and so those who long for blood
sharpen their blades, and will find their rest."
Is this a lie, is this atonement, is our vengeance a lie,
and is this what history is? The moment justice is settled –
as if the rotting carcass is ever settled – will this this bring comfort?
Will the news of this bring comfort to the victim?
"There is music playing somewhere, I hear it.
There is music playing somewhere, I hear it".
This music, full of the steel stainless wash of that descending chord,
the brass of impenetrable sorrow riding over the fleshy pulse and stink
of the sacrificial dub of sound: this music is peace, this is the music
playing somewhere, and I hear it. I hear it, I hear it.

2
I have fed on the distraction of art for so many years,
this is the truth, and my art is aslant against the heavy hand
of truth – the filter is the flawed imagination of someone else's beauty

or nightmare, I am a chameleon, a parasite, and this is how I have survived.
There is a wall of aquamarine stained with brown, like rust,
and the ceiling is the darkening of the sea, and against this wall
is a mahogany cabinet of ornate carvings; and the tiny golden baubles
are the handles for the little drawers, and the surface is covered
with elegant crochet, starch stiffened, all these wheels upon wheels.

3

*Then Mary took about a pint of pure nard, an expensive perfume; she poured it on Jesus' feet and wiped his feet with her hair. And the house was filled with the fragrance of the perfume. But one of his disciples, Judas Iscariot, who was later to betray him, objected, "Why wasn't this perfume sold and the money given to the poor? It was worth a year's wages."*
— John 12: 1-8

Every revolutionary has dreamt of the heroic act,
the confrontation with the tyrant, perhaps in verdant hills
or the pocked-marked walls of a city on the verge of liberation,
the cold declaration: "The death of anyone is a cure of the killer,
but heroes, true heroes will chance the judgment of eternity
for the sake of the people — and the tyrant will scowl,
then whimper, and the hero dreams it is he who stands
over the tyrant and calls him coward, calls him the murderer
of innocents, calls him the snivelling monster that he is;
this is how revolutionaries dream before the revolution,
for after the stench of unwashed cobbled stones,
the shit and the vomit, the quick rot of bodies left too long
because the workers are too drunk to clear the hallways
and the streets, after the confusion of new laws
starting to reek of something broken like the pragmatics of power,
after the celebration, a week of giddy drink and gluttonous sex;
after the quiet evening staring into the sunset, the body
uncertain of itself on the new day, and the broken alabaster jar
of perfume still scattered on the floor; the scene of gratitude
and mercy heavy in the air; after this come the new dreams,
the new horrors, and the new insomnia. The hero plants roses,

the hero digs into the sod, the hero spades manure into the earth
in mounds, and thinks of shallow graves; the hero stares into the blue sky,
and then rakes the leaves into high pyres, letting the smoke
rise into the sky, thinking in the broad daylight of the sacrifice,
the sweet scent of aspen leaves; and then, far off, the hero sees
the dark smoke of war, of cities burning, of retribution, of the cane-fields
aflame, and the hero understands that it is all a great vanity
without the songs, without the songs of revolution, without the songs
that speak of the colour of the flag, the territory of the liberated;
the myth of possibility: this is what the hero must understand.

4.
Neville, I know now that you imagined your revolution, and that day,
when you wrote of the death of a revolutionary, by whom you meant you;
when you asked your comrade to put a bullet in your cranium
were you to betray the people; this was more than just bombast.
I know now that you had awoken from that dream of the revolutionary,
and had asked yourself, "Am I the keeper of the perfume of poetry,
the alabaster jar of beauty in war, or am I the blood-stained revolutionary,
haunted already by the regrets of killing?" And in that moment,
you wrote your letter. "Friend, if I ever betray the revolution,
if I ever become seduced by the lies of tyrants,
if I forget the colour of my skin, do, oh, Hector, plant a bullet in my cranium,
and I will always thank you for this mercy, I will always thank you."
I have kept, dear Neville Augustus, your cabinet of perfumes,
and I have given myself to filling my mouth with its bitter astringent taste,
and spraying it out like a poco priestess over the living and the dead,
over the unpredictable earth, letting the tiny bubbles of fragrance
dance through the sullen air, in streaks of light, but mostly,
the baubles of that word, possibility, that pregnant shiny word.

KD

47.

*for Bazra — poet, activist and editor of TWOT — who was burnt to death near his shed in NSW, far away from here*

Today hottest record November since weather began
today the burn inversion of head in the sand
the land quota of here-burn to make history of ends

this historical day, this array of false apples and Sky News suns,
this star chamber of aesthetics to claim a poet's line when it suits
and damn other poets and thinkers to the pit of 'alarmism'

on a day when feature is absolving though a list of 'historic fire events'
and a snarl at those who say ash will pile on ash and point to increase of ash
in the land of 'fire and drought' they'd repossess via dispossession

their love of capital vents fuels updraft only to lose pace
through lack of oxygen today hottest record since weather began
the stooge of capital demonstrates a predictable blame

of conflagration on those who see tree script against colonial
fire usurping Aboriginal fire culture to claim pattern to claim
    'to be expected'
furious at climate activists as a poet dies near a shed died alone
    death unknown —

died alone without laurels and plaudits given out
by the machine of grace and favour wink and a nod
shadow-makers — alone with poems in the head,

liked by the community, unyielding to capitalism.
We knew him and his wild ideology, his distrust of power.
Today hottest record November since weather began

today the burn inversion of head in the sand
and we think in mirage and melt and siccative art
kept in tins in chemical factory warehouses. Ash

of denial ash of trees and body and yes even air
burnt ash wavering as the wind turns about comes
about and the don't-speak-during-the-crisis brigade
   push eulogies to ends controlled by the living.


JK

48.

*Blue skies convert all genocide into fiction*
        — Derek Walcott, from *Midsummer*, ChapterXLIII

*I prepare to take my medicine*
        — Culture

1.
I do not trust my poems, and this knowing
is an admission that I have grown to mistrust
poems, through no fault of theirs,
for mine is a pathology, a desire
of my deepest longing, and this,
poetry tells me with its lingering
after-scent: its perfume of truth,
is a delusion. But all delusions
are in part truths, and this is so,
as all hope is built of the insubstantial,
the knowing we avoid;
all faith, they say, is blind.

Today, I trust all poetry, and I trust
my poems as the only truth that will last
beyond the shadows of these winter days,
and listening to the drone of my voice,
climbing and descending the topography
of my syntax, while I walk the campus,
I feel naked, vulnerable, exposed,
for these truths are repeating themselves
like the stunted trees of this city
in ways I should not trust. And I have
lived a charmed life, for the people I love
have avoided my poems for so many years;
and in hiding, I have grown into this
livid stretch of nerves. The world,
and now I say, all faith, is blind.

"What is that smell?" someone asks.
"Oh, that is jasmine, I think…"
"No, that is the scent of poetry;
sweet as sleep, long sleep.
Is it on you? Why did you bring it here?"
"I don't know what you are smelling."
Liar, liar, liar, liar, liar.

I mourn the poet's body
burning alone in the bonfire
of neglect. Did you say, alone?
Did you say, he was alone, John?

"Blue skies convert all genocide into fiction."

2.
Needless to say, this morning
in Lincoln, the sky's blue is sardonic
as all bitter beauty. I am pregnant
with a poet's sorrow, which is
a fruitful sorrow, a fecund
sorrow. "Are you happy
with your life?" I review the choices,
and see no box for, "Read my poems,
they are beautiful, and have found
the language for blue skies,
and in this, is a certain sorrow
that is happy as all art must be."

And maybe this is how I have failed you –
that you have never learned to say,
"I am sorry," with the desperation
of someone who has sinned
against the innocent;

that all your apologies
have been forced, a kind of concession,
and you have always had the right to this,
the right to weigh the sins
you may have committed
against my constant failings.

And another man may have pushed back,
and may have even said to you,
"What you need is to be able to carry
in you the heavy stomach pain
of what you might lose
for what you have done."

With me, you have been the holy one,
a saint, one incapable
of matching the wounds I have inflicted.
You have grown used to the perfume
of my poems, to how they catalogue
my failings, and defy the wiping
away of all things; how they linger
after I am gone on some new journey.

The logic is off, I know,
because I have sucked up any right
I might feel to be hurt –
it is the way love can be tempered,
love can be retarded by peace,
by the scarring of hurt not fully healed,
how it is true that love can be
all that we have left.

It can be what has been
and what will not be.
I am in your blood, or maybe you
are in my blood. That is true.

And I have not learned how to be cleansed,
how to start again, how to ignore
the purple stain of clouds
at the back of the blue mountains.

We watched a dying woman
forgive her unfaithful lover,
and while I warmed at the mercy of her gift –
that love will balm fear –
you said, "Better she than me,
better she than me."
And then I knew what harm
I have done to love.
I knew, then, what sorrow remains
in you, and my fear was so full
that I could not speak,
could not chuckle,
could not calm the souring
in my deep, in my stomach.

"Blue skies convert all genocide into fiction."

It is true in this city.

We are so alone, so alone
in the wilderness, and my syntax
drips with the spikenard of lamentation
I smell in the rugged gravel of Joseph Hill's plea –
"Great Jah will provide bread and water for I and I...
Only Jah to vindicate for I and I...

Sing:
*"I'm alone, in the wilderness*
*I'm alone,*
*I'm alone in the wilderness..."*

KD

49.

The deniers collect dates
to make 'research' to make
precedent to work history
to their endgame to blast
claimants of hurt and damage
to blamegame via epithets
and all the while all the while
the Great Centipede comes
in early comes in and roams
the tiles and I see it go under
an elevated surface and I wait
to catch and release into
the night seething a night
already shed its ancient
cicada skin but centipede
doesn't emerge where I expect
in the false light and I sense
it will run behind curtains and work
back under the couch and as
I process routes and trajectories
the centipede is on my bare
foot my bare leg climbing
in that proverbial epithetic
liquid way where metaphor fails,
tangled in sweat-tamped hair,
where an 'extremely painful
bite' comes into play but
I love its movement and lift
it's fast but gentle this history
of growth segment by segment,
this history of movement, of toxin,
this emergence out of earthy
places into demi-earthy place
to make me aware, to make

me shift language jolt words
further out to the tip of tongue
because all words that have
pushed out of my lungs
till now have been gasps
and need substance: deniers
will deny even this happened
to me, this Ethmostigmus rupripes
declaration of body temps
and surfaces and nocturnal
moults of an aphonic human.

JK

50.

*You brought the violence in here*
         — Zonal

*amiss*

1
There is an art of silence here,
a compromise in the air.
It is catching. The art is to weigh
the heat of blood, the expiation
of anger, versus the dull silence of calm –
the compromise. It takes a cold heart,
void of guilt, doubt or regret,
a heart capable of performed love
we call politeness, to master this way
of a whole people, the middle way,
it is called – be nice, they say.

This is how this city has broken me,
how it has left me an exile of myself.
I stare at the snowfall, it covers everything,
and soon all will be white and forgotten.

We do not live with passion – we wear
the garment of a mannered living –
not even Victorian, for here we lack
the flame of self-righteousness – this is the quiet
after a riot, the bodies buried,
the world still as dawn. Now those I love
have learned to manage me.

I am to be managed I am told,
I am to be gently and nicely managed.

2
*alit*

I will not wallow in sorrow,
nor weigh me down in the mud of regret.

I will not succumb to the alien air
that presses in on me; this is defiance.

And I have no one to look to,
though I have waited for others to come
to my rescue, not remembering that I am
a crowdapeople, I am called multitudes,
I am an army, I am a nation, a peculiar planet
flawed and unreliable when seen from deep
in my blood; but were I to accomplish the magic
of distance – the thing that art has given the fortunate,
perhaps I will see this grand tragi-comedy of hope,
the rising music of faith's contentments.

I will instead laugh, fill my lungs
with the deep music of having seen love,
or held in my arms the labour of my love,
my industry and glow. There is
that photo of Neville, in his forties,
khaki trousers and a rugged cotton shirt,
tails drawn high enough to show the skin,
the rib and the hardness of a stomach strained,
his body taut with that stilled motion
of a cricket stroke, his eyes consumed
by this one act of connecting ball and bat,
of calculating the physics of speed
and placement, the body, now, remembering
with elated aplomb, the muscle
memory of its physics, and in this,
my father was what I dare to call man.

This is happiness, this is man panting,
sweating in the glowful way of health,
having arrived through the bramble
and stone-crowded path to the agreed place,
a compact with myself. And here, say,
"Oh body, oh self, how I have neglected you,
how I have berated you, how I have ignored
your makings, your finished things, how I have
shrouded every delight with the gloom of regret
or fear. Forgive me, self, you have had one honest
friend and he has betrayed you. This view,
the island laid out before you, the backward gaze
over the path we have taken, it is beautiful,
and we must delight in us; dance with abandon,
drunk as David before God and the world,
with the denouncement of woe, of upbraiding,
the lie of humbleness and laboured modesty;
I say to you, and only you, let the tight snare roll,
ring its bell of beginnings, then the short breath
of anticipation, the tease, before the one drop
buoys you, and the bass caresses, ay. Now dance!"

KD

## 51.
*incantation against being isolated*

Will I be able to find you, Kwame,
if I come looking next year, before
snow appears, if snow is to come
before the whiteness eats up difference
to make a one-sided metaphor
that blends with the prairies,
irritated and troubled but 'well-
kept' when incorporated communities
have anything to say about it?

I am good at needle in haystacks,
but only if the magnet is straw against
the inert but diffuse needle, a lack
of metallic properties, of glint.
I live among neighbours who know me
just enough, if at all, but as part
of the disturbance — I distract myself
with the focus of the rufous whistler's
wake-up call as literal as dawn.
I cut grass, I lay down a floor
of stalks and leaves and husks,
and I follow the compass back
to the house — rick, stack, hall.

Will I be able to find you, Kwame,
if I come looking next year, before
I return to the ash that falls faster
and further than sleeplessness,
or as a polite detritus in my trance?
I am lost searching for you there
in a city I don't know, so take to
the spreading world, bent on horizons,
listening out for your deep song.

JK

52.

Dobet Gnahore sings with that warm
mezzo-soprano, the aroma of dawn
and moist red clay, the melody turning
into the shape of mountains
covered in the green carpet
of jungle – there are so many tears
caught in the low mauve clouds;
and I tell you to look and see a man
stripped almost to his last self,
moving his arms and the round language
of his body, his eyes closed,
him living so deep in his blood,
him allowing the pulse
of the syncopation to transform him.
It is raining all around him,
and the small zinc shelter he has found
with the raw cement floor –
there a few chains from the main road –
that is me, and I have stripped shirtless,
and allowed this sound in my head
to carry me into the secrets of memory
and loss, to the thing that sounds like prayer.
Everything has become simile for me now,
for my mind is slowing to the place
where words elude, find deep
corners where they giggle in hiding,
and so the simile is my only hope –
the word would be sorrow,
for this deep violet in the space between
my throat and my stomach
is the colour of a looming sky
over Kingston, or the sound
of Lorna's voice conjuring a harmonized
fleshiness to an emaciated pop song –

she is sure no one can hear her.
And I am taken to the room
so many years ago, to the soft blue
of her dress, her skin brown as earth,
her smile a calming love; I am still reaching
for what the morning is offering me,
the words I have no system for,
and I will not call it sorrow,
nor melancholia, nor the thousand human words
for this moment; instead, I carry in me
a catalogue of moments, of similes,
and they will suffice, for it is not sorrow,
John, no, no, I am blessed;
but it's the thing we know in our blood,
the thing we have called poetry;
though privately it has been
our persistent curse, the beauties, the ancient beauties.

KD

53.
*the need for immersion*

Should we escape the hooks and ropes of history?
A symposium out of the ooze of lost forests, immersion
as ancient fertility, the body-tree-body, the branching
out we might leaf-tip, touching a close-cropped sky.

Why should all the intensities of joy be spectres
momentarily encountered in searching for clean water
beneath the dry – empty aquifers gasping stone cradles?
Joy is a cumulative medium, and can be stirred

by presence like the galvanic gold leaf – life life life! –
a demonstrable haunting that has us treading more
lightly, letting what was and is move through us
without blocking the way. No? We know the blessed are

offering their hands, so often pushed away, we know
the blessed sense that we want to share, to parley.

JK

54.
*For Geoffrey Philps*

And how are you? I ask, though his smile,
and the trim ease of his body
are giddy with the word "contentment" –
the ease of it, the settled music
of his calm. I envy him this holiness of soul
and this grace that covers him,
for I, the man whom he declares to have written
now the saddest poems ever,
dare not contradict, nor quibble
about the meaning of sorrow in poetry,
or about how history is a long breath
and how the tiny spots, the dark
wounds on the mango, are truthfully
mere camouflage for the sweetness
that lurks beneath the blemish, and history
is the longest breath, and my lungs have drawn
back to widen the space for its healing.

In Miami, I have lost the language of sun;
it is as if I have forgotten the guileless dialect
of constancy, the ritual of daybreak,
midday, and the long shadow of evening time.
What I covet, though some would say envy –
though none of these express the praise at its core –
what I feel of you and long for in me,
is more than innocence, for there is a knowing
at your root of your ways,
but there is no guile in you, dear friend,
and how pure a draught of water is when scooped
from cool mountain brooks.

Your friend, Marilene,
the displaced Haitian, said, smiling to you,

"In you I found a protection so familiar:
how at once, as quickly as hello, I knew you spoke
the dialect of friendship I lost in childhood,
and I became that girl, again, who came knocking
on your door saying. 'Hi, can Geoffrey come out to play?'"
And as she spoke her body reshaped
into a glow-filled seven year old,
on her toes, craning to look past the guard,
your bemused mother, to seek out the yes
of your boyish eyes, gathering in beauty
and laughter, and for your mother's yes,
so you could sprint screaming
into the guileless daylight.

KD

55.

Noongar Elder Len Collard calls it 'receiving stolen goods' — these land
    purchases
on land that's burning too frequently too fast, sold over. Yesterday, in
    ever-widening

terms of residence, at the base of The Scarp, we took a closer look
    at the new suburb of *Bushmead*,
project being 'shaped by nature'. The 'dream of a plot of land' streamed
    5G *the reception isn't bad*

in that enclave near Midland, until recently part of Hazelmere — a light
    industrial suburb
with a fair quota of contaminations — part of Hazelmere, but not now,
    not now because the name

has been changed to *Bushmead* — 'shaped by nature'. Two-thirds to be left
    as 'habitat'. The People Vs. Nature.
New Community enclosed in the frame. Not too long ago, it was — in part —
    Bushmead Rifle Range —

and fresh streets named 'Ruger'... etc train the untrained eye. Muzzle flash
    of red-tailed cockatoos.
Display home bespoke built-in wardrobe brute 'Arcadia' of home-making,
    family raising,

that disturbed feeling of desecration someone had somewhere else.
    'Defence land' brought
into action in 1915 after purchase from 'private land owner', used
    as a small arms

range and driver-training course with fuel storage depot. *Defence* noted
    the possibility
of contaminants but hadn't come across anything they were overtly
    concerned about —

'land sold on', so no probs. Hands wiped. Investors' ecologically vital
    bush land portfolio
work with parks and lifestyle bushfronting. Little chunk of Hazelmere
    ... a corner, really – Bushmead,

Perth's 'newest suburb'. Stolen goods fenced so wildlife can pass through
    *Perth Future Directions 2031 and Beyond*,
jobs shaping (biomedical – you can smell shapes) and carving out
    (workplace safety) masterplan, blueprint.

Website talks of strategy – 'Geography' (map of Australia), 'Price Point'
    (dollar signs) and 'Product Type'
(stylised drawing of buildings). Lifestyling the pristine (do people
    *likely* recognise a red-tailed black cockatoo's

take on participation by emersion, disestablishment). Community:
    'shrublands and woodlands of the eastern Swan Coastal Plain
critically endangered' greentape long lines parsed into an acceptable
    containment field of design – the *link* –

busting out of feasibility of permissions and 'opportunity'
    (submit, resubmit, succeed), of 'acceptable
balance' to make a realism of leadshot buried in ancientish trees
    (off-target, stray), ribboned

off because they don't fit the pristine *here* and will be *compensated
    for* by 're-
vegetation' decisions at the trailheads, the 'ai' of Greek, the woe
    of western

law trajectories, the dirges scripted into the act of consolidation,
    the legalising of receipt
of stolen goods. Said and done fence-ism. It takes unravelling,
    orienteering clauses and claims,

brag sheets and stock listings – copytext. Script doctors. Winding
	nature's shape, its tissues
of stagecraft and a meditative walk through habitat degradation –
	Fortitude. Barracks. Calibre.

What retrospecting defence land? Suburb. Advance, new residents,
	who will later become protesters
when further fragments of what's left is no longer 'bush forever' –
	nibbled and regazetted, attenuating

circumstance. History slogans waterways demanding *some* riparian
	vegetation
retained. No real getting around that. Consider north and south
	developments

and how inward-looking the newest compass is, folding the old maps,
	re-centering.
Heart of the remnant shrublands and woodlands cored, answers shifting
	with each tranche

of satellite photos, each history made and left behind to trawl through.
	Comparing
images and shifting access. Masterplan a trippingly long url forced into
	a couplet; and here's

the Google satellite image of 2019 cutting cloth to fit measures
	and the old patterns
prickle the new sell, the old shape stored up in stories that won't go away.
	Said. Done.

JK

56.

Here then is the book of transgressions, the secret plots
of those committed to calumny and the destruction of order –
and I, chronicler of sorrows, practice my art of purpose
in the lists I make, the laws broken, the beauty destroyed,
and standing before the notetakers, the memo writers,
the collectors of secrets, neighbours who trade to betray
the enemies of the state, and I am filled with caution –
I say I do not know the names of these monstrous machinations,
all I know is a sermon was spoken and the trees
clapped their hands. All I know is that at night
I hear the cracking of tree trunks, the felling of forests
and the clap of wood exploding in the forests where the fires
have started their deep and hungry consummation
of the earth. I went searching through old papers,
through the forest of my art – the poems I have written and set aside –
to see if I could find complaints against the destruction
of our earth, and what I found were slivers of bewilderment
and no small amount of jealousy for those revolutionaries
who wake each morning with a fire of resistance
in their bodies, who can stare at the wide complex
of human action and the decaying universe,
and found a singular narrative that somehow is able
to consume the billions of years ahead and behind,
is able to shake the Solomonic despair of all vanity,
a chasing after the wind – the persistence
of existentialist resignation, and instead plot the revolution
to change the march of the world. I envy them this,
and can only find hints of hope and faith in my words,
secreted inside the clutter of feeling and the delicacies
of language and metaphor. So, I am grateful for you,
for you who will face the bulldozers, for you who will press
his shovel into the land and do so knowing that there is a deed
ceded to you that tells you that you are truly the husbander of acres
laid out for you. And one last thing, something of an excuse,

but mostly a thought, that my father and his father,
and his father's father left me nothing, left no legacy of husbandry,
no acres of meaning, and no seed of responsibility;
and so, all I have are the long plantations of words
that I have been cultivating in my fecund heart,
and what is this, if not the scorching of all hope,
if not the great metaphor for the destruction
of all the green that stretches before us?

KD

57.
*from Schull, Ireland, knowing the fires burn fiercely where we come from*

Far from 'Jam Tree Gully' we don't know if we will have a house
to return to, a house to open out to air to sleep under tin roof where fire
sucks air out of circulation and rules all roosts we might or might
    not call home
though it is so much of what we are is house with interface between
    creatures and us,

dwelling imposition imprint troubled free of place and placement
though self-disrupted over vast curve of expansion day-in night-out
the heat-stress how much can the frame take?... the smoked air
the winged healer the messenger whose health fails straining

to get a breath of parity of nitrogen oxygen argon balance in composition
yet *here* in the penumbra of flu-fever *here* the chaffinch twisting
    the *deciduated*
tendril over a chilly stream, or the hyper-stilled grey heron so rampant
with full-on constrained energy on the retreat of the estuarial river

all that low sun gleam sharp after harsh weather all that confusing
of weather for climate which it doesn't actually do in documenting
layers of sediment, the heritage wall crashed through by car or utility vehicle
recently or since early January when we were last here extramural

almost extra but noted as demi-local at the colder time apropos 'our'
hottest time of house home this house almost home this cottage
    though not ours
but nothing is ours and each swing across the globe is the pendulum
the jiggering sway of earth via sun an expansion and contraction
    of antecedents
  and all the surfaces painted over to look different from our same.

JK

58.

And these words, *dreams, rounded* and *sleep*,
how is it possible not to envy the genius
of someone who makes language to patch up
the ugliness of betrayal, of weakness,
of how we hurt and have hurt? And I know
Neville sat in the peculiar mood of tropic twilight,
in stained polyester shorts, cutting his ten, smoking
slowly in the half dark, considering those words
turning and turning them around in his head,
waiting for death, waiting for the end, hoping,
though knowing that what would be left
would be simply the inheritance of all artists,
some will be interred with their words,
and this will be all. At eight fifteen the light
grew thick and muddy. He coughed. The island
was filled with long sharp knives.

Children in that real magical place of green
and red and brown play cricket on a red kerchief
of ground; I am stealing this from a poet who has perfumed
her metaphors and myths so thickly that her publishers
mistake her for a novelist, and indeed, it is novel as in "new",
this song, but I confess that a novel has not turned me to tears
not in years, and perhaps never, and yet this thing,
that familiar between the landscape of my making
and unmaking, the language of my dreams,
desires and the gummy stomach churn of Kingston dawns
an ailment associated with a decade, those seventies
where all feeling began, where I lost confidence
in what I knew and what I felt, when I grew to accept
that sometimes a ball could move too fast
for sight, and I, bewildered, must accept the limitations
of my body. There in Kingston, that sensation of desire,
lust, fear, joy, hope, and beyond that, the merciful relief

of faith – this is the language of the art Curdella Forbes
has given me, she in her art, in the pitch-perfect music
of her novel, and her people, her characters are aging
at the rate of my aging, a generation told as all great art
will manage to do without guile or intentionality,
but with the urgency of a body so full of music,
so long held in: a virgin saint, full of desire,
but with the fortitude of habit to keep all pleasure inside,
held there. This is what the art made here is,
and I accept it as a gift – a long poem, an epic history
of memory written before it settles in us,
and this is the great rounding, the end meeting
the beginning, the envied thing – the art
I have consummated, the flight of all true songs,
yes, this is the all of it. How often I return
to my old man, Neville, when the body softens,
I mean, and the air is heavy with the resignation
I do not know and may never know.

KD

## 59.
*transmigratory prayer*

Again, I've transplanted my head into the lantern of Fastnet
to view the migration of souls and find nothing that will let
me ride outrigger to new worlds as all worlds are made old
so fast, half-life resolution faded as vanity sparkles in embroilments
of 'race & culture' without compassion for people living next
door with different ways, crossing paths on the way to the shops,
gathering breath where they can as the great ocean bake-off
leaves fish and krill and squiggles in currents solecised
into languageless moments, the most bereft moments of all.
There are no saviours among self-declared tech prophets
and their largesse of tiny stars that are within reach of long-armed
socialites with hands laved by wealth. I've transplanted my head
into the lantern of Fastnet to escape fever by taking on more fever,
furious medium of sea that in changed consistency will still
make waves that break laws of wave peaks make rogue outside
iconic images of lighthouses to be snapped and cast aside.
Shelter with me, all of us, and let me shelter with you together.

JK

60.

The undocumented fall into single file to thread
the narrow paths of the Sierra, before the long mountain crossing
overlooking the meandering turns of the Snake River,
its deep brown calm over the land, and land that has in its soil bones
as ancient as First Nations and those before. These are the last steps
before the noise of arrival, the immigrant assured of all memory,
learning new roads, new rituals, new faces, learning to read the skies –
but the border is a false construction, we know this, that before the border,
the land continued uninterrupted, and became its own language,
a long novel of climaxes and denouements, all this before the grand breath
of the ocean. But we call them undocumented as yet another of the myths
of nation; after all, their names are written in government ledgers,
in the grand books of baptism and communion in the cathedrals,
ancient as the ships of Cortez and his monstrous agenda,
they are registered in the songs of lands that have known both blood
        and delight.
This is the documentation of our humanity – and for a brief respite,
between one calamity and the other, all that stands before us
is the untouched terrain, the land so contested it has discouraged
        the intrusion
of guns and machines. It is the interim, the moment between
darkness and darkness, where the stars spread out deep into the night.
On the edge of two nations is a bungalow of cages and cots.
Tonight, five mothers stand on the hillside with candles,
        smoking cigarettes,
repeating prayers for their dead with faith so strong it conjures
the scent of their dead children, those who crossed so many borders
before this last where in the heavy musk of detention the fevers took them,
their poor emaciated bodies hungry for the dense fortifying of peas
and bright yellow cornmeal turned with the slow rites of the poor.

KD

61.

*transmigratory prayer 2: tip of Sheep's Head Peninsula*

Between bays the narrow eye-lashed Cooltrain Lough
or smaller lens on high magnification – a road-through-lough –
Laharandota – marsh-tear adjusting a strabismus assembling run-off

from Caher Mountain and the rough edge of the Sheep's Head, the point
    of loss,
where too often someone is swept away, sudden and vanished as
    hooded crow
or seabird that doesn't settle again, just gone with lamentation

shuddering waves and shifts, foam, the swell a signature of sway,
of greater heaves and twists of land-prayer gone adrift,
or let loose in tidal currents and forgotten like microplastics

or slicks from the decades-old Whiddy Island oil terminal disaster,
those syncopating rhythms of ships and salmon farms and deathcows
grazing edges of sea green froth arising to marsh the cradle

above cliffs and walkers absent in quick-change weather
the city poets of tech sophistication barely want to know too much
of what they felt has been mapped and who'd go there

anyway at such a time other than habitual wanderers
trying to make sense of stories of cairns and lighthouses
and vulnerable if not endangered species of growth

neck of sheep projecting into water-mostly-body,
on the Way, horn of cow digging copper from giant's flesh,
bringing family here to take root in rock and find sanctuary in a giant's
head always looking out, panorama of the habitué, walker's folly,
    deep needs.

JK

62.
*A Year Later, Returning Home for Your Son's Wedding*
*For Aba*

Nearing Christmas now, the televangelists
break into their sermons with the haunting
of old seasons of childhood, flat sounding
German hymns of holy wintry night.
The air in the roots Pentecostal cathedrals
smells warmly of rum, the distillation of skin
and sleep leaves a residue, seductive as cologne,
and the men in their pastel bright jackets and white pants,
eyes bloodshot with the night's rituals;
the women in their garments of fluent praise
proudly sheathing their round bodies, close their eyes,
sink deep into the pleasure of thankfulness.
And outside, I am driving through Kingston,
its slow Sunday ambulating, the traffic sluggish
with indifference, and the hills hazy in the morning
sun-bright. We did not come for her, but in truth
we came to fill her absence and, on landing,
I promised myself not to imagine her in the cliché
of un-useful comfort, "she's watching from above, etc."
She is dead, we are none the better since — except
we hug longer, harder, whispering in low gutterals,
love: *Yes, understand, I know, I know, it dread*.
And then apart, our glistening eyes, not full enough
for weeping but sufficient to truncate our rehearsals
of how we are doing; it is hard, we say, and, no, no better.
Though, it *is* better, just a little, for then the sunny
city looked as dark as it has ever been, and it hurt
in the body — a throbbing wound. It was worse.
So, let's say we are here for kinder rituals,
to rejoice in the bitter sweetness of life —
its disregard for loss, as if it is saying, if you continue
in the house of mourning, know that the world will forge ahead,

and bodies will commingle, and hearts will hunger
for pleasure and acceptance, and the orphaned children,
as if guided by some terrible primordial gluttony
for the remaking of feeling, will hunger for love,
and seek, in their gathering, to make babies –
the world, such a callous necessity, marching on.
It is the season for love, after the grey year of sorrow,
or something worse, something unnamable,
the year of grey light. The unspoken sluggishness
of our hearts. Kingston, I have not announced my arrival
to friends, instead, I have slipped into your sepulchre of memory,
and felt in my heart an unspeakable disquiet,
as if what I can lose no longer fills me with panic,
but instead a dull resignation to the order
of our coming and going. In the soft stale light of her room,
I look away from the body of my mother
while she speaks into the darkness, repeating
the memories of years before I even knew myself,
and this, too, is a tender kind of love –
one that has repeated itself so much that silence, alone,
is its only language. She talks about her daughter,
the one who left us bereft. I stare into the green
mango tree through the louvres, where the light is delicate,
a light she can't see, and it comes to me that for these three days
of celebration, a small sermon turns in my head:
"Devour, oh you who see, every colour that rushes towards you
in this city, consume it all, be greedy for the storing of light,
for soon, this too will pass into a kind of mute twilight,
before the shadows." I would have wanted music
to mark this interlude, a music I can return to again and again,
but all I have is the quality of December sunlight in the tropics,
ricocheting off glass and shiny ways, and sharpening
the colour-drunk city with purifying light and softening shadow –
this is the strange art I carry in me on my return to the endless stretch
of prairie snow. Let's indulge, I tell my heart, and call it a canvas
(weak simile, but it will do.) Forty-five years ago, lunch time,

at Jamaica College, Snowy, grizzled shaver of ice, scooping
glittering half globes of shaved ice into our right palms,
and then painting the white with squirts of syrup –
the green always gleaming beyond all hues,
the red, the punch of sweet satisfaction, the snow
still and waiting, and quickly I raise it to my lips,
and devour the sweet cool before it melts away.
You see, no matter where I go, my heart stays on that island.

KD

## 63. transmigratory prayer 3: Lough Atalia Road, Galway City

It's not as easy as saying that *I understand*, Kwame, but I want to
and think I do more than a little, and maybe this is the privilege
of 'getting to know' someone like this, in poems, in the materials
and essences of line-casting, over a tranche of years? I think of *your*
Kingston — the way you share Kingston with me — as I walk
with Tracy and Tim facing into a fierce Galway Bay breeze
along Lough Atalia Road, heading towards Eyre Square, and
      the after-lights
of after-Christmas, the clinging on. Tracy tells me that in France the period
between Christmas and New Year is called 'le trêve des confiseurs',
and I can only imagine that when people are gorging on sweets,
the confectioners need a rest. But I am likely misreading, though
among the Christmas crowds of Galway City I will hear French
expressions mingle with Irish and with English and with Polish,
and I will think, *This interlanguage is where language resides* — where
words and phrases overlay, where something shared arises from push
and shove, the joy and annoyance, the laments and laughter.
But I am, yes, *getting ahead of myself* — on Lough Atalia Road
pathway, there are few other people, and the wind is biting,
and mute swans anchor themselves in the ruffled lough to stilled points,
paddling against blast and tide but not beyond their limits,
well within their capacities and experience, their design specs.
Expectations. And off the path into the lough, St Augustine's Holy Well
that fills when tides fulfil wishes with flow wracked in roughish
water, the crosses focusing miracles and swans turning
to see who's approaching, who makes life of now
or replaces the tide with archaeology, a need for the past.
Treading water. Wading in. Tracy has ancestors from nearby.
That comes sudden, distending a moment. *Nearby* as I pass
and brace against the cold — always underdressed as I am —
but Tracy's arm looped through mine, series circuit, thinking
of Kingston and prayer and the transmigration of souls into the breeze.

JK

64.
*bright*
*for Kekeli*

It is only in the dispassion of a photograph
recovered unexpectedly, when the bodies
must be identified, and the place and time
calculated – only then do I see it is you and us,
two men and a woman, grinning, and there is
a bright cloud of joy in the space between us –
a kind of laughing, which is another word for love.

Your handsomeness is the reminder that I love
a woman who may never know the uncertainty of a face.
You inherited her beauty – that easy face,
the kind that makes us look again. In St. Louis,
at the Mattress Barn, an old white woman
full of cheer for the season, is kind to us,
with laughter and suggestions, while your slow,
easy limbs – the lope of your walk, filled
the place; and then I recognized the strangeness
in her body, the flirtation, the constant return,
the effort to keep us around – keep you around,
so that in the end, when she said, as if tortured
into confession, "You are a very handsome lad,"
apropos of nothing, and you nodded softly
and mostly with a puzzled smile, I understood
how the beautiful ones exist with their own
skills of survival. Yes, you will suffer,
my son, but oh how warm some cold days
might be as they are for the beautiful ones.

There is a word for this reckoning, a word we relearned
twenty-seven years ago, one May day, the word *son*,
you repeating the rituals of our bodies,
before you turned into your own splendid self.

The space between us is the beauty you bring
into this world, how we have said we never doubt
your kindness to strangers, how you welcome
people into your world with the ease
of a heart full of the desire for simple fairness,
and this kindness is what you teach us
every day – you, with your head full of music,
your mind replete with the imaginings of a maker,
you who gaze into mysteries and smile,
game to know, and understand. To call you
son, is to name the blessings we have never
truly earned – a kind of grace, a mercy, love.
Bright light walking along the path, bright
light glowing through darkness, bright, bright!

KD

65. *transmigratory prayer 4: vita*

A small Swiss town's suburbs near great mountains
on the edge of a great lake with sheen that is sourced
from swans and snow melt, is no offset to the burning
in the Antipodes. We know the glare of burn — so much

of the western zone burns more each year without people
beyond being aware — it burns where fewer people
are so we hear less, but it burns and burns way more
each year in different ways at different rates…

many other hotspots in Australia know dry lightning
and other ignitions and their conflagrations are marked
in memory: ash days. But now *all* Australia is aware
of the catastrophe and its sourcings now because

the burn reaches into the hearts of cities, into
tourist zones, across farms, consumes more towns
by the day, changes the atmosphere for weeks
and offers no future relief. *Now* is yesterday's

warning — pitiless, unworkable by the evil of excuse-making
'representatives of the people'. They 'understand' firefighters
when they think of them in quasi and para military
terms, but not as people who have left behind

the government ways of talking. The people
fighting fires include many who speak of fire as being fed
by policy. Of fire they fight more frequently and overwhelmingly.
Fire that speaks more fire. That shocks — the refusal

to shake a prominent hand, to role-play for authority.
Many people were already aware, and many
had already had lives overturned, burnt out
in previous fire seasons — but now fire

is eternal, it seems, and there is no relief.
Iterations and refrains, an odd out-of-kilter
rhythm of trauma. It just can't go away, not now
when rain is ash and storms are fire making more

fire. We can't scan that metre, we can't count it out.
Elegiac metre? No — that's a celebration of in loss of what
is lost and is premature when it needs not have been lost,
and should be singing now... elegy is an acceptance

we have no room for — the poem needs to act,
to declare, to move faster than flames. To douse
but not flood. What do we call this fast-slow
pace, this resolution to change, to catch up

with what's been shown for an age, the code
long broken? *Vital* metre? Yes, vital. Of the same
energy and pace of celebrating our loved ones —
sincere, compelled — but also outrunning our

own restraints of safety and prudence, of desire
and hope things will sort themselves out. Vital
metre is the recovery, is the pulling back,
is understanding what constitutes the gleam

of the lake when the snow doesn't manifest,
when the basis of liberty is the wealth
made in 'plants' that give no air — let the planet
ventilate *itself*! Rapperswil, close to great mountains

on the edge of Lake Zurich, is a place of roses
with their own relationship to warmth, a raft for waterbirds
accruing in the hard-to-come-by reeds, the strange sight
from the sidewalk of sad llamas stomping on a spot,

resting after their Circus Knie/zoo performances,
and roses, the roses in private gardens budding
out of tune with the calendar, winterless and less,
coming forth to beg us to hear across knots and nodes

of dialect, the need – for their sakes, too –
to adopt a less fallacious poetics, to hear and sign
a new metrics of survival: a vital rhythm of restraint,
of owning only our affections and not objects, of 'less is more'.

JK

66.

I am chasing my language,
it moves with its own ease
and smoothness,

lifts like a dry leaf,
then suddenly turns heavy
and green and false.

I come close, reach for it,
and it slips away,
tantalizingly. It dances

just out of reach,
darts around tree trunks,
slips into the gully,

and turns the colour of everything.
The musk it leaves behind
overwhelms

me with the confusion
of love and sorrow,
my body too slow to settle

on the meaning of the scent.
The way sometimes,
a memory can arouse

something like the desire
that becomes fearfully made.
And even this simile

of a leaf in flight
is false – this is the taunt
that my language throws

back at me, telling me again
and again, with a sound
that I have known,

that I respond to as I imagine
a child does to her mother's hum.
You don't know

what you are looking for,
whether accent, or words,
or understanding –

meaning I don't know
what she is, the language
that carries, I think,

the musk of history,
the mud, the muddiness of my language,
like a stew that carries

the taste of mud, dark, brooding,
not the absence of spice,
but the crowding

of all shades of spice –
the language that comes
as a healing balm, a paste

covering my body;
which is why, she says,
the leaf, the feather, the heavy

lead, those are approximations
of me, but then you don't know
what she is.

KD

*67. for Tracy and Karl*

It's likely a mistake
to determine history
through documents
and buildings, through
records and intensity
of societies for preservation –
living history, eras
revisited with caveats
to now, to the future.
The fortifications
and places of worship,
the tricks of factories
in suburbs, the lake
that drowns if crossed
without firm footings,
the way of pilgrimage
high up, heading to Spain.
In the portmanteau,
as on the camera
memory chip, the
repetitions of salience –
siege, flames, bread,
windows. And contemplation.
I don't know if the weight
of a chronicle is a bell
chiming or thumping,
a long-eared owl or bat,
a canon ball or mitre,
the armies of chapels
and a bourgeoisie
or reformation, stilted
by records, failure
of handed-down or
hand-me-down memory.

What will it be used for?
Today, crossing the railbridge
of the Seedamm, into the small
town burgeoning with hedge funds,
the small town that was so small
when Tracy's first husband
was a child, so small when
he came from the neighbouring
village after his father's
bankruptcy, small before
he went into the Abbey school
for years high up in the mountains,
for years as the town grew
out of its tax laws and incentives
into the now long after his passing.
This recording, a familiar
and unfamiliar pattern
of walking the lake's edge,
always affected by the glare,
glances skating over the still
surface, full of below
and the past's remains.


JK

68.

*Between that earth and that sky, I felt erased, blotted out*
    — Willa Cather

And here on the west coast, weather batters the body in mid-winter.
And the sea has devoured so much beach – look how the waves crest,
raised in ragged relief – snow-white against grey, and the wind
spits rain like stinging sand on my face. I lean forward, feet wet and cold,
while our home in Nebraska is slowly slipping into the place of memory,
the thing that will allow me to manage the passing of time.

It happens, these days, every time I leave, even for a short time;
I am rehearsing departure and the markings of departure in the body –
how the hours pass, where the light starts, the taste of the air – a kind
    of familiar love.
In Lincoln, the weather moves with glacial authority – never fickle, always
deliberate and blunt as a father's reprimand; it stays in our blood
    for whole seasons,
and even when the warmth gathers, the bruising cold settles recessively
    in us like a clue.

I call it now the place where the nation, the nation was made,
long stretches of first shells, the fossils of monstrous fish, the geology
    of beginning
where bodies have arrived in waves blind to the cities built across the land,
where the blind and the deaf and the hungry and the god-shot believers
looked across the empty prairies and had living dreams of cities rising
    from the spongy soil,
gleaming in the heavens, places with the mystical names of tribes
    and noble ancestors.

This land is emptying itself of bodies and dreamers, and those who stay
know deep in their souls that the earth will eventually erase them.
    Whose civilization
will settle in the layers of bones above the mastodon tusks

      and the dinosaur bones,
and the precious stones, the deep oil residue of all carbon,
      the surface reclaiming itself?
The prairie grass waves in the still air. I write about this place as an alien knowing I am as alien as so many aliens who have come through and left, and this is the language of the un-nationed, the homeless, the sojourner.

KD

69.

*Mental travellers* and those of us left with tribulation after the good
folk enjoy the rapture of their own making —

These disembodying utterances of bell towers. These calls of
    *avalanche!*
where snow won't fall but hollowed mountains will — staunch

'diggers & dealers' — heads of state — extend their smokepall, and
    in a rich mall
we eat our sandwiches between mountain walls to the bemusement
    of *the rich circle*.

The World Economic Forum is brewing a couple of mountain chains
and lakes away at Davos, where the rich pay prices they maintain.

Attack helicopters try to imitate red kites but can't — there's
no mimicry of nature in their off design, their beating dead air
    with securities.

From a suburb next to a factory that is blended as reassurance,
medical products go out to world as assisted development,
    smokestacked incense.

We inhale the largesse of the human development index, and
    moles dig to autobahn edges
to challenge divides, expose contaminants, demand we acknowledge.

When bells ring deep beyond that vague cross of joy and annoyance,
    deep into the divvying-up
of forests, stone, water, air, and flesh, we might ask, *Why build
    towers to chime with the corrupt?*

JK

70.

I sift these shadows hoping to gather in small piles the distillation of dark.
The dragon barks from the mountain – if only we could make myth
    and fantasy
of the grumbling about us. I will imagine the deep sense of helplessness
one feels watching the city built on lies, the duplicity of those who
    have sought,
slowly, ever so slowly, to turn the secret of lies into the open-ended remaking
of truth – this is what we call truth today, and if you scratch the surface of me,
what you will find is what I have made, no secret, no hidden knowing.
I remake the world in my own image, and this is the order of things.
Oh, how we will miss the liars, those who knowingly present the world
with the hidden truth. Every great film, every thriller relies on
the hidden thing, the grand design of the monsters who guffaw
at how the world has been deceived – our demons, or devils are no longer
the knowing ones, the ones with truth fully carried inside their blood.
They have acted out of the manageable things, the safe things, vice,
    evil, desire,
greed, power – the things we know to be known. Our new ugliness is
the absence of duplicity – this thing is simply the remaking of what we have
always known, and slowly, ever so slowly, we understand that we
    are fighting
an absence, a void. This is the sorrow. Or perhaps, the quieter we grow,
the more settled we are in this new order of things, my love. The more
our world settles into a dull hunger, a world of nothing, a world
of bland niceness, a world of absence. The other pile is lonesomeness.
My skin is hungry for familiar touch, hungry for the hunger of a touch,
of an embrace, of something honest like the warmth of bodies
pressed together, holding each other through the storm.

KD

## 71. *900 years*

I am saddened that the palindrome
of today can't work for those in China
who wanted luck on their wedding day – postponed.

My birthday by the Australian calendar – 02022020 –
is not in shutdown, though a Sunday, isolated out here
in the bush, nestled in our stockpiles of food

and shaky water supplies that evaporate
in their hot cement chamber, nestled against
the wrap-around of hot easterlies and insane

threat of fire, the sleepless nights that make
a mockery of insomnia – you strain for sleep-
lessness to keep alert, to keep senses tuned

to changes that *presage*: odour, taste, glow.
So, on this nameday, inside this localised but also
regional palindrome that works as well

where our son was born – where you live,
Kwame – worlds in worlds – I think of different calendars
aligning, the contradictions of life's kindling, its ignition,

and the chronologies it leaves in its wake,
to get from beginning to end and back, to reread
to ensure no error. I see the moon tilted in the white heat

of daylight, and I think how far past the lunar
New Year we are, and I send best wishes and affirmations
to those locked down, putting days between themselves
and the virus. I wish them luck, the growth of the moon.

JK

72.

It is only one part of our history that eventually we choose between
the illusion of eternity – the lie that we will not be left bereft,
that loves will not be lost; and this way of preparing ourselves
for shadows. You have chosen to prepare yourself for yourself,
for the worst scenario, and to harden yourself for the loss of me,
you now rehearse the love of me – you are building an edifice
of strength against the loss of me, and here I sit with you, watching
you mourn me, then recover, then grow strong, then walk away.
I have died. I have given up on our love. I have wounded you again.
How strange it is to be alive and whole and yet to be living as if
I am dead. This is a kind of blindness. The city I visit with irritable
consistency, the city of people who feel proud that they would rather talk
and not text, who treat the ritual of muttering emptiness on the line,
complaining about the weather and the traffic, who never take notes,
who never remember what was said, and here I am again, worried
about my absence, a low-grade depression, for all that is normally
shiny is growing dull, as if a mist, a caul has returned to my eyes;
it feels like a matter of time when I will become the invalid, the one
you will have to guide about – this is not hyperbole, as you know;
my family enters its last years in darkness, the strong negotiating
the terror of dependency, how much we have thrived on third sight,
the ability to see things coming – that one stands in the face of a world
and does not know what is coming. I devour winter, devour light,
devour the lines on faces, devour the smiles, devour the crevices in the skin;
I devour colour and the absence of colour, the numbers in white
on green etched on signs, the words dancing across a screen, how
I can follow them, tell one letter from the other, the trail of song
over the screen, this is what I devour now, as if to do so will somehow
horde beauty in me for the deep, sullen, darker days when all my seeing
will turn in on my body, and how I will imagine every single cell
remaking itself inside of me – how much I will live inside me then.

KD

73.

I saturate myself in film and stick in its depths.
Tonight I will watch Otto Preminger at work
across the ad hoc arrangements of noir — of time
and space and the failure of sunlight which seems
so absurd *here*, though violence is not unusual
on farms and in towns, on the roads and along
fencelines. I will view after a stretched day during
which I bent down to study a dugite's quiet eye —
deadly if alive, and I thought it was dead till it lifted —
like hope, like necessity — face to face on a hot road,
on a hot road that was epiphany before it slid away,
and also to see the return of the brilliant red-capped
robin, light amongst the thinned swarm of gnats.
It's so very dry, condensation is a personality trait
we hope for, drinking sweat, pouring it over
the exposed roots of plants that might
only flower once, to show they existed.
I will find no answers in the film, and knowing
this almost makes watching redundant,
though I will, tucked back into place —
especially as I never wish to be 'entertained'.
I am not looking out for the flaws in a social fabric
and expect to find no consolation with their revelation.
Just sadness. The tension is not in the surprise,
but in the inevitability. Snake eye. Robin cap.
I saturate myself in film and stick in its depths.

JK

74.
*For Kamau Brathwaite*

So, John, Kamau dead. There is something deeply silent about snow
covering things and this morning, as if without warning,
snow covered things. And around the Caribbean, people
are studying the portents of the earth – an unexpected bird, a swift,
a flapping banana tree, an apparition discovered in an ancient
photograph, like the one he discerned of the face of a slave ancestor
in a photo he took accidentally at Cow Pastor, the one that prophesied
he stay put, plant there, fighting for the land – and they are all asking
what cataclysm awaits us. And it is not a fancy to say that on days
when the liars strut through these halls of power, when Trump's
contagion of falsehood and unfeeling seeps through the darkness of dawn,
slips over the soft dusty snow, that this deeper silence of Kamau's passing
is a prophecy, a portent of our time; it is how prophets mark epochs,
their births and their passing. I have stopped to look at the way these lines,
these my lines move across the page, and I think slowly, ever so slowly,
and I think of Kamau at the podium, the patience of his voice holding us
in suspension, waiting for the words to find their thorough fullness,
their shape, before he speaks them; I think of how the fragmentation
of his sentences scattered over the page are his way of saying, *Pause*,
saying, *Breathe*, saying, *Trust, poet, that these things we say, each moment
of syntax, each vowel, each breath, fills the world with that roundness
of meaning, of feeling. Trust the making of silence before sound. Trust.*
How I have stood and rushed over language as if afraid of the truth
of my words; how he would fill the hall with the deep baritone of his silence,
his breaths, his speaking, the poems taking shape before us, crackling
with rhyme and song, and it is no wonder that Derek once mocked,
the language's patient occasion – all the time in the world – of it, it, it, it, it, it.
How he mocked that which one cannot have, cannot believe in, cannot trust,
mocked with an envy of soft love and desire – the trier mocking the natural,
the one chosen to hum a deep music of our history into the long darkness.
It is enough, it is enough, Kamau. I will not indulge in the binaries of poets
gladiating against poets – after all, it bored them and should bore us,
and every side was a contradiction of sameness. They were two men

wrestling with language and the fear of silence; biding their time
with the silences and sounds before the inevitable – this long silence
before us now. Still, I say this here – a half joke, easily indulged,
fourth formers conjuring nicknames from the sky, easy teasing –
in the end, the weight of *Negus* overshadows the pettiness
of a convenient joke, and even the clown knew this well.

I have now come around to say that whenever I look at my first poems,
all I see are the stumbling steps of one trying to find footing
in Kamau's prints – how imitable he was, how badly imitated he
    always was,
such bad poems spawned by his delicate craft, the deeper genius
of his lyric architecture, the way it is sometimes so hard to hear
the delicate art of a drum beat, and we all say, beat, beat, beat, imagining
ourselves the makers of the drum, forgetting the slaughter of the goat,
the blooding, the bone-sticks left to blanche in the sun, the rituals
of rum and light, the green stain of crushed leaves, the groaning
of spirits, the rooster in the morning, the cowbell starting to lay
the ground for the muses of history, the muse of memory, the muse
of the deep-sea song. Oh, how we thought ourselves able to master
the master – fools mistaking the kindness of music's doorway, for
    its genius.
Still, without this sloppy imitating, where would I be? Where would I be,
today? Think, then, of the day in London in 1971, deep in winter,
when it did snow, and Neville had arrived to be with us, and he
walked with us through the city; and, chuckling, he gave instructions
for his African children on how to walk in fresh snow, how, he said,
we should look for the footprints of others, and place our feet in them,
and we would not slip. And how, demonstrating this, he did slip,
his two legs thrown upwards to the sky, his arms flailing,
a vision of the unravelling of a man of deep dignity and poise,
something we had never seen before – the vulnerability
of involuntary flight; nor had we seen the athletic acrobatics of him
righting himself, the magic of his ability to turn chaos to a kind of flight,
his tan coat-tails rising then settling at the planting of his feet,
    his knees

in a squat, before, chuckling even more, with the bright astonishment
of balance, he said, "Now, step where I step." And we did,
despite the hint of scepticism for what we had seen, for we knew
we could not turn chaos into dance, into flight and settling,
into a music of a body remembering the genius of its making,
despite the years on him. Though now, my poems have found
     their footing,
and my understanding of the art of deep balance, the beauty of patience,
the authority of love, Kamau, is my marker, my art, my permission,
my reggae aesthetic, my ethos, my beginning, and today I cannot
even use "lament", instead, I say, I look before, hoping the snow
will not cover completely the prints, though far ahead, his long silences,
his long deep silences into the hermitage of his last years, were
a kind of lamentation, one he granted us, granted me. Why it is
that every time I want to speak a poem, I long to find a music, a song?

Walk good, Kamau, tek time, walk good, Kamau,
no words are enough, nothing is enough, nothing
but these torn and constantly new words gathered here.

KD

75. *now was the sea*

'Consequence of fact' is an *impossible* dismissal
of what is, what was — the salty speaking whose moment

we follow, we trace, we step inside. It can't be a shucking
of a skin to lose the shape we step into, no moving

on. It's all contained, then breaks out and falls away
simultaneously — the shell we pick up from washed

sands but don't listen into, having done so often
as children, even for those kids coming from inland

to see where the world as they believe is tested,
just shells picked up to think of the lives they

contained, their nacre, then dropped half gently
back onto the sand, the briefer tide marks closer

to water at the points of going in/coming out,
and part of us still listening for answers, regretting

we didn't lose ourselves in the first encounter
with shell and the sea inside the shell, *the oceans*,

a fortune-telling as science, the collectible moment.
But they're still there, those listenings, and they are

replete with answers of lament welded with hope
because the consequence of losing focus on the horizon

is not to reach it, or to forget its possibilities if we stay still,
which is okay, too. I *had* been writing glibly

of prophets and prophecy, of the collapse
of ecological narratives, but *now* I am reminded

by loss of the facts of voice, of the followings
that open so many paths between sea and land,

the consciousness of journeys of voice-spirit,
of island and continents and currents shifting, shifting.

JK

76.

The camera follows the limping poet through the city – miles and miles –
then the sudden squall of snowfall, the whirl of flakes, the smiling
dogwalkers, and the long silence of the high trees naked of leaves.
The camera stutters, distracted by the flight of geese, and then returns
to the upright gaze of the poet – he thinks that all art preserves history
even if falsely. At the apartment, the photographer with his lanky
hungry leanness, the look of an addict still competent to create art
and care for the elderly, moves on his toes about his apartment
of Persian rugs and shelves festooned with books of leather spines
     and insides
unevenly stuffed with browning pages, this special kind of
     nonchalant wealth –
look at the address and see the height of the ceilings. The photographer,
in jeans and a black t-shirt, tells me to remove my glasses while he
adjusts the natural light spilling in from the grand park – and there is
no more ceremony than that. First I see his eyes, the way his dark hair falls
over his forehead, the worry lines on his weary face, the deep hollow
of his cheeks, and then he mists into a soft muddy shape, coaxing
with language. I am naked now, as if my body belongs to a stranger,
and he starts his causal dance around, barely speaking, lift a chin,
thanks, a polite pause, then the tick, tick, tick, then pause to see,
the tick, tick, tick. I said, "I would rather not." He said, "the glare."
I said, in resignation, that I will never use these anyway, for what
am I without sight, my eyelashes now obscenely long from the glaucoma
drops, my nose bridge, scarred by the press of the spectacles?
And he moves about me, and creates a swirl of silences. I can smell
the soft funk of my crotch, the flesh rubbed into a tender bruise
from five miles of steady walking, and the warm perfume of my armpits
rises as a kind of mist over me. He circles, he squats, he sits demurely
on a paisley-covered stool, then abruptly he says it is over.
I reach for my glasses. The room is dustier than I remembered it.
The light is sharply orange; it smashes into everything, and I understand
that history is always this way – always bodies beside bodies,
and maybe words, and a transaction of dreams, and exchange, perhaps,

though mostly, we are rehearsing how to say goodbye, after
the unremarkable helloes. I will keep walking today, through the city,
with no affection, just the sense of having arrived and left with nothing
to show for it but the desperate promises of strangers – they promise
the world as if it is the job of those who live here to promise
that dreams are real. The poet is a craftsman, a master of dalliance,
the murderer with an alibi, the counterfeiter of love:
how gracefully his clothes fit in a new country in a strange tongue.

KD

77. *history of farming in the Western Australian 'wheatbelt' as a demi-sonnet*

The photographer demanded removal of eye-glasses
in a field of wheat where only touch of sharp ears
and smell of ripeness were guides to the cradle
one had been dropped in – natural habitat
for 'rural poet', but the tint on the lenses
too much for readers with no more than a passing
interest, a flick of the page, or swipe of screen,
just a moment of absurdity – poet already
light-blown, overexposed in wheat crop, tinder
dry to be harvested any day now, crouched
to spring before the knives and forks of header
rolling to lop you off, collect and winnow, leave
chaff of lines that barely scan in the fanfare
of pastoral, farmers and farms blurred in this picture.

JK

78.

This deep throbbing hunger is my belly's elegy, and history —
I am collecting the addresses of those homes we have lost,
the mortgages abandoned to cover the debts of the wayward,
and in generations, the slow decay becomes the norm.
We never owned anything, we the socialist renters, moving
from nation to nation signing the leases, and when the landlords
on a furlough from their bungalows in Florida offered the place
for a price, the old man said, no, he said, no, and this is how we lived,
from rental to rental, middle-class educated poor, and then comes death
and the burden of all these unsecured loans — the address is our history —
Carlisle Avenue, Kings House Road, Bird Sucker Drive —
bivouacs for casual living. Now we who owned nothing, own land,
though I have not learned the art of property. I am weary, so weary
through the nights, my heart in constant doubt, as if perhaps
with time and practice I will learn not to fear the broken heart,
the betrayal, the terror of rupture. Eventually, we who live
inside history go blind to its machinations. We all, if we understood
our deeper self, long to be the harbingers of destruction;

      and destruction

is my daily state — the things that my words can say — I have
questions to ask, and I dread the anger that will arrive. I have
the brain of a playwright; I construct narratives of betrayal and dramas
of revelation, and everybody in my life, close to me, is a character
creating moments of unbearable pain; and I fear what I think I know
but do not know for sure. To think that this is the shadow that covers
my days. To think that in this epoch of untruths and lies spoken
without guile, but as if they are true, how green the grass is
in midwinter, and such the like: this is the shadow of these years. I walk
through the days with the deep hollow weight of fear in my stomach,
and I have no one to share this with, no one who has the language
to understand my stuttering words, and this is how the history
of these years, of these days will settle. "Do you have friends
I know nothing about who consume your days and make you laugh,
who have given you the balm to somehow offer me kindnesses

you have suffered to give for years? What is the difference,
how does one read the difference between forgiveness, and guilt —
how is one's kindness a compensation for the delicate betrayals?"
We arrive while the sun is still preparing for the day and, all in white,
we roam the fields, skanking to the roots-man, then the horses of white
and sorrel and red, stomping under the cypress trees; then the priest
squatted in the temple. My family tells me I must write happy poems —
every poem I write is a failure, every poem I write is a hankering
      for assurance.
*I wish it would rain, rain, rain in my brain, Father, water, in altar.*

KD

79. neither mondegreen nor oronym

Sometimes I attach myself to a musical phrase
or fragment of song in the hope of being drawn along
a different timeline – but motifs grown from raw materials
of other lives bother me, so I remember wrong, reciting
a different lyric, a slightly different tune. These are no variations
on a theme, but dysfunctional moments that sound wrong
then sound right, as if I am uttering what I heard, a mimicry
that with a little practice pulls me into a time and place
I have nothing to do with. This worries me, and I try
not to hum or sing without thinking over what I am doing,
but it gets the better of me. I learn via my mother
that my grandmother – lover of poetry – used to let
'*Epicacuanna* Wine and Mallashallahazbaz' be what
they were as sound distracted from meaning, because
it rolled beyond its history, its exquisite or maybe
terrible underpinnings. Tracy notes the plant –
medicinal for some – ipecacuanha – and that,
as they say, also rolls off the tongue in all languages.

JK

80.

She writes, "You who see me, see my body in this land,
you must know that I come from five generations of settlers."
Gwartney writes this in the untidiness of an indulgent history,
a wilful merging of the guilt that the descendants of pioneers
carry, a resentful, mealy guilt – a polite guilt, tamping down
the burning to say, "We suffered too – do you think a tomahawk
planted inside the brain of a white woman, or the rape of the body
of my ancestors and their adjacents, do you think that is not suffering?
And yes, yes, I know, I know we invaded, we stole,
but we suffered, too, and now silence is all, for those of us
who have tried to learn the names of the valleys
and rivers and mountains in the native tongue; it's a game,
a kind of false-telling; call it peace-making, call it silence."
A new book is gathered on missionary Narcissus, the persistent
martyr, and somehow defying the wretchedness of guilt, she persists.

With dates attached to their births and bloody deaths,
the slaughtering by marauding tribes, this is the language.
It is not envy I feel for the settled assurance of this blood history,
this handful of dirt, this avenue of tombstones,
this history of shame and pride, this bitter remembrance and forgetting;
nor do I feel the hunger for the legends of how we begin –
the brown, aged leaves, the handily-bound books, stitched
to last through the decay of time, the dank, the floods, the heat,
the feasting silver insects, the historical accounts that are held
in museums, the findable legacy of one's beginning; it is not envy, I feel.

But what I marvel at is how all it takes is a cluster of names
to cover a nation – how the things forgotten because of hate,
because of the burden of insignificance, because of the lack
of arrogance, or because their faith does not allow the rescuing
of the dead – the lineage of ancestry to be restored to a holy land
by the rightful naming – as if that which was bound in name on
the earthly plain was sealed in the heavenly realm. I marvel at how

it matters only that one small tribe is remembered, so that the unnamed
tribes will be footnoted. This is unfair, we must add – that the enslaved,
the brutally broken tribes, the slaughtered nations, have been left
to gather dust in the forgetting of history, and this is the cruelty of history.

This is the terror of history. And in this, in the words we share, John,
the legend of my past and your past, the aroma of what we are
collecting here, the names of acres of land captured and stolen or
returned or settled or left unsettled; the names of the bodies here
with us and gone; the stories of our hearts, our fears, our loves and desires;
in this, I know, hidden, perhaps in a kind of embarrassment
that am defying the great disappearance, the expunging of memory,
the emptying of those shaped like me with voices tuned like mine,
with eyes dark as mine, with swollen ankles, and thighs
defiantly swollen, with hair densely matted, we with the genetic selves
kept – a cousin, I would say, or perhaps a nation's imprint of some kind
of being, some kind of belonging.

It is this I am seeking to keep – yes, what my old man called
the perfume of history – or was it of poetry? The perfume of poetry,
when he could have chosen "stench", the foul canker, the rot, the souring,
the funk; but instead offered the soothing perfume that poetry is,
that aroma that will cover history and its multitude of sins,
a multitude of festering wounds, a multitude, my friend.

KD

## 81. *some family albums*

'What if?' cannot let be collapsed
into anaphora – no repetition
in beginnings to commence
down same paths, no repetition
absolving the guile of questions
providing no answers. Those tricky
cameras with their tricky shots.
The false eye of a well-ground lens.
The portrait painters, the sketch
artists. Newspaper column inches.
Telegraphic economics. As one story
prompts another – *all of us –
I can relate to that – so close
to my experience – it's hard to imagine –
empathy – sympathy – unable
to relate – disconnect – nothing
to do with me – don't hold me
responsible… I was born here,
what am I supposed to do – culpability – blame –
denial – refusal – we are all in the same
boat – together – we'll all suffer
if…* positioning around the gaping wounds,
the desolations, the endgame…
responses, consequences –
but each moment, each life, each damage
is unique in its horror and loss
and not to be deleted by the blocking out
that comes with confronting
the massiveness of the crimes,
the bloodbath that is teased out
into 'history' – into different strands –
overlapping, interactive, but separable
to get something absorbable
and processable and consumable

out of it all. To make something
out of the 'here and now'
to build on, to learn from, to front
up to as legacy, to refuse, to lament.
*Art* adds curlicues. It sweetens and salts
according to taste. The art of the photographer
is discovered in family snaps. But those stories
hidden within stories we so often want to forget,
don't we, really, at least temporarily, or till
the appropriate time, or until we break out
of the album, struggling
for clear air, to get a breath out
of the happy-sad-occasional fallout. I've
searched out redemptive qualities of memory
and know they're as selective
as the pages of old photo albums –
the mounted corners left in place
with the brighter patch of card
where an unwanted memory
was lifted. We're talking old school,
historic mode of presentation – 1980s
back back back… to a beginning,
to plates, exposure, the world
standing still, families unmoving.
This can be – is – simulated electronically,
but the visceral quality of removal from time
wouldn't be the same – adapting
to the moment, all inappropriate
portrayals excised to avoid having
to make awkward explanations:
personal histories that could have
gone any way, but went this or that
way in particular, now best re-
routed or even forgotten. Adjustment?
Adaptation? Rectification? Idealism?
Respect? Appropriate behaviour?

Morality? Redress? Amelioration?
A relative or ex- or friend
no longer wanted, but the rest
of the image just fine? Excision.
'What if?' cannot let be collapsed
into anaphora — no repetition
of tactics of evasion, of *where
can I go* in the mess that is both
heritage and inheritance, which
can be cherry-picked or have
the eyes picked out of it to make
it palatable as ancestry? Yes, dear
friend, to let the perfume rise
out of the stench, but different
flowers are likely being talked about,
and *the stench* can be decorative and baroque
in the retelling for some of those
who'd lay claim, who'd buy
into stories without suffering
the consequences — what if
the colonists and the slavers,
the colonist-slavers, deploying
their manners to pass on the patterns,
had said, No, this is no way
to go about making our future,
mapping an inheritance for our
progeny. What if they had *said*,
what if they had *pulled back*,
had *shared their bread*, given
back *what they'd taken*? Asked
for sanctuary rather than taking
and re-scaping and fencing? Learned
new habits? Imagine the 'great poems
of the self' never reaching the shores
of 'destiny', and the tones
of poems rustling leaves,

proud of every photo taken
because it can be shared
without shame, without
answering for crimes
of effacement, denial.
The art of perfume,
the flowers that were.

JK

82.

*But someone will have to pay*
*for all the innocent blood*
*that they shed everyday,*
*O, childen mark my word,*
      — Bob Marley, "We and Dem"

On the dreary trudge — the frontier begins. A hundred years later,
almost two, a woman says in the way of appeasement,
"Perhaps it is true, that for us to live so well,
some of them had to die…?" The question suggested
by the nervous lift in inflection at the end of the phrase —
and who is this "us" who have lived so well, who are living
so well, and how well — so that there is a peculiar
justification, a terrible logic, and it is a haunting
confession buried deep inside the book, though, in truth,
there is no question there. This is its own duplicity, this questioning,
this effortless way of speaking the tragic: there has been blood,
so much blood, and the rituals of bludgeoning,
of rust-tanned white men, clichéd westerners, hunters,
the stereotypes, the killers of vermin rabbits
under-wheel of trucks, the people she knows intimately,
like a daughter knows her father, knows her brothers,
knows the scent of Scotch on her grandfather's breath,
knows the comfort of their manliness, stoic as stone — they will kill,
as easily as threaten even the softer bodies of their women.
It is a logical equation, a management of ethics,
and who are the dead, the slaughtered and the erased?
Tribes and tribes whose faces I do not know,
though I know the logic of this pragmatism,
this expiation of guilt (but the embrace of guilt,
as a kind of penance) is familiar; and the faces of those
bloodshot eyes, skins chalky with deprivation, the weary look
of slaves, those faces are as familiar as the panting bodies
of the football team strewn on the wide grass, undressed

in the heat, sweating, bodies broken after pleasure, the familiar look
of black bodies coffered by desire and violence, as familiar as this —
and that saying, that Darwinian logic, offered in the soft voice
of a mid-western woman who never rushes her words,
who carries in her throat the secret to receiving mercy,
a kind of forgiveness, an expiation of guilt,
who we count among those in whose mouths ice couldn't melt —
mouths of tender duplicity. Perhaps, perhaps for us to live
as we do, and by this, I mean me, today, perhaps,
it's true that someone would have to pay, as we say.

KD

## 83. historicising

History will give nothing back — it takes and takes
and builds structures that crumble even as they *offer*
shelter. Taken to court, the shoddy builder who has taken
short cuts and scoured a conscience with aggregate,
argues, *I provide housing cheap for the poor, so*
*corners have to be cut to make ends meet*. Or the state,
housing en-masse: to the benefit of the many the towers
tumble and are cleared away and built over. History
of title deeds and planning permissions. An expectation
that history teaches us: *that we improve generation*
*by generation, contract by contract*. On stolen land
pegged by timeline-and-map history, I cherish the arrival
of rain, a damping of the spirits to lift prospects, and the rub
of incompatibles — thunder over wet dryness, an odour
of contradiction. It's selective from the relative isolation,
but where, say, fire can make death its common purpose,
epitaphs form in common across the vast differences.
And so, I look down into the valley, as if to look
up at the heavy clouds over the hill is embarrassing,
a coy moment of watching rivulets make erosion
in older and older erosions to reform like an origin
I can't see — so much is affected by fenceposts,
so much by gravel driveways sheeting down
to cottages and shacks… the gravel scooped
out from laterite hills that are still brazen bush
and forest. So much unspoken here, and yet
it shrieks, like the slow steady hum of rain:
what you hear is not what's being said.
But looking down into the valley I saw
a doe and its joey watching me through
the rain, perched on the edge of the skinned
firebreak, and I smiled and said to them, What
lessons from history can we share? And they looked
away, ashamed for me, registering my embarrassment

with the clouds over the hills I could feel
and wished would stay for a good while,
      a good while yet.

JK

84.
*Postlude/ Prelude*

And what we have not said, John, is wider and broader
than what we have said, and yet we have said so much,
and yet in the much there is hidden the grace of the little things.
For to say *pebble* is to say the beginning of all things,
and the end of all things. I admit that every morning,
the news wafts into my half sleep and fills me with the weight
of unknowing — and it makes me wonder if all I need
is silence, perhaps the sound of the sea, or the relentless
grace and prayer of an island spread out from the vantage
of the green and thick-treed mountains full of the mist.
But there is so much that one must call history, and it is true
what you've said, that history is the organizing of memory —
was it you? Perhaps I said it, and I may have also said that history
is what we keep and what we keep is not all, and what is left,
perhaps this is the history that you and I have sought to return to
again and again. And this is why I feel inadequate hearing someone
speak the words: "they disappeared in a pink mist" —
which is half remembered — but I do recall they were speaking
of four men dying with bombs strapped to their bodies —
oh such a fanciful detail, something like the petals of hibiscuses,
things that multiply in their beauty again and again, so ordinary,
and to think that somehow this image was never part
of my reckoning with history, not until this accidental hearing,
on a day that will be obscure and mean little for me,
though each day I know that history is being marked somewhere,
somewhere else. Poetry is our art of multiplication. It sits
in a bowl and grows like yeast, the leavening of feeling,
and this will then been carried across borders, across hearts,
across centuries, the sustenance of bread, the sustenance
of decay, the disease of rot that feeds us. I know now
that scattered across the incidentals of my daily alertness
are these reckonings with history — as if the artists have left us
with these clues to unsettle the ordinary rituals of our days.

You will, I know, understand how we are made by what we know
and what we barely know, and if we are honest,
by what we do not know, not in the old ways of knowing.


i)
After Lalla Essaydi's *The Silence of Desire*

Two woman, naked, casual as an accidental sighting,
the bodies turned as if there is no gaze, as if they are
looking in on themselves – the way of thought, two bodies
framed in four frames – not a fragmenting, but an isolating
of the calm desire of bodies, standing there, one
penning on a wall in henna the lines of an old holy song
so long memorized that it becomes as holy as grass
or sand, or the ordinariness of water – the holiness
of words remembered as words and without meaning;
the other creates tender henna markings on the soft
folds of the other's back, at the right side, above
the clavicle, there where no eyes will see, not even
hers, not even those of a lover, as secret as desire,
and what she writes is a whisper of something tender
and hidden, the lie she has kept secret, the act she
will never forget, but will never speak, though she giggles
and answers the question, "What did you write?":
"A thing I will never say, but you will carry on you
until, in the thirteen days have passed, especially if
you do not place the rough cloth on it when you wash,
especially if you let only water and dollops of coconut
oil tenderize the place. You carry my secret on you."


ii)
Two women fully clothed, but not clothed at all, for what
spreads like unruly ocean waves about them is the calico
spread of cloth – the garments to make make garments,

they are stitching, their fluent lines of dried blood, making even
circles, and the blooming of flowers multiplied, and multiplied,
naked for the domestic vanity of their hair, black, unruly,
carried as if someone has told them that this is their pride,
though for every bolt of dark I imagine the absence of crowns,
the last vestige of all humanity. Two women sit, circled
by cloth, oh cloth, oh cloth, the bolts of cloths that the hands
of Accra women will gather in bundles for all rituals, all births,
and weddings, all deaths – the cloth stained with the blood
of all rites of passages. Two women make lines of grace
on the off-white fabric, imagining the secret gathering of their bodies
the face covered, the hair covered, the body sheathed
in the suggestion of flesh – the flesh covered, and the nakedness
hidden. A silent mouth suggests an army of words.
Why take me into this deep sacred courtyard, why hold my hand
and guide me through the oasis of green, to the sand garden
where these bodies draw lines with the soft thin brush
dipping into the clay bowl filled with blood, crushed henna,
the broken leaves that turn all skin into stain, deep stain?
I close my eyes, but these eyes cannot undo the din of silence.


iii)
I am a witness to the transgressions of art – I stand aside, taking
glances, a *prips*, as we say, though if you looked my way, my eyes
would avert to the sky, my lips moving as if in prayer or thought,
for the closet of women, the sacred rooms where the bodies
allow the sun to feed their skins, where heavy palms full of oil,
and cocoa butter scooped by generous fat fingers, and smeared
on the bodies most private secrets, the firm massage of oil deep
into skin, these rituals among the discarded fabrics of the undressing,
the cloth, wave upon wave of fabric, caught in the camera's attraction
to the movement of folds and curves – the kinetic grace of cloth,
these are the secrets that the gallery opens to me and my transgression
is to study the shape of these bodies, as one seeing for the first
time, searching the backdrop for the thick intensity of forests

beyond the walls, the tropic sky, its blue brilliant as hope; and art,
the art of women defies the prison's muting tones – into the secret
garden, into the secret courtyard, into the casual way of bodies
so varied and complex, the feet, the feet, bare on the tiled floor,
the feet moving across the room, the dance of feet, the art of feet
leaving only the oil residue that only ants notice, how they move
around the prints left behind, how they worship by their reshaping
the contours of feet – the ants know that these bodies have been here,
and this is what holiness can be in the white halls of all secrets.


iv)
If then there is a body liberated from the prison of cloth, then the barrier
is a flimsy as love and, at the market, the women let their fingers
flow through the falling bolt of cloth as if gathering the fabric
to form a pool to wash the face, to clean the orifices, to cleanse
the eyes, to remove the residue of sorrow's tears, with Nina Simone
talking robots, talking to the people, her southern tones growing
deeper into history, into Senegal, talking about tear drops of love,
the language of stains, not so much the tears for the clearing of splinters,
not of laughter, or perhaps the tears of laughter like the tears of sorrow
are the tears of a body broken for you, and for me; and the women
in the market place, the fluid fabric against their skins, and you read
into the patterns the rituals of the prison of the veil, the prison of the covering,
and then only then, when covered, as the growing girl into women will
be covered, she discovers that what is not seen, what is not conceived
by the lazy eye is the true liberation – and in the shelter
of the fluid fabric, its spill to the floor like a rippling pool, there
in the harem, there in the isolation of a man's economy, there,
her fabric, her ghazals, written into the cloth with a brush dipped
into the blood of henna, and the henna, like tears is heavy
with protein, and the proteins of sorrow and the proteins
of the laughter – the one open field, beyond the courtyard, the stretch
of the impossible free into the sea, or towards the mountains,
this is the healing that the women lounging in the harem – the chaise,
the cushion, the carpets, the rugs, there on the waiting place,

drunk with black thick tea, drunk with waiting, there the rituals
of clothing, of the veil, of the cloth falling gently over the hair,
the last prisoner being the eyes – the last jail, and then in absence
she is free. My friend the Iraqi poet says the artist does not know
the prison of the harem, and this is what we lose, what is lost.
Outside every shelter of women and their bodies, every prison
of cloister, outside the rooms where stitching and cooking, and writing,
and singing and the planning for factories and bridges and churches,
the world continues in its mangy march. If there is a body liberated
from the prison of cloth, the barrier is flimsy as love.


v)
After *The House Is Black*, film by Forough Farrokhzad

Who living in this hell is praising you? Fearfully and wonderfully made,
Mother God without labour you have given birth to time, and in this
dispensation of faith we ask no incriminating questions – and love is
the acceptance of miracles, of great miracles. These bodies never enter
the harem – they are broken bodies with the deep wrinkles of leprosy
and the wounds of skin hardened by the calcification of decay,
though the mouths speak psalms of praise, the flight of doves
to the desert lands a shelter from the eyes of the disgusted. I ask you why
you punish me with evasions, knowing full well that in my worry
I bite my tongue fiercely in my sleep and wake with my heart
a-flutter with dread. I ask why is there kindness after years of bruising anger
and I imagine that the sinned-against has now sinned against
and offers kindness to mask guilt. Is this paranoia, my love,
my nation, my exile land? Will you be there for me
when I am suffering? Will you be at my side when my body
is failing – to whisper, "Home" into my years, to usher me
into our history? Or will you leave me to the technicians and the faceless
staff, their rough hands, their impatience? Will you take my hand,
walk me through the deep wounds, the forest of aromas,
naming each scent for me, humming the melodies of birds
and the groan of engines, teaching me the shape of a mountain

by the echoing of sound? Will you be the comfort in my darkness,
oh my love, my nation, my exile land? Over time, I calculated
how I have wounded others into a silent detente, how they wait
for the ordinary way of retribution – no conviction; where once
there was love, now there is care; and care is practical,
fickle, and never desperate. To my love, my nation, my home, I ask,
When news of my near death came, how soon did you ready yourself
for mourning, how quickly did lament pass into the romantic
beauty of elegies? Deep into the night, I watched an actress
shatter the calm of the night, her voice breaking through the cocoon
of my private watching, her wailing, in hiccups and then louder
and louder, at the news, the invention of a daughter's death –
her face a perpetual crumbling for the rest of the film,
never returning to its former shape – and in this I imagine
what mourning is like. I wanted to ask my love if her body collapsed inside
at the prospect of my passing. But I feared asking. I wanted to ask
my nation how soon was the obituary drafted, who was selected,
and what will be the ritual of my homegoing – have you rehearsed
the language of mourning, or are we now impatient with the waiting
– too soon, too soon, too soon? But as you know, I dare not ask these things.
I feared asking, for love, like history, after wounding, is pragmatic –
after labouring with the lepers, is pragmatic, after forgiving
and re-forgiving each day, after muting the tart of betrayal, is pragmatic;
"You fight the urge to do wrong, and when you fail,
you ask for forgiveness, and then move on."

vi)
The forensic artist leaves the labs and enters the abattoir
where the stench of death returns. She studies the art of rotting flesh,
the preservation of heat and dry air, the patterns of desert sand
on the pelt of the cow. She is a matador, she is a bold body
cast in bronze; cover me, she says, in the thick grease
and lay over me the clay of our beginning,
and leave me like a corpse to settle into permanence.
Bronze is the power of memory, bronze is our last art,
and in the Benin foundry: bronze, bronze, bronze.

*We, jah people can make it work...*

If you are hearing me now, says the poet, if these breathless lines,
stumbling through language, these borrowed words, these words
caught in the swirl, caught and planted here, and now spoken; if you can
hear me now, neighbour, you were brought to this, which frightens
the dry bones, and so many dry bones, and I, the preserver of pelts,
I the maker of this fabric of gathered wayward words, I am doing
the work prepared, prepared, prepared before me and you.
The forensic poet covers his body with the cast of clay, and then fills
the crevices with bronze, then sets me, wrinkled and worn
in the gleaming sun. Study, I say, the contours of tumours,
of wounds, of blemishes, the pores of skin, for in this brokenness
is beauty. Somewhere in the Old Testament there is an account
of artisans making tumours and deep festering wounds
of bronze, an entire exhibition of the decay of the body, the things that kill
with steady efficiency, the boils, the distended growths,
shaped with such precision and detail, and then shelved for all to see,
as if in this some kind of ritual of resignation is made. It is true
we make art of the things we fear, and we build shrines, altars
for the things that terrify us; we make songs to confront the canker
of history. The analogy is crudely obvious, but at times the obvious is art.

KD

85. *respiration*

I am listening to Jimi Hendrix's set
with his 'band of gypsies' at Woodstock,
specifically to 'Izabella' whom, we
hear, the persona will soon
be holding instead of a machine gun.
Vietnam. Vietnam. Vietnam.
Song tautens the ear with the jags
and cascades and eschatons
of battle and love, with passion
and lust, with the incursions
of death-rents, as he tears apart
the 'Star Spangled Banner',
replete with every injury,
every torn body of either side,
of the absurdity of war. This
Hendrix is also, in *some* ways,
in some ways at least, the shy Cobain
who worried about the way men
treated women in the rockworld,
who loved peace and 'blew his brains out'.
In some ways. In many ways not.
And history resides in the not,
in some ways, in many ways. Favouring.
Funerals are for the many ways.
This corrosion of breath, this end
of respiration, the sounds of breathing,
the rasp, the sweetness we inhale
from those we love, of those
we desire. All this makes
interstices in the history
I construct, feeling guilt
that goes nowhere. I used
to work it out on the drums,
now my son does, and he's

so much better! Each roll,
each accent, each double-kick —
an organisation of mood, of impression,
of call and response, of moving
with history. I say to him, You
are in the history of now, trying
to find a way through. Why
would anyone condemn such
release? It is an act of breathing,
it is life coming back against
pandemic, it is healing and restoration.
It is health, it is community, it is alone
and of the many. It undoes the binaries.
I am thinking of Isaiah's rant against
the trinkets and adornments of women,
a special damnation in his condemnation
of departures from the way of the Lord.
I am seeing his rich language, his
embellishments in a fury of deliverance,
the warning that demands to be taken.
But for me, the women implicated
in the story lift above the decay,
are the way through, have answers,
ways of communing with the spirit
Isaiah is asking the Lord to bestow
on him. Messengers that need to be heard,
already trying to say something about
gaze and control, about liberty and art,
about choice and deprivation.
I climb and fall with the glissandi
out of markets and 'entertainment'
into a profound welling-up of text
and singing, of timbrels and cymbals.
Why is it that Tobi Vail, drummer
of Bikini Kill is discussed by some
in terms of her relationship to Kurt

Cobain? We will discuss Kurt Cobain
in terms of his relationship with Tobi Vail.
We will talk about acts of 'influence'.
Of cross-pollination. Of privacy.
The ease of answering such questions
is the ostinato we roll with so readily?
Listen to Vail's drumming to understand.
I am sure Kurt did. I am sure. I follow
a drumline and find voices,
and shudder with fear and joy
and disturbance at the sources as I
envisage them. That sound of the stomach
of mother, the testing to see what's going
on with you so close to birthing,
I remember that – a piano moment,
a percussion instrument, a reaching
back as past's presence is felt,
emerging from the ocean, breathing,
hitting the high-hate stars without violence,
ringing with a love for time passing,
and for remembering, for remembering
that 'Purple Haze' was always
a love song for Hendrix.

JK

86.

*After Dionne Brand*

On Sunday, I walk out of her many paragraphs – her versos –
with my body bruised with beauty and pain – what they call
a lashing in Trinidad – my muscles throbbing with the ache,
as if we have been quarrelling, or rather she, my friend,
has been lashing me with her tongue. How she dares me
with her assured polemics – she is a revolutionary,
she will remain a revolutionary, not a witness to war,
but a witness to the effect of war; and I know that what she offers
in the considered gait of her intellect is beauty, though
she scoffs at this, and beauty is what throbs through my body.

I tell a thin Nigerian poet who walks with the jauntiness
of a settled immigrant – I explain history intimately –
that I know my grandfather lived in history because
in those days when a ship arrived, the broadsheet
newspapers would record each passenger and the same
when they left, and so each day the waiving of kerchiefs
and tears formed an image tucked into the deep ink of dailies,
and my grandfather's name is there. He left his village
and walked into history. It is a kind of way to remain,
the ship's ledger – the names of those who were to set sail.
"Bon voyage," they say. "Bon voyage." And in Brown's Town
and Kingston and Mandeville, someone says, is Englan'
dem gone, is Englan', Dover, or Portsmouth or Liverpool.
"What a ting," they say. "What a ting." Though among
the congregation in the early dawn, those who stood
at the cusp of the hill and watched the dray and cart
bend its way around the narrow mountain lanes until
they vanished into the thick trees, those who stood
in the dew, and then walked slowly back into the chapel,
to kneel and finish the prayers, they know it is Africa,
they know it is Nigeria, they know it is Warri, words

they have come to know as they have learned the names
of the prophets and the obscure personages of the Holy
Word, and so they pray against the haunting of the monsters
they fear, and embrace the promise of homecoming
that my grandfather would have offered, that man
of broadness, broad shoulders, broad forehead, broad
nose, broad lips, broad language, broad arms, broad
faith, that man dark as all our ancestry, who smiled
and strolled through the village, saying farewell, walk good,
write me, write me.

                "I am writing my way out of a nightmare,"
says my friend to herself, or to her Clerk, as she calls her, the Blue
Clerk, though in time the self is not a poet, but an author,
and she is the one before us, accounting for, in her chronicle
of unforgivable things, the outed rogues gallery of genius
white men, Locke and his Africa Company shares, and Eliot
with his drowning negroes, and Plato and his mansion
of slaves — they with their humane contemplations, their books
the edifice of this civilization. And she says, "I cannot bring
myself to forgive them"; and she says, "I am just a lover",
which she does not mean so much as "Can you forgive?"
She is, then, our friend, and so is Brathwaite, and so is Césaire
and Morrison and Mackey, Morejon, and Harris, and Wynter,
and so are all those poets who once lived as hermits
in the deep dark catacombs of the empire's libraries, the archives
of cruelty, the evidence of their great sins (though she does not
believe in sin). Like serial murderers, they have kept keepsakes,
mementos of their crimes, leaving them for their coughing
descendants to unearth. "I can't bring myself to forgive,"
she says, as if she does believe in forgiveness, as if what others have done
is forgive, as if Caliban's compromise is forgiveness, though
all of this that we do is not forgiveness, which is not ours
to give, nor is it ours to withhold, as if there is power in this.
Rather we reckon this is all, we contend this is all, we expose
to the air the heavy perfume of history — the stench of it.
In the half light of a March morning I intrude on myself,

my naked, shadowed body moving across the mirror,
a kind of strangeness, familiar as memory; there is comfort
in the revealed secrets of my body in half light. And as I read
over these our lines, I intrude on myself. This is our art,
two men intruding on themselves, intruding on their own lives,
intruding on each others' lives, with the interruptions of our words.

In his weakest moments, my father was beautiful, with
the old doubts of a young man leaving the familiar earth
of a village that held the spirits of old slaves, old Africans
taken into the terror and lamentation of exile – this before
the bolstering faith of his mento-Marxism, the dreams
of revolution, the rum and gin and tonic, the colonial embrace
and resistance – oh, the dreams, the dreams, before that return
to the island, to the deep whispers of doubt, to the broken-
down Ladas, to the rent and the loans, to the silence of nights
waiting to hear the news of the polls, the loss of friends,
the dying, the betrayals, the ones who announced that they had
outgrown conviction – and in that softness, the clerk and her author
would have called him weak, broken, lost, but I remember
him as tender, and a complete poet, his tongue reaching for words
that could turn the twilight into a kind of hope – and yes,
it is true that for months he listened to the sweating radio
preachers promising damnation, though what he listened for
were the occasional bright slivers of poetry in the blues
of the moment, the jazz of the moment. I say the broken
will chronicle our history, beautifully, and this is my hope,
dear, friend, this is my hope for the days left to us.

KD

# II: A CODA TO HISTORY

## INDEX OF FIRST LINES

1. It's a long drive along the valley past struggling patches   199
2. A vision deprived of hope may be just a cliché – which is itself   200
3. No poet can serve the state and tell us a truth   202
4. They will call it hope, they who say, look to The After Earth,   204
5. I didn't think I'd have the strength to write this today,   205
6. Then, let us chant against *have not charity*,   206
7. Yes, Kwame, charity is beautiful and charity is a tissue, a web,   209
8. In these silences, the bubbles of hurt are indistinguishable   210
9. There are rumours of a better humanity after this experience   212
10. In Kingston, the sirens fill the twilight air –   213
11. We are not writing our elegies, but we are writing   216
12. And the good news is that there are friends who will tell you   218
13. So caught in the local which stretches so far   220
14. More than a coda, this interim is now turning   222
15. I watch birds divide into flocks of beginnings and ends   224
16. A glimmering streak of laughter falling from the upstairs room   225
17. There is too much space around my making of poems.   228
18. Thankful for the way the wind carries words   229
19. I woke to the madness that is 'Liberate Michigan'   231
20. A poor joke which is not a joke – this is our corona,   232
21. Just back from another food drop and an encounter   234
22. Somewhere in the catacombs of those four quartets   235
23. So, in the dream, I met you and your son   237
24. In the deep night, I find a Jamaican station,   238
25. My maternal grandmother, child of the goldfields   239
26. I sip sorrow. It will arrive in waves, but I have the tool   240
27. I don't know if Australia can have a fully 'natural' disaster   242
28. It is not as if I have not been thinking this,   245
29. It needs to be blunt and said as you say it.   248
30. Eventually, I will learn the dialect of our time   251
31. The 'easing' the 'relaxing' the 'opening up'   253
32. On such mornings, the dead speak back to us,   255
33. We speak across each other but not at cross purposes,   257
34. My son is a year older. He draws the foundations of buildings   258

35. Your celebration is the street of history I would like to follow    260
36. Poet Robert Lee through his fisheye lens, his face a talking head,    261
37. I risk withdrawing into myself and in wishing to become    263
38. It is not cross purposes, this one saying this    268
39. Another one of my dream impositions, Kwame    270
40. The stanzas, the rooms, the dream, the way bodies    272
41. I am too rapid too ready to leap too ready to respond    274
42. A poet painted the picture of doctors wearing beaks    276
43. I am writing 'Earth' in a drama and trying to let earth have a say    278
44. I repeat these lines as a kind of meditation, for their wisdom    280
45. I don't think 'uncanny' works for anything other than    282
46. And I can tell that the quarrels will begin. I can tell    284
47. I always believe no one needs to die    285
48. There is an art to sorrow, the way the mind builds its citadels    287
49. I am exterior – outside the silhouettes, viewing small    288
50. "The unbearable whiteness of being," sings Double Ugly    289
51. How much less of ourselves we know long separated    291
52. Before the game, the Philly Eagles chant,    292
53. I am entangled in 'experimental' fictions of collapse,    294
54. A deep grotto, the mist softly rising, the dense mountains    296
55. See our way through. See history's way through    299
56. There is in the labour of those who have learned    302

1.

It's a long drive along the valley past struggling patches
of bush and brazenly 'clear' paddocks to deliver food supplies
to elderly relatives who hold a hospitable THANKS! sign
up against a window pane. Glass is such a strange concept:
clarity of distance sound almost carries through, a living
picture of circumstances. And waving back, the bags are dropped
on the seat outside, and our smiles and greetings are festooned by white-
browed babblers quick throughout – garrulous and group-orientated,
shaking the leaves of sheoaks and olive trees, jam trees. Leaf-feathers.
These are our closest people behind that glass but love means
distance. They have done so much for us across lifetimes.
Isolation of preservation for people so loving the world.

JK

*2. remnants found in ruins*

A vision deprived of hope may be just a cliché – which is itself
a hopeful saying, and so one leaves through the words gathered
and ordered and wonders: is the sum of my art hope, a kind of possibility
in a time of mounting chaos? If Milosz is right – that we do construct poetry
out of the remnants found in ruins – then why would we the chroniclers
not be secret scavengers, hungry for catastrophes? But this is not who we
are, not who I am. Here in Lincoln, we are waiting for the law to arrive;
still, the sun batters the last snow and the air is crisp, a gentle distraction.
How well tuned are our times to the prophecies of division and chaos,
how the youth in Berlin, Myrtle Beach and Miami frolic,
spring sunlight on their gleaming skins in giddy defiance,
while the aged and elderly huddle in our closets, envious
of the things left behind – all these lies forged in the bucket of myths
hurtling across borders in the digital freeway. What do you know,
what do you know? I have lost track of the mountain woman.
She is off the grid, will remain there in the blue light of the forest,
fully convinced she is a lead in that great epic film of our demise;
she will survive, and she is prepared for it. She says, "Leave the best
of your recent poems where I can find them, and I will build a cult
around your prophetic art, which we shall call 'The Beginning of History',
and this will be enough; it is what I have been called to." Of course,
I am inventing things here. The truth is simpler; we are shut in.
I have not reached out to anyone, I have turned to the unfinished things,
the stacks of futility we might say, and this, too, seems enough.
If there is calm, it is the calm of resignation. The gods of this contagion
spoke to me in a dream, and said, "Stop calling us Chaos, for you know
the art of this pall is in the quiet wisdom of its order – how the old and black
will be culled first, and the young will find their strength. Is this not the order
of our ancient selves?" Admittedly, the anger of the elderly is grudging
and unreasonable; we secrete it in our frightened bodies, until we grow
resigned to the saying, "We have had our time." And what of the rich
in their mansions, and the poor in their cities, and the oppressed inside
their borders, and the hungry and the broken, and the vulnerable?
Chronicler, speak it, do not accept the resignation of your greying hairs .

Instead, say that the equation of survival is the diabolic discourse of the oppressor. May we seek a fairer music, even in these times. On March 20th, a poet wrote: "Open your eyes, Dad–/ please. There is still time to see/ the first days of spring."

KD

3.

No poet can serve the state and tell us a truth we can do anything with.
I say this because in the same way the seeds for the crumpling of now

were laid a fortnight ago, and then a fortnight back, so 'will the official poet
of the crisis' emerge reporting in the name of the people but acting

for the state and their footings in big business. They are the secret agents,
the encryptors of control that isn't about collective well-being, but about

the protection of economics, of systems, of property, of wealth-accumulation,
of capital, of bigotry, of privilege, of class, of keeping masses impoverished.

And there are the compounds of paranoid righting apocalyptics,
those who won't share but 'with their own', who look for 'opportunity'

in breakdown. There are many versions of this and some don't know
themselves until such moments come. So, these are the decaying planks

across hell we can fall through, but won't. We won't. And we must
look after the spirits of the fallen as well — they live, still, and always will.

Because poetry can't be contained doesn't mean it should destroy
as it goes, not in its essence — it needs to lift above the controls

and make its own isolations that are community. Not splendid. Not
marginalising, but allowing space in imagination. To garden. To increase.

As mixed messages are compelled by a weird militarism
that is about soldierly romantics in which death is the signing off

of courage and glory, so *this* state is ruled by a soldier premier
who says the show must go on, and his medical officer suggests

everyone go to the pub. And people who have panic attacks
in the aisles of supermarkets are mocked, and the home affairs

minister says he will go after 'hoarders and profiteers' when this
entire stolen colonial country is built on hoarding and profiteering.

This is a brute reality people adjust to because the rhythm of a poem
is heart and lungs and stomach and sinew and bone and
    the communication

of organism in itself and with others. Always others. Separating off for
    a while
refocuses the organics so they can come back together. Love all elders. Protect

and nurture and allow room to grow old. Older. In drought-
conditions, we set a new organic vegetable garden in place to share,

tapping emergency water because people will have to eat
and every trick learnt across decades in different countries

under different growing conditions can come into play. Play –
a learning mode, a necessary mode to grow through stages.

No poet can serve the state and tell us a truth we can do anything with,
but that can be a conduit for the organic and inorganic and help create

a health of body and soul and biosphere that will withstand the sudden
decline, will not call it 'incursion' or lay blame, but let language

break free of syntax and grammar and still pave with commonsense, logic
which is a phantasm that lasts, and show the soul is what we

sing in every movement of our bodies, thoughts, how we love
the birds and animals and insects and reptiles and rocks and plants.

No poet can serve the state and tell us a truth we can do anything with.
No more 'in hindsight', but now, in the present tense of an ancient
    universal mode.

JK

4. *the after earth*

They will call it hope, they who say, Look to the After Earth,
the End of the Plague, The New Age Returns, Post-Viral Nation,
The Survivors, The *New* Survivors. They have titled speeches, songs
and grand epic novels in this way, and most are whispering
of the boom times, the times of plenty, the triumph of the survivors,
these are the sermons of hope, they say. I have, in these days of
long walks, considered the meaning of art, the promise of art for
lasting meaning — how the century before was the century of despair,
how great art cannot exist void of hope, how the death of God
and the authority of scripture, of the classics, the brittle paper of archived
scrolls with their arcane languages, has meant the decay of genius — for art,
they say, must triumph over the squalor; that because mankind has
a poor tolerance of reality, the poet should know to be judicious
in the prescription — starve despair, sing songs, offer hope of resurrection,
revolution, a future. The President is the prophet of hope, he says,
with his scowling bark, his body growing stronger, as if he feeds
on the offal of fear strewn across the nation. He says, Look to the end
of the plague, when the rich in their mansions will feast on the plenty,
and the losers will be culled from the human economy — and who
does not want to be among the winners, the gloating triumphant?
You and I, dear friend, know that beauty will come only when
we face a tomorrow with blunt honesty; this is the beauty we wish for,
this is the path of the poet, kerchief over her face, walking through
the silent city staring at the cranes, in their ritual of ancient passages,
bodies alert to the change of temperature, before they lift themselves,
circle the Sandhills offering a soft farewell, then head towards
the sun's path, against all chaos, against all calamity, against
the world's determined decay. And here returns old Derek's wisdom,
that "blue skies convert all genocide to fiction."
You see, we island people of forced migrations have long known
the futility of fighting contagions — the duplicity of promises,
the lie of blue skies, the art of blues skies, the seduction of blue skies.

KD

5.

I didn't think I'd have the strength to write this today, Kwame,
but I have found it because it is necessary and it is the purpose
of poetry to speak when it feels hardest to speak. I am too
judgemental, Kwame, (repeating your name is a balm for me,
sorry), and as I say, error after error made and wrong directions
taken or no action where I feel it should have been taken,
I find I think and speak harshly. I am trying to pull back
this urge, not to go quiet, as I am not capable of that, but
to leaven my response with compassion. Planting a new bed
of the drought garden today, hoping seeds will find enough
moisture to sprout, to grow, to yield, I work with a dirty
sweat where each drop of moisture falling onto the hard
clay I try to break strikes me as a rain from inside, my inner
self speaking out, breaking out of its constraints. I want
to feed people organic vegetables grown from rocks,
Kwame. I want to forgive others and myself but never
forget any of our failings — my failings manifest,
our failings our togetherness. A strange sight
out there in the heat — two willy wagtails working
insect dropzones with two grey shrike-thrushes —
in synch, moving on fast. It was weird, and though
I am the insect of this garden, it was wonderful, too.
I am writing garden poems and the virus is in the air,
riding eddies in the district, inventing its own science.

JK

6. *and have not charity*

*They spoke the stilted French*
*of their dark river,*
*whose hooked worm, multiplying its pale sickle,*
*could thin the harvest of the winter streets.*
*"Then we can depend on you to get us those tractors?"*
*"I gave my word."*
*"May my country ask you why you are doing this, sir?"*
*Silence.*
*"You know if you betray us, you cannot hide?"*
*A tug. Smoke trailing its dark cry.*
    —Derek Walcott, "The Fortunate Traveller"

Then, let us chant against *have not charity*, even though we lack strength. The woman drifts towards us smiling, she stares at the dog, then closer, and closer, on Pine Lake Drive, with its lake-front quirky mansions, tree-filled yards, the facades of the houses mute, stoic as Nebraskans facing calamity. Then, having broken through the barrier of six feet, she expands her smile, eyes bright, breathes until she says, "How are you?" and places her open palm on Lorna's shoulder. And we chuckle with charity and hurry forward, her words fading quickly, and in their soft lingering is aloneness — a sense that she has waited at the driveway
for the tenderness of bodies, for the sound of words to come into her radius and settle like neighbourliness. And we make mental note to disinfect our fears; the air is crisp with a kind of cleansing; it is the first day of spring, we are told, and the haikus come marching across the miles stretched out across the globe pinging with news of people cloistered in their care, their carefulness, and the word *spring* rings hollow; the trees, they say, are still naked with the stark emptiness of this plague. And in the markets, red circles, our marks, line floors of the aisles, a kind of warning and guide — six feet apart, the length of a body fallen prostrate and stretched out — the distance from the living to the dead. I must admit that the balm of not knowing has been stolen from us; oblivion and belief in the spirits of fate have been yanked away, as the bodies of the dying shuffle across

our daily screens – the image of those about to pass – and how normal
it all seems. This morning I wake with a sweat and imagine the beginning
of all endings, though the heat of the house is another comfort,
and I imagine that soon we will be the chroniclers of yet another
catastrophe. How quickly the monsters rise up, how they speak
with petulance, searching for some diabolical scheme, like the President
who curses the hurricane, the earthquake and the tornado for seeking
to impoverish him, or the contagion for daring to defy his pronouncements –
what kind of world do we live in? The last century's survivors of dictators
chuckle, ask if we thought all those epics of absurd power that
appeared in novel after novel, translated with alarm and incredulous
wonder, were mere fictions: "Now you know what we have
lived through – that we were the roaches dressed in top hats
and high-collared coats petitioning the courts of the world,
asking for those reading to know that what we have written
are not allegories, not fables, but the plain truth of our absurd struggles.
The stories we told were not fancies. How is it that a man looks enviously
at parishioners kneeling at the altar of a god of trees, a god of the sky, a god
of the seas, and wonders why he cannot have such devotion?
We told you this, we showed you the word written by their hand, we
chronicled it all, that this is the true disease that has festered
in the blood of the world for so long. There is no lie in this. And remember
how we laughed at death, we the dissenters, we the dissidents, we the rebels,
we the satirists, we the tellers of secret stories; our task was to remind
our friends and family that somewhere in our past there existed
a world in which the logic of love, kindness, and beauty existed."
      And yes, it is true that if you live in a world
of impossible happenings, a world in which we grow slowly tired of saying,
*This can't be real*, of saying that *One day, someone will stop this*, that
some voice will rise up and say, "We know it is all a joke, a grand farce
played on a nation of starving silent people!" But soon, what happens
is more than resignation, it is the cool adjustment to a new world,
and we, too, lost all conviction, turned it into the fiesta
of the absurd. Each day, John, I look forward to the long walk
through this suburb, to get lost in the maze of interlocking streets,
(how odd, that wherever you turn you find yourself where you started,

panting, bewildered, and yet comforted). This is what it means
to imagine a kind of normalcy – as if all around us, a world
is not unravelling with soft muteness. How does one protest
without breath-filled lungs? What does one protest without a clear enemy?
Tomorrow, I return to the music of the dead: Lucky Dube, Peter Tosh,
Bob Marley, Joseph Hill, oh yes, Joseph Hill; they have laid
the foundation of the end of things – we are dancing, people,
we are dancing, with charity, with the entanglement of charity in our hearts.

KD

## 7. *wayfinding*

Yes, Kwame, charity is beautiful and charity is a tissue, a web,
a maze of influence and loss of affluence and poverty, of goodwill
and commonsense, of being and absence, of presence and distance,
is as if to reach without satire and chatter into a kind of *malgré lui*,
into the pool of available best responses, though we fall
at every step, those stones across the dusty pond of clichés
rescuing a way through, wayfinding. All this active in isolation,
all of this 'a sign of the times' however regions try to reconfigure
their relationship to existence. But then a shock — a full page
advert in a Sunday paper from the gun lobby, telling the Premier,
himself a war-talking military man (anyway, also), to 'rein it in/before
we are all sorry'. This unthinly veiled threat was laid out like poetry —
and decoded it means, *Don't block our supplies of guns and ammo.*
And yes, it's like the run on weapons in America at any time of crisis.
*De rigeur*. And today, the spokeswoman wards off the accusations
of threats with declarations of appropriateness in 'raising heads
above parapets' and 'before the horse has bolted' and that gun
shops are 'mostly mums and dads businesses'... to paraphrase,
but not much. Charity of the gun lobby. There's that charity
to contend with as well, and the overlap with 'God-fearing'
is strong here, too. Not exclusive, but strong. And as the Sunday-
shooter down the valley rapid-fires at targets (we assume),
picking off the points, dead-eyed, we embroil ourselves
in garden more than refuge, and we relish messages
of love and sharing and empathy and hope as they
germinate, find ways around a drought that is a deluge.
Thanks Kwame, thanks. Thanks, again. Here, in the vocative.

JK

8. *How I pray in the plague*

*I was rehearsing the ecstasies of starvation*
*for what I had to do.* And have not charity.
*I found my pity, desperately researching*
*the origins of history, from reed-built communes*
*by sacred lakes, turning with the first sprocketed*
*water-driven wheels.*
    — Derek Walcott

In these silences, the bubbles of hurt are indistinguishable from
the terror that lurks in the body – the phrase, "ecstasies of starvation"
will have a music that lures us to peace, but how do I stay with
a tender heart of peace and calm when I slow in my walk in the face
of an old saying that has hidden its conundrum of theology from me –
perhaps not hidden, perhaps what I mean is before I found my pity,
my charity, my love, I could slip over the conundrums, lead us not
into temptation – that imperative that has no sensible answer,
for is this the way of a father, and what kind of father must be asked
not to tempt me? And what of the mercy of temptation, and what of
the lessons of temptation, and what of the diabolical cruelty of testing?
You see why I slip over this with the muteness of the faith that must grow
in increments of meaning? In these silences, the bubbles of anxiety,
the hurt I cannot distinguish from terror is my daily state,
and you teach me to pray in this way, and in this way you teach me
the path of being led into terror. I will say this and let it linger,
what I mean is that this is the way of poetry for me, for much
of what I offer; I am sure of nothing, the knowing or the outworking,
but the trust of its history of resolution, so that I will say
this is the origin of history, and by this, I mean this small conundrum:
"Lead us not, lead me not, lead them not, lead them not." And what is this
but the way we know the heavy hand of God, that to pray
"Lead *them* not into temptation" is a kind of mercy, and to say
"Lead *us* not" is the penitence of a sinning nation desperate for
the lifting of the curses of contagion and plague. The subtext
is the finger pointed at the culprit. So what kind of father do I tell

this to? Might I have said, "Neville, please, lead me not into temptation"? What would it mean to tell my old man not to lead me into temptation? Would that not be the same as a reprimand to my father, a judgment on his propensity to fail me? Do you want answers? You have come to the wrong place. I am selfish with answers. I am hoarding all answers. Go, instead, to the prophets and the preachers, the soothsayers and priests, go to the pundits and the dream-readers, to the pontiffs and kings, to the presidents and mayors, to the brokers in answers. But me, I hoard the secrets of my calming beauty, and I walk this road, not as a maker of questions — that would be a crude wickedness — but with the fabric of our uncertainty, a net stretched across the afternoon sky. This is beauty and in this I will trade until all music ends, and the air grows crisp as airless grace. They say that if you find honey in the stomach of the baobab tree, you must leave the better part for the spirit of the tree, and then share the remnant sweetness with your neighbours. And what they say among the reeds, what they say in the arms of the trees, what they say in the shelter of the sky, that is enough for the days of terror and sorrow. Amen.

KD

9.

There are rumours of a better humanity after this experience,
but humanity's foibles and failings and vulnerabilities
seem unlikely to be reset by rumours. All the well-meaning
pleas and exclamations that this 'event' will act as a guide, a template,
a lesson, a way through a reflection is to believe in the force
of one's arguments and hopes. What we can be sure of is that
empathy and compassion are the strains of being that bring
worth into being, against the argument. And by argument,
I think of Tracy's poetry book *The Argument,* and the tensions
between soul and self, between life and death, of the beauty
even the dying will remember, reach for. In this moment
and these moments, loss is the answer to moving on,
letting go — but it's always the wonders between, the memories
of sensations so alive it's a promise of reset that the rumours
are true. I've never believed in a separation of Heaven and Earth,
and will never let go of a pantheism that will divert the rabbit
from the much-needed food in the garden, rather
than trample on its existence, call it a plague.

JK

10.

*The heart of darkness is not Africa.*
*The heart of darkness is the core of fire*
*in the white center of the holocaust.*
    —Derek Walcott


In Kingston, the sirens fill the twilight air;
the curfew begins with casual ease
and the slow emptying of the street
before the staining of streets
with the mute lights of a city hiding from itself.

The people are stoic:
"If a dead mi fi dead, den a dead me mus' dead?"
Or perhaps this is resignation. Down in the market,
the strugglers announce themselves.
They say, "Look around you, look around you,
who do you see, face-to-face?
Is it not we the strugglers, while the safe
hide in their mansions and wait."

This did not begin as a song of class and power,
it began as a pastiche of sorts,
a strained pastoral of an island waiting for the chaos
of bodies falling away. And the older women
are in their gardens gathering
ginger root, cerise, thyme, mint leaf,
shame-old-lady – and the poetry
of invention in the names of the leaves
that will stave off death:
Leaf of Refresh My Lungs, Leaf of Woman Power,
Leaf of Forgive My Sins, Leaf of Charity and Grace,
Leaf of Africa Vengeance, Leaf of Fall Back and Rise.

At dawn the roll call – the ritual of obituaries.

The men are slipping away,
the veteran artists; it is as if their persistence
is an affront. Ellis Marsalis, Bob Andy,
Bill Withers — the mourning arrives in feeds,
tiny bytes of dispensable lamentations —
blue lights, green lights, white lights,
the scrolling screen of images flashing,
the truncated sentiment, the pocket grief.
Where will the slow march to the funeral be,
and where the high-stepping,
the weeping, the performance of joy
under spinning, gleaming umbrellas?
This is how a culture is made.

"Bring out your dead!" Ecuador, Iran, "Bring out your dead."

In Kingston, they have taken to calling
the police *The Virus*, and, "it a come, it a come,
it a come." To think that beside the dispatches
from Kingston, Aba, did you think
it could come to this?
Did you think it could come to this?
I read Saint-John Perse's lament to Friday,
and pray never to be an alien to the earth
I long to rest my soul in. But all of this is vanity,
a deep misguiding vanity, while the world
collapses around us. All these contagions,
and the American president chuckles at his soaring numbers:
"My TV Ratings last night were higher
than the Super Bowl, did you see that?"
What monstrosity have we wrought
that we have no language to speak of it?
And here come the sirens,
the Virus are turning the corner
in their masks and with their batons.
"Ba-by, Ba-by-lon, Ba-by, Ba-by-lon, Ba-by, Ba-by-lon."

Here, in the cave of my study, here where I study
the necromancy of verse and horde my secret fantasies,
I can't share this hidden ration with anyone.
I simply hide and chew, lick away the residue
and face the family. Here on the soft fabric
of paper pulled from wood, preserved between
sheets of soft-beaten cotton strips,
I confess that the virus may have arrived
in the tender embrace of love, a friend
or a stranger, or a tainted breeze
in the daily rituals of labour and living,
and I search out the economics of death:
Will my family owe the taxes I owe?
Will they be free to step out into the new season,
protected, kept, debt free?
What must I do to prepare?  What instructions?
How to be clear that these are the orderings of a life,
not a note of a suicidal depressive?  You see why
I dare not shout this from the roofs?
This is what Babylon the Virus has done to us.

April 2020

KD

11.

We are not writing our elegies, but we are writing
an elegy – the boundless and endless statistics
that bind us to our houses, our inner sanctums,
the ground around us we can tread without
seeing others, or seeing them further off
than we're used to. In the close places,
in the 'high population density' places,
or here, in a disturbed low of post-post-'settlement',

inside again from the garden, out from which I scanned
the acres for magpies and gerygones, and heard
a distant human voice contracting. I worry
the snow peas refuse the endless heat, holding
out for an ashy winter that will give them nothing.

Tracy is baking again – her soothing mixed
with pragmatism, an eking out the stores
and the Amish recipe she adapted and used
daily in Ohio those years we couldn't buy
vegan bread, comes into another actuality.

In the bread is world and its suffering
and solace, its need and its release.
Hot days of sun are days when the yeast
will rise to its own drives, beyond specifications,
a foaming, a different usage of air. Less
sugar used than Ohio families use off-grid,
separated but close, never other-wordly though –
really, intense of the world. And Tracy adds a little
seitan powder to give that gluten-bind that even
Australian hardwheat doesn't give completely.

Once, decades ago, I was a protein sampler
on the wheat bins further north, looking for that bind —
the bread that pulls apart and doesn't crumble.

In many ways, a bread poem is Tracy's poem,
and she knows how best to write them — her
labour, her love, her patience. But I act by proxy
here and now as so many have to everywhere.

Everywhere really means something now — carries
implications beyond idiom, beyond the colloquial.
All the names I know will come that have floated
free from the body count — family of friends
around the world that will become part
of my glance out across the garden. And so,
the sundering skies, the proving of bread,
the eclogues I write to all those voices of world.

JK

12.

*"It had two gentlemen in the village yesterday, sir,*
*asking for you while you was in town.*
*I tell them you was in town. They send to tell you,*
*there is no hurry. They will be coming back."*
— Derek Walcott

*I*
*must be given words to refashion futures*
*like a healer's hand*
—Kamau Brathwaite

And the good news is that there are friends who will tell you that they came,
those two gentlemen dressed in their uniforms of brutality,
who will watch the coming and going of the strangers and the familiar,
who will record in their smiling faces the secrets of their cordiality
and see the daggers there, and who will say, they said he will be back,
and you know for what, ready for war, or to run, which is what the artist
will do, or better still, fester in the rich mores of paranoia, and build epics
of terrible silence, haunting fear, and the relief of secrets kept, held
and then shared. And you should know that this is the epoch of viral
pronouncements, the contagion of gurus leaning into their upright phones,
their hands reaching forward to touch "record" and then the release,
people planting images of their revelations like low-stake gamblers –
the broadcast will scatter to the winds and perhaps some will not return
void. And so the bodies pile up, my friends. This is merely a metaphor
for the clinical acts of death. We will wait until the storm has passed,
when we will pick our way through the battlefield in search of clues,
(another metaphor), and what we will find has not changed since
the last catastrophes, oh prophet, for the rain does fall on the wealthy
and the poor, but the rich man has an umbrella, and poor man gets a fever
and shivers his resilience to a noble death. This is what it feels like to learn
you have won some celestial prize. On the radio, they say this sickness
is killing the old. And you whisper to your cowardly heart – ah but I am
not old. On the radio, they say this sickness is killing men. And you whisper

in your callous heart, ah, but I am a woman, and I have been prepared for this equation all my life; I will miss him. And on the radio they say this illness is killing black people, the descendants of that mercantilistic monstrosity of the wide-open seas. And you whisper to your crabbit heart, ah but I am white, and the world is a cruel place – I will send some coins of indulgence to appease the spirits swirling in the wind. You in your small corner, and I in mine. Such Calvinistic resignation: the world is charging, and charging and charging us for every easy breath we take. And on the radio they say the illness is killing those with sugar lurking in their blood, those with hearts dancing rapidly through the veins, those with terror in their skin, and our Fit-Bit blinks out our reward – the pulse tracking our living, tracking our triumph and tracking our failures. I will never make another song like this – it is lacking in the salt and ice of predictable meter, it is lacking the comfort of rhyme, the chorus of the ballad, the rise and fall of all great artifice. I blame the absence of art; I blame the comfort of the gallery with its long corridors of hung art; I blame the reassurance of art I have taken in as in prayer, every day. It has been months since the static of colours, soothing, layered, drawing me in deep into the geometry of beauty. I blame the closing of museums; I blame the distance that soon grows between bodies sequestered in the same space for days and weeks; I blame everything, and nothing. What lies before me, the promise of my sanity, will be to return to the song of Césaire, to the dialogue he has with his island – the one he abandons every time he sips deep coffee on the streets of Paris, to whom he promised like a chastened philanderer, "Embrace me without fear… And if all I can do is speak, it is for you I shall speak." How lovely the songs of the exiled poet, how bold the pronouncements of fidelity. You see, John, I am constantly looking ahead as a way to ward of the battering storm of memory; and here at the door, I carry the song of my old friend, Kamau, in his soft stammering tongue, "it, it, it, it, it, it, it, it…."
Open the way for me, please, open the way for me, *ouvri bayi pou moi.*

KD

## 13. An Anti-History of 'Surrealism'

So caught in the local which stretches so far, and yet against
restraint people huddle. We deliver food and speak through glass
which forms an impermeable membrane between
generations – that is, we talk, perform, emphasizing with hands
and body. Theatre of life. As if we'll never be too close again.
As if the propinquity of greeting is the body's over-active
imagining. After all, what is warmth on a thirty-nine degrees
centigrade day, the river bed exposed to the constituent
ingredients of dust, and pelicans gasping, unable to lift,
to gain any clearance. Plumes of smoke from burn-offs – sickness
of the surreal as reflection of sickness of peoples' worldliness.
And we wonder why *even* the brazen would leap to fill gaps
in exploitation at such a time… across such times… in such times –
clearing away trees blocking a view to entitlement, to the cloud
of breath, the moist particles of speech evaporating off lips;
future investment in future not to lose too much momentum?
Stubble-burning out of control, as always, each year –
'out of control', a lend-lease of war that is the charred heap
of war talk, the battle by any other name authorities foist in the latest
PR-controlled release – compensating for the fall in burglary
in the region, but 'offset' by the rise in domestic violence,
the attacks on one's own treelines, the raising of a 'vacant'
piece of land just around the corner? Surreal adjustments?
So we move through the surreal landscape that shifts surreal
from human conscience into something spontaneously surreal
erupting out of the land with its own surreal calling cards, and I realise
that surreal is the techno-euro-modernist appropriation
of elisions in art and culture, land and catastrophe
and slower healing than the flash of screen imagery.
It's completely rational surrealism. 1927. Coinage. Beyond realism.
I am still trying to correlate Tracy's experience of encountering
(at a distance, at a distance) a very elderly lady in the aisles
of the small rural supermarket almost in tears and saying
over, 'But there's no flour'. In this land of hard wheat in dryness,

of wheat silos and demi-endless flow of tagged railway wagons
to take the grain from the great sidings. Surrealism at a tangent.
Months after harvest finished the surreal grain keeps surreally flowing,
spilling. Like the police car that followed us down backroads – our usual
route through the valley to the elderly – then hesitated and hooked
towards-behind us at the T-junction, ensuring we stayed 'in region',
kept the side up, behaved as we are expected to behave.
Surreal, these coppers, also worried, but vigilant
for certain things, driving past others, oblivious.

JK

## 14. *Last days*

More than a coda, this interim is now turning into the dark haunting
before disaster, and I wish that the shadows were as simple
as contagion's sickness and death. There the accident of fate,
the ill luck of bodies passing the wrong bodies, is a kind of comfort.
Here, I am heavy with the old betrayal of language – how in my life
the spoken thing is the deepest wounding. I will find no comfort
now. The day is slowly drawing dark – the evening is golden
and the city has grown naked and silent in its obedience
to fear, to the rituals that have become a way of living now.
We walk past each other, wave hands, nod, keeping our distance,
and yet keeping our connection. The novelist in me will ask
the question he does not want asked of himself: what silences
haunt the lives that move slowly through this city where the dead
are being counted with no reference to the simple truth of mortality –
people die, people are born, people live, and all at the same time;
people hurt each other, people break hearts, people live with the weight
of failure, of guilt, of regret; people sing, people grow numb
to the battering of the heart, people lie awake deep in the night
wondering when the day will arrive – and the promise is that ahead
of us, new contagions will come upon us? My daughter asks,
the one whom I promised never to hand a fist full of bees, the one
I fear has been stung by a wayward bee, allowed to slip through
my fingers; she asks, "Are these the last days?" She means
the Book of Revelation. At least she did then. But today, though
she does not ask, she means the comfort of childhood, the part
of us that should remain with us despite the years, in spite of the years.
We say these have always been the last days; we say we are
closer now to the last days; we say, do not worry about the last days;
and we continue to eat, to smile, to ritualize our comforts.
In the store, my one weapon of peace, my reassuring smile,
is masked by the homemade mask I wear; I am hiding my fear,
I am hiding my sorrow, I am hiding the churning inside of me;
I am hiding the lie of reassurances. "These are the last days, my love;
but I promise you this, that I will fight to let the day last

and last and last, holding back the coming of dusk, my love, it is all I can offer in my desperation." This is what I say through the muffling of my mask. I hope she will believe this; I hope she will give me this last morsel of trust in these times.

KD

15. *no real poet could speak these words (lapsus linguae)*:

I watch birds divide into flocks of beginnings and ends.
    So many people are finding 'solace' – and that's a word
with qualities of high flight – in poetry. They are returning
in multitudes to what they had forgotten to notice at all,
sun-called. And then there are the poets, digging deep,
sharing the abundance. I love them, the poets. I wanted
to be a poet since I was five because I thought I could
learn to love what matters within – in the gut where
words are made, fed through the mouth. I was a child
of nursery rhymes and can still quote all of them – I think
all of them… Yes, I am confident what was recited
over and above was digested. Then I read them
myself to match print to sounds, but also handwritten
rhymes inside birthday cards. I even ate paper solipsisms
for a while as habit, hoping rhymes would grow
inside me. Chirography and a story of lives wrapped up
in half-song. I watch birds divide into flocks of beginnings
and ends. Embodied, feathered, clawed – sustenance
and waste, the demands of the sun, privations
caused by a moon with a chary or even cynical look.
    So many people are joining the flow of lines and ends,
so many en-jamb against endstops, scanning for solace, flight.

JK

16.
*I do not find you in the morning dark*
*when houses one by one awake*
*and might as well be empty*
        —from "Sehnsucht" Kate Ryan

A glimmering streak of laughter falling from the upstairs room
is a calming gift – something that settles my heart which has been
in tight constraint of fear and sorrow for days. Each morning,
I wake to the litany of deaths and the new inventions of power
by an idle dictator. I admit that in half-sleep, I dream of spaceships,
things I have never found interest in, and the last leader
ruling an empty planet with gusto and delight – and when asked,
who he is speaking to, he answers, "When I speak, it is enough
that I speak." A nation watches the dismantling of its leader,
a man whose mind is wide open before the world –
the embarrassment of the unhinged. All is possible now
while the world recognizes its chaotic absurdity.
This is the nightmare that falls over me in the new
mornings. And I think of the rows and rows of houses,
and imagine them peopled, though haunted by a sorrowful
fancy that they are emptying. And though it is not news, the stories
of black people in this country dying at alarming rates drops
my gut – that familiar hollow-belly sickness. I don't sense that reporters
speaking understand how this retelling is so familiar and so terrible,
that people like me, like my son, like my daughters, like my wife,
are falling away. And so my days, my friend, are hungry
for that sharp dart of laughter – something like light at midday,
something like a bird crying over the wilderness, soothing like music
suggesting itself from afar, growing familiar, a kind of air, and calming.
The tiny bell of laughter from the upper room is a balm, a healing.
I am searching for narratives of greater tragedy turned to art,
stories of how people built like me have found comfort, and do not
die alone, do not die far from the hand of love. And then I come
across this, which is both a comfort and a warning: "Built in
is the possibility of it all going instantly." Which is a true as one

can manage, as real as we can bear. And what we do these days
is bear what we can. I promise you, my friend, that we will laugh
again, and that I will write songs that will be laced with gentle
jokes, the love of food, the body finding pleasure in its strength,
its flexibility, its fidelity. This may not be tomorrow, it may not be
in a year, but may it come soon, may it come upon us quickly.
I, too, want to end a poem "before that, another land, one day".

*"My uncle died over a week ago in Texas. He was already dying but they think
COVID hastened it. He died calling for his wife, who hadn't been allowed to see
him since March 17. His daughter picked up his ashes via 'curbside delivery'."*
— Leslie Reed

*For Michael Gilkes*

The hospitality of old West Indian men, those of leather sandals
and raffia-littered bungalows with Japanese courtyards,
parquet floors and the scent of pipe lingering in the air,
men with airy slacks, roomy short-sleeved cotton shirts
and cigarettes ritualized in the art of cool, the kindnesses
that multiply with age: I mourn you for it is how I have known you,
you of books, gentle conspiracies, golden rum, hi-life
and ska, jazz as intimate as your big brains – I stereotype you,
I class you as one, old campaigners, quoters of Shakespeare and crude
jokes. I mourn your generation passing today. We last met
in the toy land of Bermuda, in your very English dining room
for a meal and long talk about theatre and the calculations
of publishing. Michael Gilkes, they tell me this contagion
has taken you. They did not tell me that in your last hours
you were alone, that the ventilator swallowed your words,
that all you had was the dream of that courtyard
the memory of a time, another time. But I know this, I do,
for Kalamu Ya Salaam sent a digital post of grief for Ellis Marsalis,
a missive sent from the dense streets of New Orleans.
In that city, the jazz folks walk the wounded, potholed streets,
a single horn playing. There is no other music to capture

the lament and broken joy of the centuries of a people's making —
how each day the world tries to kill us, and the doctor senator,
he of the old plantation, lists the black bodies he has treated,
the mammas and uncles he has admonished about their swelling
ankles, in his patronizing, buckra massa tone of caring — the language
of the property holder who knows the cost of each burial, the price
on a head gone gray and broken. Ahhh. I have to interrupt myself,
to say that I know there is some residual memory in the body politic
of the pragmatism of the slave economy, the rituals of putting the old,
overworked and limping bodies out to pasture, the gospel of peace,
contentment and love, the tender homily of the spent years, the full
life, the quiver full, the diligence and labour, the homily spoken over
the disposable bodies of the grey-haired — to say that it is still with us,
that terror, that softening brutality. And I fear we have grown so pliable,
so tender in our bodies to mute the blows on our accommodating
souls, and this is the sorrow I interrupt myself with. How easily
we accept the passing away of those who now bear the burden
of a nation's history, of its memory, of its story. This is not alarm,
nor shock nor revelation — nothing so hopeful. It is resignation
to what is lost, and what we must rescue and keep in the songs
and poems, in the letters, and the proverbs. The line outside
the funeral home is long, a drive through, filled with ordinary cars,
the pick-up, the rusty Toyota, the gleaming Lexus, the leaning bike,
and at the curb, they lean out, call the name, and a masked attendant,
in a too tight, ill-fitting suit, places the copper, porcelain, gold,
plastic urns on a small pedestal and steps back, for the unceremonious
exchange of remains. Bless you. Restless peace, uncle, sister, brother,
cousin, restless peace, poor lonely soul, Restless peace, Amen.

KD

17. *'sitting in the morning sun and watching all the birds'*
   — Peter Tosh

There is too much space around my making of poems.
I have been thinking a lot about the nature of prayer
   (as I often do, which is no virtue) — if sin
is the propellant of prayer, then maybe hope for
something continually better is the atmosphere
in which it can plume as rain. We need rain here.
Others want it to stop where they are. Prayer
   is everywhere but is never static, and 'believer'
is just part of the growth cycle. Tracy calls
the compulsion to blame each other rather
than the agglomerations of power 'horizontal
resentment' because she loves the people
   above and beyond, and knows cloister
and sanctuary and presence of many birds
is a condition of people and a love of people.
How we bury ourselves in the lost burials
of a people, all people, our burials of selves.
   At night, prayers don't travel any faster,
I'm sure, just reversing day's exposure, it's 'space' —
the elision of song which some birds liberate with fear
   of night, the exposure that provides esse.

JK

18.

*She finds words are hard to say*
*so she prays everyday*
      —Ziggy Marley, "Looking"

    —After Bahman Mohassess

I'm thankful for the way the wind carries words we have spoken into
a sweet oblivion – think of the wounding and oddity of a track thick
with every spoken word – the things I may have said: "I rebuke", "I claim",
"I cast you out", "Heal, heal"; and that rush of the tongues of fire,
their familiar cadence, how the vowels repeat themselves, how they dance,
how they find their true healing power; or the secret expletives in the dark
night of my private basement home – the almost quarrel with pleasure,
the taboo-breaking shout, the permission of pleasure – things I never say
into the ears of the living or the dead; the dialogue of characters
I am making – women whispering their longing and fear – the way
I repeat their words on my walks in the hills; and those prayers
falling from my lips in such retreats, those early morning
drifting walks to find the holy, and there to find my language
a bumbling of words, inadequate, the confessions made, the lies told,
the fears whispered, the jealousies spoken, the words I shout
into the wind. It all comes down to that moment in Shortwood,
in the gully of thick bush and trees, the alarm at my pleasure,
and what words I howled into the air from fear, from shock,
from the bewilderment of transgression, for the soft, private place
where secrets begin. "I love", "I adore", "I want",
"I hum, I hum, I hum!" The snow is the trigger – how it drifts
across the window, carrying the delicate secrets of all confessions across
the landscape, soon to fall, soon to melt – what was whole, hot as ice,
becoming water, becoming air, becoming nothing.
Lately, I have taken to the unsettling art of the self-portrait, etchings
in ink, trying to repeat the shape and turn of an eye, the turn of lips,
the curl of my face crowding with the hairs of a hermit, and soon
I understand that I am learning myself. An old Iranian artist,

a drinker of Italian wines, and a man carrying in his brain the chaos
of unspoken dreams, whose every figure is a swollen distortion
of beauty so beautiful it startles me each time – I have never met him,
I have merely arrived on sombre nights when my throat is full of my heart
of sorrow, when in my office, with its shadows and orange stale light,
I try to take some kind of flight, and there he is, the debauched, the strange,
the dissident, the maverick, whose art is strewn over these pages.
And I sit in his room, waiting for him to bring me aromatic teas,
and to whisper to me in English tossed through the grater of sorrow,
terror and desert storms, arriving in distortions . So, I focus on his hands,
pointing to the images he has made, the colours, the bodies – bloated,
obscene, beautiful – and I ask him, "Do you pray," and he says,
"I do not know that language." So, I wait for him to leave the room,
the lights in the house slipping away, and there, under lamplight,
I turn the pages, each image a soft intake of breath and indulgence,
and then the comfort of prayer. I have taken to making portraits
of my face, my hands, my feet, and I wish I could turn these lines
into the abandon of a mouth released to speak in the flame
      of unknown tongues.

KD

## 19. *virologists*

I woke to the madness that is 'Liberate Michigan' — the rightwing
militias deploying 'liberty or death' against virus, stoked up by
their pseudo-Biblical king, bearing arms in the streets, blocking
hospitals and thoroughfares, out in force. This is what bewilderment
does when arm sales are threatened, and the 'world order' doesn't
align with their version of tribulation. The pundits are burning-up
the conduits of Instagram and Twitter, searching for each other
in the crowd. This is why gunshops were closed for the duration
in Australia, because blame is just below the surface — though
with a much lower guns-to-citizen ratio. And sitting on the arsenal
to end all arsenals — national and commercial and religious pride —
what happens in America is local news to us in the Western Australian
wheatbelt, where cars working the darkness bruise night with their
longings, breaking curfew and causing the hairs in our ears to shiver;
even out here in the shutdown, the idea of America is biospheric.
Someone writes to me and demands there be no mention of the virus
in my reply, or anyone's reply, not now or ever, that they don't
want to know; another writes to me trying to find a way out
of a paradox, of 'keeping going' despite being overwhelmed
by grief; another wrote when things were starting to get bad
in their region, far far from here, saying it was nothing, really,
then they fell silent for weeks to re-emerge promulgating
a new vision of resurrection, an artistic intervention in the sacred.
All of this against the backdrop of the greater dissolution
of habitat which is an epiphany that can't quite take root —
I hear and see this in the conversation between bush and garden,
between native kangaroo and introduced rabbit; I see and hear
it like news I know before an opening, that surprise-package
that brings no surprise, is made at front doors, 'based in science.'

JK

20.

A poor joke which is not a joke — this is our corona, after all, not a coda —
how the footnote consumes the page with importance until the first
text is the footnote, the dizzying commentary on the commentary
that becomes the language that demands us, that arrests us,
that promises us something we might call truth. And this, too,
is the kind of madness that surrounds us, though such delirium
brings peace in the mornings — a crown of fighting peace. Each day,
the normal settles on us, and we have a new language of silence,
a new weight of anxiety in our bodies. When the summer arrives,
bodies will step out into the light, and we will not know how to touch
one another, we will have throats so clouded by silence that the words
we say will startle us — how our voices sound different when the air
between us is troubled. I know that the sentences that I repeat each day
in my head are corrections of the same singular fear of what has been
broken by the histories that we need not rehearse — the tremors
have now grown heavier than the initial quake. This is how
my immigrant heart has been changed by these prairie lands;
for the first time I suspect that there is in those who know me,
a quarrel — delicate, muted, and stoic as these people are — that says
I should be this way, I should speak with the restraint of managed
feeling, that this is a better way. I know now who I have always been,
and the sentence I keep failing to write is the one that says I no longer
have the bravado of one who, after being known, is loved without
a list of things to change — a short, terrifying list. These lines
will embarrass me when the light changes, or when the summer
arrives and we step out into the uncertain days before us. I have
lost all assurance — that which allows for a body to enter a new space
at peace with the backing of adoration. I knew that this is how
my grief should continue for Aba, what she took from me, what I meant
to say when I said the anchor of me has been taken away; and this is grief,
though it feels like a quarrel with love, a quarrel with silence,
a quarrel with the years of restoration — messy, uneven, ugly as any nation
after the rupture of revolution or war — of the restoration of the brokenness,
the thing that will never be the same, for it must not be the same.

This, then, is why the rituals of performance and deadly machinations happening each day in the new television series, "The Tale of a Man Who Plays Dictator on Television", have moved slowly to the back of all alarm. One day, we will simply grow up, either that, or we will allow that these daily acts of a world of technocrats and publicists is what Truth looks like, what Reality smells like. I could say I do not know myself, but this is a lie. What I mean to say is I have lost confidence in myself – and this is hardly public, hardly what will be seen by those who read me each day – in the rudderless sorrow of the grieving.
So, I, happily a witness and not a maker of this history, at least I have the freedom to ignore what I will not un-see – isn't it peace, after all, that we long for? Last night, on the elliptical machine – these breaths coming as elliptical pauses between breaths, between seconds counted, between heartbeats – I listened to my own voice reading *Prophets*, recorded in Grafton Studios, another kind of reggae mecca of the soulful ilk – all voice, all tremolo, all sweetness and faith. And the sound I hear is the deep mourning in the wetness of my voice. It was, you see, a month after Aba's harrowing and death, and I took shelter in that tree-hidden, cypress-framed, warm-wombed studio
      in Vineyard Town.
In that cave of sound, my voice speaks that long elegy for my city, Kingston, broken by its own errors, a recitation so gummy thick with the uncertainties of death. There is a strange sorrow that sits between each breath, and I know I have recorded my Lamentation. Afterwards, near midnight, I climbed up from the basement, sweat covered, searching for light, trying to touch this present moment, a kind of touchstone to the hope that indeed, we continue, we live on, we love and are loved.

KD

21.

Just back from another food drop and an encounter
with a winged crow that rose again, and reset the day,
I share the confidence that came with this, *here*, Kwame;
and though I know it cannot heal the loss and hurt,
and that it will seem only a gloss to the anguish, it *was*
a moment of such rectitude in the weird slow unfurling
of day where paddocks are still burnt and last trees downed
while 'CLOSED' signs pop up just outside small towns
as essential services repair a damaged road edge,
that in the compulsion of movement and the fear
of stasis even in the sparsely populated regions,
there is a retuning and a different receptivity
to some music, to some songs, and maybe
a lot more than might be envisaged. It's as if
the tuning forks are all out of pitch, or if the delegation
of flats and sharps of the relationship between note
and sound has slipped or been reset; or an illusion
of such grand or monstrous proportions across
versions of geography, versions of topography,
versions of history, versions of community,
versions of society has been shown up with
a stain, a dye, a new histology of solo voices –
while we hear the choral works, the backing singers,
the front person of the serenade of continuance
as well as the dirges, as well as the dirges.
I realised this really with the crow's anguished
caw, which was also a determination: I will recover!
And quickly. And *it* did! And in realising that the dirge
and the song of assurance share so much we don't
hear, though we know how to sing them, to listen –
yes, people all separately playing pianos and guitars
and drums and listening to stereos really loud,
and singing against the wind, harder than it dare blow!

JK

22.

*As the fever of History began to pass*
*like the vision of the island's luminous saint,*
*he saw, through the Cyclops eye of the gliding glass*
      — Walcott, Omeros

Somewhere in the catacombs of those four quartets, the world-weary poet,
seeking shelter in faith, arrived at a holy metaphor, the disease of faith,
or perhaps it is the disease of history, its fever, and then the slow
invasion of virus in the body, feeding on the mutation of cells, so that breath
is compromised. After each epoch, we learn, a wasting away, or a cleansing
seems prophesied, and only those who survive the end of things, those who
carry in their flesh the seeping wound of memory (the place where faith
was extracted and then tossed into the midden to be buried
with the unclaimed bodies), those who stay, amputees of belief,
though somehow rich with love – that surface of survival – will speak
as pundits about the march of time. And they will write book treatises
of existentialist despair as old as the mountains and their promise –
old Solomon wallowing in his brain saying, vanity, vanity, vanity.
And despite the testament that follows, all faith is built of despair,
and that is what we find in the underground channels, bodies
lain out, fevered by history; it too will pass, it will.
What I have not said yet is that yesterday, while gazing over a copse
of thick green, I spied a spot of sky, emerald green, like an accident,
glowing there despite the heavy clouds and the more ordinary sea-blue
of other patches, and I was about to ask Lorna, *Can you see that?*
but somehow feared that in sharing this seeing, it would vanish,
lose its magic. What I mean is that the relics of faith are
deeply personal things, secrets that lose their potency, as a prayer
of a sole witness becomes the sermon of multitudes.
Every day, the earth keeps repeating its beauty, and this despite
the bodies carried out to the empty graveyards, the prayers spoken over
these crowded deaths. There are no concussions of bombs falling,
no machinations of bloody limbs, or even the thick sweating
of bodies seeking peace in the concentration camps – not yet anyway;
but the daily count continues. And this accounting is not for consumption,

it is for memory, it is for history, it is the kept tenor of history's fever,
something that we may return to in better times, shibboleths of faith,
or the loss of faith, the things that will ground us in gratitude.
Think of the slash of emerald in a greying sky, a miracle, if you will,
and beyond that the calming pace of bodies moving on.
For days I have carried in my head the prophecies of lamenting ancients,
their words fading in and out of meaning – the ink has gone dry.
It has been weeks of pent-up sorrows. I have imagined my body
curled in on itself, every failing leaving circles of growth in the hours
in my head. Call me a goat, call me a body built with stone, call me
the unction of a soulless animal, call me a man who devours the bitter
word of the Lord, and who spends his waking moments waiting
for the shadows. I carry in me a singular prayer: Teach me, dear Lord,
to joy in my days, teach me, again, to wake each morning with a bubble
of delight in my heart – teach me to laugh at light, all that offered light.

KD

23. *visio*

So, in the dream, I met you and your son
outside a block of flats in London, though we
didn't know we were meeting each other. I was
talking to a woman about a small dog she
was holding, and how its eyes wouldn't
let me go, as if it knew me from somewhere.
She was laughing and saying, *She's probably
just bewildered at seeing a living thing
other than me for the last few weeks!*
And then you were there with your son,
and we were all laughing together,
and your son was saying that he was
going down to the river, to the embankment,
to hear this new busker who was sure to have
manifested as a response to the overwhelming
quiet, and as augury, as vision of future,
a singer of vision who loved the world
from a distance and could freshen
the air with every note. We were amazed
at his words, and wanted to follow him,
but you, Kwame, you said, *Not yet…
Let my son go alone and report back.
Let him show us the way when
the time is right. As it needs to be.*
The woman laughed and the dog barked
once and we all nodded and went our ways,
away from each other, towards the innominate.

JK

24.

*And the people started to pray for sweet soft-summer rain*
    — Andrea von Kampen "Rainmaker"

In the deep night, I find a Jamaican station, and allow it to play,
licking the edges of sleep — reggae circa 1968-72, that gummy
tender cadence that carries me into the upheaval of a body
learning a new language, the sweet alarm of desire, the terror
of parental death, and the long silences in the house after a fight,
waiting to hear that all the things we have come to trust will be gone;
and there is that music, heavy with feeling, and still ended
by the casual light of mornings. On this island, death quarrels
constantly for being ignored, for having to battle for the space
to be taken seriously, to be lamented and mourned,
for the dawns arrive with an indifferent beauty — the trees,
the sky, the earth, and the sea that keeps on going and going,
and the mangy dog, slinking along the side of the road,
surviving yet another night of hunting and fighting those wars.
I enter sleep and then exit its softness only to find myself
travelling along the coastal road, my fingers smelling
of scotch bonnet and curry goat, my dreams still intact,
my eyes practising the shape of leaves and mountains,
and houses perched on the edge of hill slopes; or better,
rehearsing each ball of an innings, how it came at me,
how I moved, how I calculated, how I miscalculated —
the broken heart of the stumps knocking against each other;
and inside me, in the wet, groin-brown womb of me,
the faces of girls, of women, the scent of their presence,
all in the bass-line, in the succulent spaces between
the third beat of this sound. This is why I find myself leaving
this country, sometimes, when my guard is down,
and when the light has turned just right, and when
the air outside is in that uncertain place between seasons,
and when I know I am hungry for affection.

KD

25. Matthew 6:34 *for the detached and unlauded*

My maternal grandmother, child of the goldfields,
who lost her father to dust on the lungs, was a witty
woman at no one's expense but her own... *and* occasionally
her loved ones like me. Complaining I'd got nothing
out of a day but work, she'd say 'Let the day's labour
be sufficient', and now almost forty years later
and over twenty since she passed, I connect
across to Matthew's 'Let the day's own trouble
be sufficient for the day', and laugh because I'm
weary from cleaning the gutters on the diminishing
promise of rain, the outlook of forecasters stationed
far from where *we* live. Each day the predicted falls
trickle away — from 20mm down to a possible
5mm, down to a wing and a prayer and a feather.
I drop to the ground from the ladder but it won't
make land — swept away on a wind blowing
with limbic clarity, a draft sounding out
the cleared gutters like a neurological horn.
Cleaned the gutters, swept away the residues,
watered the garden with the last of the spare tank,
noticed the first potato plant rising out of the dust
to test the puns the wordplays the ludicrous
elements of hope and faith and love, the bizarre
registers of labour to replace sleep, wakefulness.

JK

26.
*How young we were, how ignorant, how ready
to think the only history was our own.*
　　　— Eavan Boland, "Domestic Violence"

I sip sorrow.  It will arrive in waves, but I have the tool to hold it
against the flood, and sip. I hide under the rock of unknowing.
The last draught, the British, shell-shocked in their stoic silence.
The peaking graph of death is persisting; it will not bend downwards.
My sister lives in her own shelter, and she will not say
if she has seen the flowers shocking the empty city – the English
garden, she says, already looks like a city abandoned to its wildness,
and even along the high street, the wild abandon is there. I am afraid to ask
her how she knows, what secret trips she makes away from her other self,
sheltered in, eating pasta, devouring scriptures, receiving the words
of the Lord, prophecies which she chronicles in her long, tidy hand,
a meandering announcement of the end of things,
free of the constraints of the immediate. These will be stored
in the stone vaults of the cloud, and will be found – this is the prophecy –
years from now, to be charted, marked by the graphs of mysteries
un-coded, so that the light that will blaze through the days
of fulfilment will be shocking.  And she will be remembered.
But even the prophetess tires of herself.  I know she is walking in
the deep sunset among the flowering bushes, certain that her invisibility –
that of the eccentric – will keep the authorities away. She checks the fish
and chips store. It is closed. A car rolls down the high street. She cannot make
out a face – the shadows are heavy in the dusk. Today's sip is toxic,
burns going down. I sit and wait for night. Tomorrow she will send me
her account of today's reckonings, and I will read dutifully, but without
thought, just tracking the words, evidence that she is still breathing,
though alone in that great city. I am searching her prophecies for that line,
"First the rats lined up in single file, stumbled into the waning light,
then fell softly to the ground, fat bulbs of blood covering their mouths.
This is how it begins." She does not write these words, she is not there yet.
We are not there yet.

And yet, this state carries the strange magic of a second dusk;
first it arrives ordinary as the changing day, the clouds gathered above us,
and the night settling in on us, the trees growing deeper
in their stark covering, while our bodies soften for the evening.
We droop, a gentle fatigue moving around us, all sound
a kind of moaning in the half light. This is the first dusk. And just
when we are settled for the night, a sharp explosion of light brightens
the blinds, the silhouette of the trees imprinted, dancing shadows,
and when we raise the covering over the windows, the second sunset arrives
as a long stretch of laughter, and everything, everything is golden
in the late evening, and the sky feels full of portents.
My daughter, her eyes ironic with a kind of glee says, "The last thing
we need is some strange natural disaster now." But this is
with giddy amazement, for there is no other way to read
the second sunset, the second twilight of these early
summer days, except as a kind of promise from powers beyond us.
We drink the glow of soft tender golden light through our open pores,
there on the deck, and wait again, this time, our hearts
assured of the second promise, the hope in better light, for night.

KD

27. Eavan Boland, great poet, died suddenly after a stroke in Dublin where she had gone from California to be with family during the crisis — aged 75, she still taught at Stanford; in another reality, Nobel Prize Winner of Molecular Biology at Stanford was reported to say that at 71 he is willing to die due to Covid-19 because he's had a good life for the sake of the 'economy' and 'future generations'.

I don't know if Australia can have a fully 'natural' disaster
as the colonial state has instigated so many of the disasters

we have here so 'regularly' and increasingly. Strangely,
the closed borders, the closed regions have made for more

freedoms of family and community if *at a distance* while impairing
other freedoms (the xenophobia, the abuse of refugees, the coveting) —

the irreconcilable contradiction of folding-
in on ourselves as we find ourselves in *the moment,*

the distending, oscillating, fluctuating moment; people working or
reworking *not* to infect the vulnerable, comprehending that there

are whole communities without infrastructure to take
the impact, and that older people are not to be dispensed

with in (as) the grotesques of 'herd immunity', the sort of brutal
dismissal of wisdom that those who value themselves as wise

beyond their years — such as Nobel winners for molecular
biology who feel they can say at 71 they've had a good life,

and that's enough, which I've not doubt they have had, mostly
at the expense of the poor and the exploited the world over,

however much they blame 'their' generation for the damage,
admitting collective culpability as a strange exoneration

of self, of all that one has individually accrued from 'success',
when it's the rich and the privileged such as *himself* who are far

more than a set theory of an age-group, a *generation* — easy
to take the blame as one of the select, the wealthy, when the poor

of the same age — if they have managed to reach an older age —
have struggled to survive: why shouldn't they live on to hope

for better than they have been left with(out)?). I love *all* our
elders, and I learn from them constantly, and know their paths

are their own and not for others to take away by proxy,
or treat as less worthy by association, as with the younger

who are vulnerable. That crisis should bring out the worst
in and of ageism and ableism shows the crisis is also existential;

and though it seems too easy to deploy this notion as a fadism, it fits
the epic fail of faith yoked with materialism, with intellectual

greed that replaces spirit with a 'spiritual' economics — 'religion'
welding itself to the peaks and troughs of markets, 'the curve'

shadowed or being a shadow of wealth and prosperity
which so few of the world's people (or *life* in general)

have had a share in — across recent history, across
all 'history', into history as post-virus economics

would project with brazen confidence, trying not to realise
that which *they've* inbuilt — that this crisis

will unfold into crisis, and that an *only way*
is surely for all to have less, especially those of us

who have had more than those who have
had *so much* less. In the spirit, there is limitless

wealth as we are told – so let's make do
with what we know, with what we tell others

to make do with? It is immense, if fragile.
Rain came, Kwame – not a lot, but some, and enough

coldness kicked-in to ask for fire to warm, give light, not burn all away –
a fire contrary and not a complement of the fire that burnt a continent

to ash, still on the winds, cold or hot, and yet, it is – also, as well –
still wrestling with nature and crisis and what will come as we heat up

again, bursting out of isolation, ready to take on the world, history
to be made. The visions are tinder, and we need them still, always –

and we need poets, Irish poets who travel to the far side of America,
who spoke with her students till cut off from the crisis, the body's fire,

all so far from here, fused in all ages, all ways to communing,
hoping for fewer natural disasters, wondering how we can palliate them.

JK

## 28. It Is Not As If

*It is not as if I have not been thinking this,*
*and it is not as if we have not been thinking this.*
For what I mean when I will say *whiteness*, when I will say *white*
people, when I say *the whites* with such seeming assurance,
with such total confidence in the clarity of this locution,
as if we all know the etymology of this word's genealogy,
the lie of a cluster of marauding nations, building kingdoms
by destroying kingdoms – we have heard this all before, O Babylon.
So, yes, when I say this, what I mean is *Babylon*, as the Rastas
have constructed the notion, in the way of generosity,
in the way of judgement, in the way of naming the enemy
of history for who he is, in the inadequate way of symbols,
in the way of the bible's total disregard for history, and the prophet's
dance in the fulcrum of history, leaping over time and place,
returning to the place where we began, having learned
nothing and yet having learned everything language offers us.
*It is not as if I have not been thinking this.*
*It is not as if we have not been thinking this.*
And I want to rehearse Jefferson and the pragmatism
of cost, the wisdom of his loyalty to his family's wealth,
the seat of the landed aristocrats reinvented on the plains
of the New World, the coat of arms, the courtly ambitions,
the inventions, the art, the bottles of wine, the French tongue,
the legacy, the faux Roman, faux Greek pretention, the envy
of the nobility of native confederacies, their tongues of fire;
the land, the land, the land, and the property of black bodies,
so much to give up, and who bears the sacrifice, who pays
the cost for the preservation of a nation's ambitions?
How he said no to freeing the bodies he said were indebted
to him for their every breath – the calculus of property.
Oh, the rituals of flesh-mongering, the protection of white freedom.
*It is not as if I have not been thinking this.*
*It is not as if we have not been thinking this,*
And Bartolomé de las Casas, Bishop of Chiapas,

and his *Memorial de Remedios para Las Indias*,
the pragmatic use of Africans, the ones to carry the burden
of saving the Indians, to save the white man's soul —
this little bishop of pragmatic calculation, correcting sins
with more sins. And the bodies of black slave women,
their wombs studied, tested, reshaped, probed, pierced, tortured,
with the whispered promise: "It will help you, too, it really
will and you will be praised for teaching us how to save
the wombs of white women, for the cause, all for the cause".
And Roosevelt and his unfinished revolution, O "dream deferred",
O Langston, you tried to sing, how long, not long, how long,
so long! And Churchill's rising rhetoric, saying that though cousin
Nazis may ritualize the ancient blood feuds by invading Britain,
her world-wide empire will rise up and pay the price for protecting
the kingdom, the realm, liberty, and so on and so forth. Everyone
so merciful, everyone so wounded with guilt and gratitude,
everyone so pragmatic. What I am saying — and I am saying
nothing new — and what I am singing is, *Babylon yuh throne gone
down, gone down,/ Babylon yuh throne gone down.*
*It is not as if I have not been thinking this.*
*It is not as if we have not been thinking this.*
For no one is blessed with blindness here,
no one is blessed with deafness here.
And this thing we see is lurking inside the soft
alarm of white people who know that they are watching
a slow magical act of erasure, and they know that this is how
terror manifests itself, quietly, reasonably, and with deadly
intent. They are letting black people die. They are letting
black people die in America. Hidden inside the maw
of these hearts is the sharp pragmatism of the desperate,
the writers of the myth of survival of the fittest,
or the order of the universe, of Platonic logic, the caste system,
the war of the worlds. They are letting black people die.
*It is not as if I have not been thinking this.*
*No, it is not as if we have not been thinking this.*
And someone is saying, in that soft voice of calm,
"Well, there will be costs, and those are the costs

of our liberty." Remember when the century turned,
and the pontiff and pontificators declared that in fifty years
the nation would be brown, and for a decade the rogue people
sought to halt this with guns, with terror, with the shutting of borders?
Now this has arrived, a kind of gift. Let them die. The blacks,
the poor, the ones who multiply like flies, let them die, and soon
we will be lily white again. Do you think I am paranoid? I am.
*It is not as if I have not been thinking this.*
*It is not as if we have not been thinking this.*
And paranoia is how we've survived. So, we must march in the streets,
force the black people who are immigrant nurses, who are meat packers,
who are street cleaners, who are short-order cooks, who are
the dregs of society, who are black, who are black, who are black.
Let them die. Here in Nebraska, our governor would not release
the racial numbers. He says there is no need to cause strife;
this is not our problem, he says. We are better than this, he says.
*It is not as if I have not been thinking this.*
*It is not as if we have not been thinking this.*
And so in the silence, we do not know what the purgation is,
and here in this stumbling prose of mine, this blunt prose of mine,
is the thing I have not yet said, "They are trying to kill us,
they are trying to kill us, they are trying to kill us off."
I sip my comfort. The dead prophet, his voice broken by cancer,
his psalm rises over the darkening plains, "Oh yeah, natty Congo",
and then the sweetest act of pure resistance, "Spread out! Spread out!
Spread out!" We are more the sand on the seashore, so we will not
get jumpy, we won't get bumpy, and we won't walk away. "Spread out!",
they sing in four-part harmony, spears out, *Spread out! Spread out!*
*It is not as if I have not been thinking this,*
*and it is not as if we have not been thinking this.*
It is how we survived and how we will continue to survive.
But don't be fooled. These are the betrayals that are gathering
over the hills. Help me, I say, help me to see this as something else.
*It is not as if I have not been thinking this.*
*See? It is not as if we have not all been thinking this.*

KD

29.

It needs to be blunt and said as you say it.
I can see and agree and am trying to act, too,
but am embroiled in the whiteness I detest.
Yes, as a pacifist, I detest that whiteness
and see it as the bleaching of shrouds.
It makes me ashamed and angry and I fall
into nowhere and have no feet and can't find
my way out of it. My hands are the wrong
shape to hide behind. I see the murderers
and stand in front of them, refusing
everything they are. I am weaponless.
I know guns from my childhood
and know their sick laugh, their
self-certainty, their imitations of 'sound' —
their chatter. Yes, of course it's death
they make, even when the target
is a symbol or a bull's eye — names
say it all, underneath — target shooting,
but it's not selective at the end of the breathing,
the last bottle of O negative blood, it takes all
in its recoil as much as its impact; it kills
life and it kills death and it is given
an 'out' through Keats's white as death
'half in love with easeful death' —
a poem I have recited since I was
sixteen, have recited on the verge of death,
as if it was a way through when it wasn't.
The poem separated from the hand
that wrote it makes a travesty
of reality — the corpses piling
up in the *feint* light of whiteness.
The poem was part of the problem
born in the eye of empire, the smell
of hospitals and anatomies, and yet

I lament his terrible, tragic passing.
I have stood in his deathroom
and only thought of a young person
and their overwhelming death,
the steps flowing with people
as now they are empty of both
in Rome and the world. I think the same
in the acts of medicine, the acts
of insurance and discrimination,
and those who take the brunt of economies,
especially in Western economies
that live off the labour of re-arranged
and redecorated class alienation.
What you say is true and needs
to be said in such a way, Kwame.
I am saying, as an aside to all tyranny,
that using the methods of the tyrannical
will lead to ongoing tyranny. Refusal
to do anything for them, to stop using their goods,
to stop giving them anything at all, will soon bring their collapse.
Total and utter refusal. *But then*, they are
even prepared for that – bringing
it all down makes the suffering
suffer more via the the pain 'brought
on themselves'. That's tyranny's propaganda.
    White bigots and the bigotry
implicit in any notion of 'whiteness'
search for validation even where
it is bluntly refused; they enforce
their validation, legitimise themselves
in every conversation. I guess
that might be what Spike Lee
and Chuck D. have been saying
forever – the very notion
'white folk' have any rights
of control or even say in other

people's (and peoples') lives needs
undoing. Your poem helps protect
and thwart the murderous, confront
them with its declarations of blackness,
and that's as it must be, and as you must say,
given the traumatic reality, Kwame.
So I listen to Sly Dunbar
not to absorb into what I have
been made from, but to reflect
against and learn from – to learn
is to respect and not just
be awed and *entertained*, those
shrouds across creativity,
those thefts as deadly
as going armed
with intent. I have literally
placed flowers in the barrels of guns.
I will stand between the gun
and its victims; I will
bury the arms
deeper than rust,
the corrosion,
beyond even air
of the grave, beyond
anything organic, living.
People are meant
to live! I march with you,
I am with you, I stand by you.
    I am not you. I know.

JK

30.

Eventually, I will learn the dialect of our time —
and by dialect, I mean the system
of apprehension, a system of tools to locate
the heart and the mind, to position fear,
delight and sorrow in the places where they belong,
not to bar them in, not to quarantine them,
for this would be cruel and futile, but to keep track
of their movement, their slippage and seepage,
how they move into each other,
how they move around. The terrible truth
of isolation is that it shores up the meaning
of mourning. Alone, we human beings
must enter a kind of neurotic indulgence,
the absence of empathy, to mourn —
and for most of us, this sweet horror arrives
in spots, moments, and then the bodies come
to crowd out our pain, the noisy mob, the neighbours,
the relatives, the mailman, the boss,
with their tyranny for attention, and soon,
we shift in our hearts, we allow the muscle
of empathy to calm us, or to consume us,
or to distract us. In this ritual of our hermitages,
we have no respite for our sorrow and fear;
there is nothing left but the imagination.
How does one eat a mango, relishing its sweetness,
while the news announces the numbers of the dead
across the world? And soon, and sooner, we cannot
carry the world in our heads, so that the periphery
nations fall off the edge of value for us; we learn
to excise the noise of nations too far from us for meaning,
and this is how we become monsters in our quiet,
comfortable sepulchres; there are no worms there.
Yesterday, a poet reminded me of ambition, his hunger
for fame, and I wanted to embrace him and assure him

that all is vanity, but looking in his eyes, I knew
he had never been as alive in this moment, ever —
love, looking forward, hopeful, hungry, envious,
covetous, restless, hubristic, those gloriously enlivening
sins of the artist — so I listened to his prattle and giddiness,
his complaint and desire, and remarked how alive
he was in that instant. Eventually, there will be a language
system to locate our hearts, which, at some unsettling level,
is what poetry becomes for some of us; poetry
being the system, the physic of language to help us find
our way through this deep miasma of silence.

KD

## 31

The 'easing' the 'relaxing' the 'opening up' —
market economics finding wild-card variables

of suffering *and* well-being *and*... life... *esprit de corps*?
Astonishing — compassion and economics, *parlez-vous*...?

Economics is a conversation among 'peers' but baulking
at peer review where things get empirical

again, and where the elegantly rich expect tax
offsets for their remission, their... sacrifices?

I vanish into the largesse, along with
the demographics of being, the curve

of presence — I am still here, and small
parcels of words spill *plein air*, canvassing,

and I take it into my head that I am a painter
of leaves, of foliage, of humus and the spectral

carapaces of dead insects. I am sidetracked from my
own purpose, my affirmation of a free prosody

as a system to *live and let live* by: vanishing
up my own arse, as the the guy who

is pushing roadside bush into piles
for later disposal (chipping, burning) says.

Across the distance, which doesn't actually
exist in the 'sparseness' out here anyway —

where being vaguely known to each other
we are expected to be like-minded

in our 'us' and 'them' existence –
never was true, never less true,

and that's no answer,
even where we view from – *where?*

JK

32.

On such mornings, the dead speak back to us,
and what they whisper, we receive with such devotion
and delight, and promise the world, we do, we say,
*Oh, I will never forget this, I will place this on my forehead
and it will guide my path*, and the dead say words of comfort
like, *I miss the green quiet harbours of your thoughts*;
which is such tender love, and it makes us think that despite
the horrors of the world, or the pressing needs, or the message
that comes from a living soul saying, "I felt you could give voice
to the people that are afraid to speak.// Oppression
is a disaster/ and that is what they are going through."
And I think who are "they" and who are you, and who are you
to name me a prophet or a speaker for them,
and what stops you for being that person?
And this is the irritation of the living, while the dead speak
from the better place, and send us words we hold to our heart,
though in a few days, they, too, are forgotten. The sun batters
the world as if the world is renewed, and the sufficiency
of the evil of the day makes us dumb. I am lying,
of course, for there is no "we", there is no "us", not in this.
There is only me, here in this moment, in this consideration,
there is only me – I dare not presume to speak for us.
At the artist's bedside, a green notebook, leather-stained
with the colour of fields, revolutions and ancient cities
garlanded with copper and brass – their elegant rusting,
turning everything to the colour of the sea of a brazen sky
of renaissance tinctures. The pages of handmade pulpy paper
overfeed the leather cover, roughly cut, ripped quickly, passionately,
each page covered with runes of the living and the dead,
sketches, colour swatches. Beside the book is an oil lamp
set inside a soft powdery-blue porcelain vase; and always,
always, a saucer of lemons, freshly picked, with leaves
that never wither before the fruits are devoured,
eaten with generous sprinklings of sea salt. The room smells

of the open fields of citrus farms, and when he dreams,
he is transported to places where the living dance
in the rising sunlight, fabric loose as sheets billowing
in the wind, and bodies giddy with hope.

KD

33.

We speak across each other but not at cross purposes,
our lines reaching out over the distance, but also twisting
off towards their own admission. Like broadcast, yes, but really
like nothing but themselves reaching out through sound & light
but not at cross purposes. A movement beyond senses.

We visited Mum and Guru day before yesterday —
first visit in ten weeks on the same side of a window;
and we were fourteen days without contact with others
before doing this even now, just to be extra safe, cautious.
And we sat distant enough, speaking… or unwinding.

Mum recited Eliot's 'Preludes', Tim played the drums,
Tracy and Mum talked over schooling issues and other
stuff, I looked over new garden beds with Guru — his
potato plantings and cauliflowers are doing astonishingly
well… and even newer beds are ready for seedlings we offer.

Under the eye of the squat mountain, we live history
at a tangent, though this interregnum changes nothing
of the colonial echo that falls on all country here.
Awareness isn't suspended and all that is known —
that truth outside the organic and inorganic, beyond viruses.

It was good to see them — I for one had forgotten
how to *look* at people other than Tim and Tracy, and spoke
like a bird, no doubt, as it's birds I mostly converse with outside
the house. We spoke across each other, and to each other,
but not at cross purposes, searching for the wavelength.

Mum played jazz and boogie-woogie piano for Tim,
but I was outside at the time and didn't hear her play.
Though I know how she *would* have played it —
a lifetime's hearing doesn't unravel with distance,
and the way we send out lines of connection stays robust.

34.
*tributaries*
For Kekeli on his 27th birthday

My son is a year older. He draws the foundations of buildings
to rise along the south Eastern coast of this nation of tawdry histories,
all that blood, all those compromises — he, I know, carries
in his head the calculations of hip hop, the reams and reams
of histories of these places, the stories of buildings raised to divide,
to separate the bodies of black people from the bodies
of the white architects and planners, and he slowly arrives
at this place of knowing that in time his mind will be able to organize
the many histories in his blood, the great grandfather
he never met, who set up camp on the delta banks of Warri,
the great grandmother of Clarendon, who cultivated and cared for
her acres of herbs and medicines, who would walk through the bush
in sandals, picking leaves, whispering to the spirits of the cotton root,
the ancestors in Panama, the ancestors in Cape Coast, in Lomé,
in St. Ann, in the dark soils of these places where the blood of chickens
and doves have been shed, where the incense has blown into the wind,
where tongues have been spoken, and here, in South Carolina
where his own birthing took place deep in May, the heat already
full and muggy while the dogwood bloomed on the avenues of that city
with its own wounds, with its own history; this city where the old
Lincoln High School, built to separate the bodies of the children
of the enslaved from the bodies of the children of the enslavers,
was already in disrepair, abandoned after the ending of the official
rituals of segregation, progress of destructive sorrow, where Liberty Street
still divides the city, where the last vestiges of black survival persist,
though barely. And he is the child of the diaspora, a child of so many
sojourners, a child carrying the blood of survivors in his veins.
My son, I know, is the carrier of a terrible beauty, and to watch
his easy gait, his eyes alight with consideration, the tenderness
of intelligence and wonder, is to believe in the persistence of a race,
a nation, a people, a family. This is how I welcome his twenty-seventh year,
how we return to those early poems, the prayer I prayed for him,

for his frail body ravaged by chicken pox, and the fevers, for his healing,
and revival. How could I have imagined this man, this man-body
standing here before me, beard and voice deep as a grotto
of valley green? How could I know that is what we prayed for,
this embrace, this bright light along the path, Mawuena, carrier
of his mother's inventive spirit, the two who know the deep love
of a people who would likely have met on a street in some strange city,
and laughed at the glory of buildings and the taste of fried fish –
the way that our bodies are a replication of what has come before,
a fulfilment of so many histories, carrier of the things he does not
even know, carrier of beauty in these times.

May 24th, 2020
KD

35.

Your celebration is the street of history I would like to follow, or visit,
     Kwame.
With my own tangents, with respect to the different ways we all walk a given
street that we know is not actually given and those who would most
control it have no idea of what has gone into its making, not really,
not in its essence; and I mean a street more just and affirming
     and conscious
of the impacts of every building, every fragment of every life that leans
into it, from all carried on the soles of our feet as much as where our
feet have been, where we intend them to take us. I walk a lot out here
where firebreaks are streets to keep fire and its fuel apart, or this is
     the hope,
but too often the embers leap and not only leap one but many firebreaks
further on. Even today, in the damp after rain, on the verge of 'winter',
I cover ash from the fireplace out of a fear that it could rise up, alive,
and burn its own path to the lines of demarcation, to the points
where we'd have to ward it off. Unlikely, given the damp, the slight
tinge of new green growth, but still… but still. Good habits?
And while your son carries our hopes – his, yours, and ours, too,
in many ways, in vital ways so far away and with such different lives
and histories – so does our son in his loving the birds and the trees
and 'his music': we hope for 'the same'. What they spread is
     not something
corrosive to health, but ebullient, is hope, is the allowing so many
stories to co-exist without malice, without usurping, with gentle zest.
Your son with his chicken pox and our son with his scarlet fever –
our fear and our love and our wonder as they know streets
better than we ever will, whatever 'sort' of streets, wherever
they run and at whatever angle to the sun. We know they will know.

JK

36.
*Rome burns and our slavery begins*
    — Kamau Brathwaite

Poet Robert Lee through his fisheye lens, his face a talking head,
a mouth deep whispering and rounding out the vowels, reading *X-Self*,
possessed by Kamau, possessing Kamau, dreaming ancestors;
all that history, all that poultry, the nightmare of Herman Cortez,
the metaphors of underdevelopment, all those letters from Rome,
and in the background, a chicken crows time after time, and this is how
the world communes with itself, for forty nights of lamentation
and celebration, dreaming manuscripts for Kamau B, the poet, the griot,
the ancestral dove. That when Kamau, who told me to call him "Kamau"
when I called him in reverence, "Professor Brathwaite", and then,
"Prof B", which is where we settled, me being well-trained in the rituals
of eldership, for what do we call our teachers, those who teach us?
And when he went to Rome, he did not think of glory,
but of Babylon burning, and blackening and Amsterdam rotting,
and the economies of electricity and coins, the myth
of heaven, the money of heaven, see the pennies dropping, of ships,
ships blessed at the docks – they were sent out with papal blessing,
to slaughter, to destroy, to commune, to enslave, to rape, to pillage,
to collect, collect, collect; and when he came to Rome,
he did not write lyrical paeans to a civilization, or speak
of being broken, being torn between the classics and the present existence
of black people, African people, and this seeped in me like a quiet
disease that has inoculated me from the pathologies of twilight.
I see no sin in bringing up the ugly thing, the bones in the corner,
the lies they tell, and though they call me unfortunate,
this has long seeped into my belly, my bones, my skin, my blood;
oh Mont Blanc, meaning white mountain, and that pun is meant
for what it is, that pun is meant for what it is, buzzards gathering
over the world. Uncle Kamau, I come to your back gate
in tattered khaki, like a garden boy, and I offer to clear the bramble,
and you warn me to be watchful of the dark green leaves,
and the purple-flowering vine, and to stay far from the floor

covering of dainty lime-green leaves, how precious they are.
So, I labour and Kingston sweat, and when you return
as the sun stands tall over the day, you carry a sweating glass
of ice-water, and offer it with a nod, and I drink the long draught
of the labourer, and out of respect and honour, I leave a mouthful
at the glass bottom, roll it around, and throw it out over the yard,
with that quick wrist gesture, ancient as the act of all labourers.
I return the glass, and we talk of the colour of *yoyi* leaves,
how in Northern Ghana the spirits dance through your malarial
forest, Beethoven's *Missa Solemnis* – have mercy, have mercy, mercy –
bringing sweat and the breaking of fever and a new music
that will grow in density and light – mercy, mercy, me.
And I told you of the tart sweetness of Lomé fermented porridge
with groundnuts at dawn, as we stare at the mountains over Irish Town
in the silence that settles over us. Then you pause and say to me,
your sleep-lidded eyes bright with wisdom: "Since solstice,
I've been wanting to say this. Babylon, you inheritors of the ruins
of ancient philosophies and cities, you who have consecrated
the mythology of the colour of your skins, I don't want
to hear you say you can't begin to imagine what black people
are going through. Because you are lying. You not only can imagine it
but you expect us to imagine how it is possible for you not to imagine
something as simple as this. Say you are ignorant. Say you've been selfish.
Say you have fattened yourself on the compromises of your humanity,
and have weighed us in the balance and let us be the price, Babylon.
Say you have protected your self-interest by wilfully ignoring.
Say you are daft. Say you have no imagination for anything or anyone
other than your people. But don't lie. And don't ask me to feel
that pain of yours. Imagining is not hard. It's human to imagine,
to empathize. It is inhuman to say you can't begin to imagine.
It is so because it is a lie." I am still clearing the ground
you started to cultivate in the way a poem grows, abandoned
with love, and stared at with awe – the raising of the jungle,
from dawn to dusk, and when the light starts to fade, I walk
through the land, and we talk as ghosts talk to the living.

KD

37.

1.

I risk withdrawing into myself and in wishing to become a honeyeater
I have fixated on a diversion to earth-air to allude and analogise

actually becoming one and perishing with the disgrace that was
my human form. But then I know I won't and can't and air won't

admit me that way – even when I compost plants they won't always
grow 'properly'. But that's as the case itself. I think over Gandhi

apparently answering when asked what he thought of Western
civilisation: 'It would be a good idea'. As each mountain

splits as we heat, as we head into what would have likely
been another mini ice-age but will now be a conflagration,

I know that every soul of the one soul (I sense it, I do) will suffer,
and teargas and rubber bullets from the factory, to worker, to point

of sale, to 'under orders' delivery will be another breathlessness, less
of what's been built as world soul particle by particle. Lost in this.

2.

Where a log train's
past repetitions ghost the asphalt
of joggers and dog walkers
and semi-immersionalists

where its tracks were grass trees,
Christmas trees unflowered again,
though passed as if a name will
come forth, so capital disposes

of their slender but uneasy
leaf-fingers, parasitic and life-
loving every disclaimer in a field
of exposure alone and parted

and knowing taller trees risen
gone as I listen and file voices,
translating, fearing how they
come out listening to Ginsberg

as demi-troubadouring Blake's
'Tyger', sung syncopation maybe closer
than it should be to slithers
of universal movement gone,

forests gone and family waved
and waived down lines to speak
of overheating and ice age
and costs of artificial illumination,

of shared candles to interrupt
night, no vision as love all
votive as no one denied when
hungry and lost and hoping;

divisions in memory and neurones
leave us blanker than science
which is sheen of wandoo
and light absorption of jarrah

and why nature poetry robs
the air of space for sap-blood tales
cycles nations fallen into god's gaps
which can be explained many

other ways by the language
coming back here and gathering
air and intensity of what's there
already by many pretending it's not.


3.

Honeyeater starts draining nectar
inside small red trumpets of filaments
that's not red in itself not a version
of sap that single-mindedly plans

a nesting future knowing more
than us falling apart in failure's
solidarities as repetition of withdrawals
of ground covers all elements lost as

Gondwanaland supercontinent shifted
generally single-mindedly, though intermittent
hesitation left loved ones of imprint
behind a quality of shift and alteration,

boldness of divided air and aeration.
Plead with honeyeater to remember
back through geological time's frayed ends
for constancy so long before it could be.


4.

It doesn't matter that I am alone
next to Tracy as we wait, but it matters
that she alone believes what I say, when I weep
as a honeyeater wanting to believe the koan.

Leaves aren't covering but exposure
via broken shade leaves me with more
skin cancer to have cut out of destiny
that felled forests and remade prayer

as something that doesn't require
even a glimmer of an answer,
in fact, they are secular feathers
of communalism wherein I exist

alone with family wondering
about the range of choices
the hakeas' unflowering or delay
leaves sharp metaphors lopsided wavering.


5.

Why doesn't the Bible burst
into flames in Trump's violent
soft workless hands! Has it — as *incident* —
been edited out and the forest fires

digitisation causes be forgotten when
rains come seeming to say, *You can
rely on us like tear gas in this
atmosphere of combustion?*


6.

We protect the children
and know they might
grow to be better than us
though disbelieve as

shown by how we treat
the adults they become.

Time knots our efforts
and the bottlebrush-
flower – one-sided and yet to bristle –
actually calls to the honeyeater,
even as it makes a first flight
whether or not seasons accord.

JK

38.

It is not cross purposes, this one saying this,
that one saying that, but perhaps one song
of outrage and alarm and one pondering
the ethics of looting, and the epistemology
of violence and repudiation, and noise, the art
of noise; and while we mourn, we stand in the street,
and wait for the pepper of gas — open our lungs
and suck deeply, counting, everything happening
at the crossroads. The plague is still in the air,
and I have stayed in my shelter; this is at cross
purposes with freedom, and yet, even in this
moment, I am at cross purposes with silence
and fear, and I have not looked at the video,
I will not look at the video of a man dying,
I have not developed the appetite for such seeing —
these crosses, these avenues lined with the crucified
bodies, someone saying, look, look, look, feed
all anger, look — I have not looked at my brother-
man's death in real time, the image growing every time.

Anne says, "Every morning, I open the screen,
and I look at this, and mourn, and I lament, and I grow
angry, and I garden in anger, make quilts in anger,
and I clear the garage in anger, and I hide my face
in anger, and I hide my face in shame, and I batter
my body, I batter my eyes, I have found, I admit,
my soul, and I batter my soul, the soul I thought
there was no language for, and now, I bruise
my soul, each day with the sting of this, these
minutes of reality — and what do I show for it?
It is too early to say. Each day, I drink coffee,
then I watch a man die, there, murdered, there.
And I write on a sheet of loose leaf, 'I have found
my soul, the one I did not believe in, and I wonder

now if the location of the soul – like finding
a lost cell phone, or some missing keys –
is the beginning of salvation; that is what I wonder."

There is much at the crosswinds of fear and loss,
but there are the crosses we talk of in Jamaica,
how we see, see me crosses, and look pon
the crosses you bring to my door, and what a crosses
we dealing with, and such the like, for it is Jesus
and it is the death and it is the blood and stones,
and it is the mark of penitence and the stamp
of Easter worries and the dark path
in the middle of the crossroads where I know
all country folks take a soft breath and understand,
even without the sermons of history,
that here is where the spirits and the bodies
have conversation in the dusk light,
and these are the cross roads and those are
the cross paths to our arrival and our departures,
and this is the crosses, these are the crasses,
which in Jamaica is the same as one's dying trial,
as in, "you ever see my dying trial?"
Which is the language of these days, these days
of crosses, of crasses, of crassness. But how bruised
am I, how hungry for comfort that on the night after
the memorial, the night after the gathering
held its body still for eight minutes and some seconds;
that on such a night as this, a mere familiar
palm on my skin, a gentle pressure is enough
to lighten the soft gloom of our long
and ceaseless fence of crosses.

KD

39. stanzas are rooms

Another one of my dream impositions, Kwame –
I dreamt that I was in a city march, a gathering in protest
and was trying to convince other activists to place space
between each other to understand that the virus is real
and I found myself trying to shift stanzas across the field of the page because stacked on top of each other, pressed
close together, they were a 'spread risk' and that justice would
come if people could protect others by protecting themselves
while standing up because there's no pretending that lockdown
means a cessation of injustice and exploitation and the ongoing

cruelties… but the stanzas kept shuffling themselves
back into shape denying the field of the page the possibilities
of different configurations to say the say but say differently
as well and in the crowd I saw so many masked and unmasked
people many who didn't want others to think they wouldn't act in the moment though probably would have preferred
not to be feeling the need to act but so many things bursting out
in them that work at a tangent to the real and murderous truth
but what matters as the state and corporations ponder the opening
bells of stock markets of balance sheets and I think of Richard

Wright's *The Long Dream* and the morgue scenes
and of every time death has come – again and again –
and so few have turned up here at least to say the wrong
has to stop and I wander holding out the stanzas which
now fall apart as if that's the only space they deserve because even in my dream I was unable to appreciate the work
being done within the stanzas themselves and all the separations and isolations that had been forced upon them or
coerced by writing workshop or anthology or management of language via marketing of bits that make up symbols
that equate people with words that make poems out of angst that are best kept in the dreamspace where they will
disperse and be forgotten even by their author. But why, Kwame, do so many colonists 'immune' to the agony look
for The Moment to finally speak up to act to burst into history

masked or unmasked as if they are cleansing themselves?


JK

40.

The stanzas, the rooms, the dream, the way bodies
are risking the plague, the wave of "action". This is why
I privately vowed not to look at the video. The first
is I have always felt sullied by the impoliteness,
the desecration of watching the sacred moment
of a stranger dying. Even now, I am haunted by photos
of Mexican executions, the frame after frame of radicals,
revolutionaries against the wall, the discourse of photos,
how they capture the moments of permanent record,
so vivid in the eye, the gaze of terror, the despair
of realization, the way a face hardens and then softens
at the realization that this is not a dream; the speed,
the violence of the moment, the cloud of smoke,
the crumpled body, the contrast of postures, the broken,
disjointed awkwardness of the dead, the unnatural
placing of the limbs, the dumb confusion, the nonchalance;
and then the firing squad, their cigarettes, their awkward
moving away, the casual gait of the leader, or the one
chosen to check, and then the close-up of the noble
campaigner's face, the youth, the oblivion, the look
of death. And I stare at these images, filled with the selfish
questions of the fearful, and in awe at the final gestures,
at the language of death – how ordinary it is, and yet
how extraordinary to consider that this is for good.
I imagine that this awe is a gift, this amazement
is a delusion, a delusion that the comfortably living carry;
and once I stared at the quick execution of a national
leader, the way his face was animated with pleading,
and then he too was dispatched, and the rejoicing
of his killers. There is no nobility here, the death is squalid
and what we can't know is the smell in the circle about
these players. I have stopped looking at the moment
of death, I have stopped intruding on the one instant
of sacredness. This does not make me a saint, does

not make me noble, but it teaches me the logic of faith.
It is clear but it is mostly a sense of intrusion,
a terrible rudeness. When Emmet Tills' mother said
"I want them to see his broken body, to see what
they did to him," she was giving us permission
to enter the sacred. It is a monumental, extraordinary
act by her and I imagine that those who looked held
the moment sacred. But this peculiar defiance of mine
is personal, a kind of religious fasting. I do not look
at it so that I can remember that I have believed
without seeing, which is the gift, the sacred gift, Black
people have not had. And everyone I know has looked
and seen. And that is right for what it has done.
But I have preserved the imagination. I am preserving
the sacredness of the imagination. I am preserving
the sacredness of faith. The substance of things not seen.
And yes, this is how I do not break bread, how I do not
drink the wine, this is how I choose not to discern
the body, for I do not know who sits at my side,
and I must wait for the season of mourning, first
the nine nights of our lamentation, and then the forty
days and nights of wilderness-walking, our heads
covered in ash, and only then will I know who sits
beside me, only then might I allow my guard to fall;
to then say that what we eat from the deep pot
of soup, the slippery flesh, the vegetables and the found
subsistence of fufu, how we eat together, squatted
there, our breaths between our swallows, our bodies
in a kind of prayer, but really a communion. I know
that this is my private ritual, my private pledge,
my private covenant, and all I ask is you know
that such is the caution of sorrow, our true mourning,
of hope in the change. This is the ninth night,
sing me a shanty, then, sing me a shanty, now.

KD

41.

I am too rapid, too ready to leap, too ready to respond
at the moment of seeing, at the moment of taking it in
but it's never all taken in and what I see I have seen
in the moment. A splash. But there are some things
that even a glimpse, even a flash across the scene
will go so deep that what is stirred is as close to the truth
as will ever come, that whatever song rouses up and bursts
out will know more than me, the singer or mimic, more
than I can contain. Not my song, but a song
that finds its way through and is made lousy
with my hyped-up alertness, my expectation, my anxieties,
and then I try and call it back but it won't return
because it wasn't mine in the first place, just its
actions, its working my pain centres, my reciprocities,
all the childhood moments we hide even when we're
trying to talk about them, because we are being
pulled into lines, given a 'nature'. But I have more
doubt now about nature and especially 'human nature'
than I've ever had even when — at eight or nine — I spread
out, stomach to the ground, not giving a damn about dirt
or vulnerability or passers-by changing the setting,
and studying the movement of an insect or a spider
spinning or seeing if the reflection in a blade
of grass was something of *myself* or the inflection
of *something I would never see*, can never see,
bothered in my excitement. I have never been
divided as myself, though I have been divided
against myself. Dualism couldn't make sense
as I was lopsided, uneven, not made up in the best
way possible, I don't think, not really, not as *anatomy*,
though I have stood outside myself watching
and seeing, consigning the worst thoughts to a museum
of thought while distrusting everything a museum
is or even might be. There's a new colour

on the visible spectrum if my eyes are true
to human biological specifications: I saw
it just now over the south rim of the valley —
because I lack language where it matters,
I called it *natura naturans* and maybe
it could best be described as a plutonic
wasteland mixed with green and cerise
with a promise of growth and harvest
of some sort, even if sketchy and odd-shaped.
There *would* be a name because I know
so many have seen better than me
the consequences of surveying
and marking-up and selling off,
though I rush in and announce
things just like that. I will look
sideways to find out, but know
what I see won't be easy on the eye.

JK

42.

*But if I don't get my desire,*
*then I'll set the plantations on fire*
      — Gregory Isaacs, "Slave Master"

A poet painted the picture of doctors wearing beaks, though the poet understands the nightmare of old art – the darkness of galleries, where only the slashes of white against the grim dark charcoal and blue of the night can be seen – and this slash is the beak of the doctors, they who must touch the dying, and who, too, will die softly, as they have all their lives. Another poet, one who is now dead, is teaching us of love in the midst of history, and I continue to find a strange kind of comfort in the repetition of history, though my neighbours tell me that I sound jaundiced, jaded, my asking, *What is new, what is new*, while people quickly resign – they won't wait for the tumult – but resign from high office, giving no explanation, and the horde of poets are hungry and sense a feast, though the jaded sit in the shadows, waiting for the hot iron to cool, to see what will be left. You and I have danced around this business of the urgent, this art of the prophet, this role of the chronicler, and you, the hopeful one, you believe in the word, you believe that those who you know, those who will read your word, will be changed by it, and I say how long have I spoken to them, how long have I lamented, how long have they heard me, so that after readings, they ask me, "Why are you so angry? You smile, but you are angry, your words?" And I smile back and say, "Angry? Me? Do I look angry?" Which is how I read fear, and they walk into the night, and the world continues, me watching for the siren, the tense dialogue, the awareness of fear; so yes, I carry the spirit of Jonah – not quite the same, but shall we say, "I understand", and yet who is to tell when the revolution will happen, and who is to know what it will look like? History does, dear one; Sam Sharpe knew he would die on the gallows, and yet he vowed to spill blood, and he knew that the soil is a fecund place, and it takes its time, and soon, perhaps in a month, perhaps in a century, it would sprout that freedom tree, but that Christmas the planter ministers preached of peace and of protection and of order, and they held their bibles

aloft in the church yard, while abroad the news of slaughter. By then
the enslaved already knew that the proclamation was redundant,
that freedom arrived before the Queen sent her letter, and this is the way
of revolution, the way of history. And so here we are, we poets
who write the footnotes to history, the footnotes that spread like
ground cover, like wild vines, greening the page, greening the pristine
script, covering it with the feeling of history, with the pulse of history.
We are the makers of all codas to the chronicles of the powerful,
we are the song of praise Sammy planted in the earth, we are the whisper
of the wind, the part of the telling that bleeds and sweats and weeps;
and this is who we are, or who I imagine myself to be, the poet
who sings, "Every time I hear the music /and I move my hip, my hip/
Slave master comes around/ and spank I with his whip, a whip."
That coda of the Cool Ruler who makes his own decision, and this
is the art of our coda, the bass-line, fat and full, subterranean and dread.

KD

43.

I am writing 'Earth' in a drama and trying to let earth have a say
but am blurred by my own image and in any image I make.
I cut myself today on rusty wire in the garden and wonder
how long since I've had a tetanus shot and tell myself,
this earth you love could do that to you without a care.
I am sure it could, but am not sure about the care, because
I believe earth does care. My verse play is about fire, really,
and Earth, the character, is beyond my tread though I
keep writing lines that echo something… in my veins,
now, but it's not enough, whatever comes to me when
my time on earth is done. I say this because I want
*fruits of liberty* and I want no more blood shed
in getting what must be had — no injustice
can maintain, no life be lived in the acid rain.

Each day I go to pick up Tim from the school bus —
his final year, an interrupted year, a year that doesn't
add up to a calendar year but will be a year of history
in which so much is hidden, like all years in their
different spaces, placements — each day I go I pass
at the same time precisely, the sun almost on
the horizon as 'winter'solstice draws a line
around this region, names itself and is named,
each day I see a young person, maybe twenty,
with his car parked, hazard lights flashing
on a dangerous bend kneeling or sitting or
crouching by a roadside shrine, a memorial
of footy jumper and treasured objects
and signs and notes and illuminations
to mark the tree a pair of youths careened
into in their vehicle a few months ago
and died. At night. It shook the town
and young people will grow old weeping
in this dangerous spot where in the setting

sun they too could become fatalities. Statistics.
It saddens me so deeply that I want to write
a poem, pull over with hazard lights on,
cross over in the glare, and offer it,
saying, I see you every day during the week
and I write poems and this is a poem
I hope might help in some way — though
I don't really know how. Not really.
He and I would likely have nothing else
to say and maybe he'd find it an invasive
act, a suspect gesture, an intrusion
into this unsafe most public-
private grief. I hesitate. And I worry
for his safety because I can see high risk
on that bend at the great flooded gum
where death is still possible and the signs
of impact linger through all weathers,
eternal souls outside the dogmas.

I am writing 'Earth' in a drama and trying to let earth have a say
but am blurred by my own image and in any image I make.
I read histories and lament all the hiding places history
can make. I am wanting poems of rage to make a peace.
I will never write histories because I will not be a hiding place.
Remembering out in the open with the intensity of solitude, loss?

JK

44.
*... And then in dreaming,*
*The clouds methought would open and show riches*
*Ready to drop upon me, that when I waked*
*I cried to dream again*
   — William Shakespeare

I repeat these lines as a kind of meditation, for their wisdom and cadence,
for their uncertain truth and their deep warnings, and a refrain
is the kind of grace all my words need, for they remind me, John,
of our noises and our sounds and sweet airs, and so I say again and again:
"I read histories and lament all the hiding places history/ can make"
"I will never write histories because I will not be a hiding place."
And I know I have lived in the hiding places of history – this is not
the over-drama of protest, it is the frustration of the silences
in history – me searching back for beginnings, as if beginnings
will ground me in the present moment – and the hiding is the imagination.
"I read histories and lament the hiding places history/ can make"
"I will never write histories because I will not be a hiding place."
I must always return to the imagination, and history, and the art
of possibility, oh revolutionary. The words we fear, but the art
of hope is the art of imagining; to think the unsettling of the world,
the desperation of abolition – how a system, so rooted in the imagination,
so founded on the myth of order and the godly ways of the human bodies,
how this thing could be imagined, the plantations returned to open
fields, the factories dying, the economies collapsing, the diets changing,
the order of the Lord, God's promise of obedience and decency,
changed, unsettled, destroyed; how to imagine a morning coffee, the syntax
of language; how to say *please* instead of *or else*; how to consider the obedience
of animals, their loyalty, the long history of its construction; how to
implode buildings, what to do with the rituals of inheritance, and all those
bank accounts; how to rewrite the language of laws, the legislation,
the gobbets, the maxims, the charters, the ordinances; the edifices
of philosophy, the meaning of free, the etymology of colour, of skin,
the shape of the head, the jaw, the limbs, the size of the penis, the labia,
the breasts; the monstrosities and the beauties, the fables, the myths,

the warnings, the shadows in the dark, the bodies dancing,
the bodies twisting, the voices, the sound of the voices, the definition of noise,
the definition of harmony, the long, long, construction of shades and shades,
the math, the physics, the physic, the chemistry, the blood,
the blooding, the blooding – all shattered, all dismantled; how to imagine
God, how to imagine Jesus, how to imagine the continent of darkness
and the continent of light; how to conceive of wealth and poverty,
the tomes of history, the lies and the truth, the sound of a woman
crying in the wilderness, the sound of a baby weeping in the reeds
and rushes; the meaning of nation, the meaning of loyalty,
the meaning of war, the meaning of peace, the meaning of peace-keepers,
the meaning of police, the meaning of policing; the edifice of insurance,
of health, of medicine and the hordes, oh the hordes now let loose
on the world – the hordes, the unchristian, thieving, feckless hordes,
without knowledge, without beauty, without grace; how to release
them, poor creatures into the staid and ordered world, o merciless
disruption; how to imagine that the small sin of withholding of patronage
can warrant such terrible dismembering of the edifice of all morality?
This is history. This is the business of Christmas 1832; this is the violence
of June 1865; this is the chaos May 1888. And I will say it plain and simple,
the sufferahs have always had the capacity to imagine the disruption
of their oppression, and here is where we are now, asking what
must be destroyed and what must be torn down, what must be wrecked
and what must be dismantled, and at what cost, and at whose cost.
And I say that this, too, is the poet's art; this, too, is the poet's vocation,
this is how we measure the poet's achievement or the poet's failure;
this is the morality of art, the truth of the imagination – of the nightmare
and of the dream; this is the poet's charge, or perhaps what I mean
is that these are the tongues of fire flaming on my head.
This, our coda, this our shelter, this our footnote,
this our hiding place, this our un-hidden place.

KD

45.

I don't think 'uncanny' works for anything other than a comparison
that slips away into disconnection, Kwame, but while you utter

days of pivot, I am working through the lies and shirkings of Scorcese's
*Gangs of New York* and its hiding of the brutality, the Irish famine migrants

fighting emancipated slaves in New York, burning an orphanage,
lynchings, and an entertainer's history in deep denial. And I am also

talking over Heaney's great poem 'Bog Oak' with Tim, who is writing
on the Heaney bog poems, and I am discussing the irony of you and I

pushing against the constraints of the Spenserian stanza,
because Spenser needs pushing against as do all restraints – his devastating

policy views of Ireland, that those Irish people who would not
succumb to the Crown, would not Anglicise, should be starved out

and, as had happened before, they would be 'creeping forth upon
their hands, for their legs could not bear them…' – this brutal man

of crown and fairy queens, of the most pliable stanza imaginable
in English, we pushed up against stanza after stanza, swapping

and flowing against events and wrongs and our own inner
tensions and convictions. And now we are here, looking

for a way out and a *shelter*, or shelters, and those lines
you quote of Shakespeare's that open passages into the dream

we have left but need desperately to return to, upon, rising
out of forests we have cut, dropped and smothered, the roofs

over our head that cannot last forever. Uncanny? No. As each
liberation needs a sustaining lyric that can carry more

than its own shape, its own form, we look to the dates
of liberation and oppression, of loss and jubilation –

a calendar of stanzas whose rooms are built
from ordinary gestures of familiarity through difference.

JK

46.

And I can tell that the quarrels will begin. I can tell that the quarrels
will be about dying and contagion. I can tell that one will say,
"I am a prisoner," and another will say, "I live in shelter," and soon
all covenants will strain. The bodies will whisper, "I have survived
in my hermitage, and I can survive beyond this." One will say,
"I have long satisfied my hunger for touch — I have learned to steal
touches from my own hand, and this is enough." I, prisoner
of affection, know that all affection sours to duty, and duty
is the burden a body will eventually resist. Around the world,
the hunger for risk grows, and we have grown weary of prophets,
of the doctors with their beaks, of the warnings and pogroms,
so, the quarrels will begin, and in the same castle, shelters will be built,
and some will hear the moaning of others and weep in sympathy,
and others will recognize the cadence of the sound of sobs,
and admit that eventually the heart grows cool to such noises.

This is how the world will slowly fall apart, in silence and quiet
desperation. This is how one knows that prayer is an act of silence,
a desperate desire unspoken, the thing that we fear saying
for the fear of not having. And as summer gathers around us,
the light stays long and longer, and the quarrels begin in deep
silence; no one speaks, no one offers a dream, no one hums.
Instead, the shelters grow thick with the order of resignation.
To live through the contagion, says the prophet, is to study
the art of selfishness, to master the quiet gestures of the hoarder,
to keep secrets, to hold onto all language that reveals the heart,
that leaves wounds open; to build tall bulwarks of silence.
This is how we survive the plague, how we settle inside the seasons.
The family gathers at dusk, and the floor is strewn with eggshells,
and we all know how to step delicately, how to circle the white
fragility of these times. We are, in this, a praying people; this is all.

KD

## 47. *accommodation and disquietude*

I always believe no one needs to die,
that it is not inevitable, certainly never
necessary, and that the true value
the overwhelming magnificence
of life lacks expression in literature.

In our second bout of high winds
within a few weeks — a remorseless
drive against the flexible and uprootable —
we listen for the strains and fractures
of structure, the house more than materials.

And the worst of it will arrive in a few hours,
running down its corridor, doing the body-
imaging of walls and windows, eyes
into the night, the taunting of 'what will
morning' reveal to us? In this, we keep

to ourselves but ensure some kind
of lightsource is within reach, that we
have a supply of fresh water, that if the roof
goes we know where to shelter — the strongest
part of the house, the frame within frames.

And this all works as analogy
and correspondence and homology
and metonym and allegory, maybe,
though this is extracting and lavish
to the hillside we sit on, so we will let that go.

I always believe no one needs to die,
that it is not inevitable, certainly never
necessary, and that the true value
the overwhelming magnificence
of life lacks expression in belles-lettres.

JK

48.
*To My Brother*

There is an art to sorrow, the way the mind builds its citadels
against despair. I have not found the word, but the deep abyss
beyond the rim is the sadness of helplessness, a body held back,
strapped in, the mind reaching, reaching, as if desperate to find
open sky but only finding a long channel of entanglements, shadows
of terror. There is the dream that repeats itself, the body moving
so slowly while the horror hurtles towards you, towards me, coming
down upon me. I have learned to find sanctum in forgetting, or perhaps,
the art of dwelling on nothing. I have not spoken your name in months,
not really spoken it – there is a sea between us, borders, the cost
of flying, the reason to travel, the ritual of shaping the mind to ask
how are you. Even here, I write as if to you, but this is not what
I will write to you or say to you, for the last time I dared to ask, I was told
you were in Ward 21, again, and there was talk of another woman
waiting to see you, and of policemen, of the strange grace you seem
to get, though I have blanked away the scenes of your body
unwashed for days, or the condescension of government workers,
of people who chuckle and shake their heads. How easily
the news could have been of you, stretched out, your body
now cleaned of the blood and the trauma of its wounds, your face
upright, the sharp lines of your handsome dignity. You see
how quickly one turns to the morbid? That story of your unwashed
self is decades old – these disruptions of your days are now quite
ordinary in their quiet ritual. You are well, I am told, and this
if good. My brother, like seasons, the sorrow returns to me,
the mourning of those years ago, the knowing that this was merely
the beginning of a new terror, for I have always waited
to be the one to say your eulogy, the one to tremble at the pulpit,
the one to ask the dark sky, did he come to you, did he wear
his batakari of white linen, did he wear his chokota,
did he call my name, is he angry, is he sad?
Such arrogance and unreality in that, for it is likely you
who will speak over my body laid out as a memory of something

old and intimate. It is you who will find the dignity
to speak of love, to speak of affection, to speak with humour
and grace of the complex of our making and unmaking;
it is you who will send me off into the good night,
praying for my journey back to Accra, to the red soil
of our beginnings, to the welcoming spirits in the village.
I have not allowed myself to enter into the slippery grotto
of your daughter's heart, how she walks through this world
knowing and unknowing her father, and how we love her but dare
not sit to talk to her. Not till now have I allowed that perhaps
she wants to sit before me, woman now, to ask, what is my father,
what is a brother, what is history, what is history? Not until now
have I thought to break the casual silence of memory, to think
how a daughter might want to know the secret sorrow of her father –
the one who sometimes walks the Kingston streets late at night,
each step a risk of calamity – what is his deep complex of memory
settled on the soft tissue of his mind. This is the art of sorrow,
the art of memory, the art of our wounds. Here, I say it in these
lines, that who I am, what I have become, what I am becoming
is shaped by that which comes upon me on deep storm nights,
the heavy stone in the stomach, the tears with no reference,
just the valley of the shadow; and this is how I have been made
by you, my brother. To think that I have yet to ask you how
you are faring with that old Virus and the army of its pandemic
in Kingston's damp air, how are you doing, my dear love,
my other self. This is the confession: my calm is the foil
to your dizzying days, your voice, sweet as grace, riding the air,
riding the air, heavy with hope, ambition, beauty; my counter self.

KD

49.

I am exterior – outside the silhouettes, viewing small
songbirds return after the *reign of the three kookaburras*
over the last week, with their perfectly tooled beaks.

But the silhouettes aren't of any life form in particular,
but of pneuma, or a presence I can't articulate,
being limited in my language and its effects.

I am tongue-tied and my words don't fit any
but an ultra domestic speech – I have lost contact,
but somehow this enhances the silhouettes,

and I force back the urge to walk through them –
doors within doors, this going-nowhere-view
of interiors, that enrich and deplete with respiration

of histories I've read into and have overlaid
with snippets heard as, say, Chaucer recites in the Red Shed:
'Or stele, or begge, or borwe thy despence!'

and wonder what law pertains, fixed and adrift,
as I lever and work the rocky soil I should
probably stay out of, and yet… biology…

the historicism of body and compulsion
trying to grow with but through the silhouettes.
Barn-owl-moon is delineated as I am inside, failing.

JK

50.

"The unbearable whiteness of being," sings Double Ugly under
the mango tree. "Try to understand," says Okra Slime, "dem tings ya sentence
inna my brain". Meaning, these sentences are laid out in my brain;
meaning, these things have been sentenced to my brain; meaning, this is
my life sentence; these words are my sentencing for life, these stories,
these things hidden to history, are sentenced to silence unless I speak them.
This is how they spoke until someone announced the arrival of barrel jerk
in the courtyard, and only when they left the hallway, emptied it
of their flamboyance and man sweat, only then did we notice
Mercedes standing beneath the eye of the needle, her face softened in the low
light, her yellow frock the colour of the smooth stucco, staring at the dark
shadow of Fidel the revolutionary hero in the photo on the wall, only then,
in the silence did we see the portent of the star of David, of elegantly
wrought copper, set against the holy brightness of the white sky, and then,
there against the ornate tiles, worn from years of feet dragging, these
musicians stepping and skanking to the rhythm, the two chairs where
Double Ugly and Okra Slime held forth – only then, I mean, could we tell
that this studio, this casket of sound, is the domicile of hardworking
people, the ones who sweat in the sun, who count their pennies,
who have travelled with their rituals of sabbath and un-forgetting,
their God replanting his voice in the thick grottos of the tropical mountains,
the dense green of the mango trees, the audacious red of the flame tree,
the poinsettias waiting like small bombs to explode come year end,
when the island cools gently for the feasts and fasts. Mercedes sweeps
the stray pieces of herb, the peanut shells, the grass, the crushed
foil of the cigarette packs, the spill of beer, the heavy trace of a bassline
that will soon shudder the lattice and doors. Soon the men will return,
replenish, and grow ready to chant down Babylon, ready to sing
in the gruff tones of the walking prophets, the locusts eaters,
the downtrodden and the beaten. "By the rivers of Babylon," they chant,
"By the rivers of Babylon", they groan in this land of strange sojourners.
Yes, yes, chants Okra Slime, the reptilian deejay in always green gaberdine
stained brown in various wars – his mother comes from country
every month and washes the bad man's clothes while singing songs

of redemption. Okra Slime opens his voice on the mic, stares hard
at the producer, Mr. Hilton, and reels off an introduction, "This one
call the unbearable whiteness of being,/ life and direct/. Who de cap fit/
Let dem wear it!" And Mercedes sees the nervous sorrow in Hilton,
how he likes to say this the case that consumes my universe,
this is the complaint of the record producer handing them small bills
for their art, having heard of how the tables have turned and how
the throne of his ancestry has gone down to rot, though in his belly
the rumble of roots fills him with something akin to epiphanic delight,
and the weight of history settles on him, this unbearable whiteness,
this invention of decay. "Come, come come," says the temple flipper,
come into these rooms, these poems, these different poems, the renovation
of memory; see that piece of mantle that came from the termite-devoured
floorboards; it is what remained, a remnant, and with a little paint
and a little love, a little sweat and a little grace these rooms, these mansions,
these caves, these songs, these poems, will say, "Welcome stranger,
welcome family to my house of rooms, my many mansions."

KD

51.

How much less of ourselves we know long separated
from those outside immediate circles, how much less
the stories that find a way in connect to experiences
we might draw comparison with, might juxtapose, make
analogies, draw up tables of similarities and differences.
And you'd think we'd – *I'd* – get to know the spirits
that both trouble and support me all the better, more
particularly, but it's not the case. Nevertheless, emanations
of life do intensify and, as always mentioned, the birds
and animals, trees and rocks, the lichens and fungi,
all of those answers in themselves. And the sky – day
and night and especially during the merging, the crossovers.
I am convinced this is the time of owls. But I am *removed*.
I have a new vocabulary, a new way of reading poetry,
a new way of listening to the same music over
again that makes it different every time no matter
its composer's or composers' intent. I have a new
understanding of punctuation, and I go through all poems
and either re-insert 'I' or delete it entirely, systematically.
In the East of the Continent, the 'second wave' –
a term that bothers me in way after way, in wave
of the hand and wave that sweeps over, and disruptions
to sets and harmonies, and collusions with patterns
already in place, *wave on wave* – has taken hold,
'community transmission' a shockwave, a shock
and a wave and sign in a highrise window and degrees
of pain and trauma and fear, reaching through separations,
drawing us near near near, saying we are part of this breath
of earth, this exchange of particles, this singing
out of confusion and contradiction and complication
and questions and searches for origins and blame
and cause and effect and and affect and relief and *promise*.
How much less of ourselves we know long separated
from those outside immediate circles, how much less
the stories that find a way in connect to experiences.

52.

*I attest to this, the world is not white, it never was white, cannot be white. White is a metaphor for power and that is simply a way of describing Chase Manhattan Bank*
 — James Baldwin

Before the game, the Philly Eagles chant, "Burning down the ships, we burning down the ships!" Such nobility, such bravery.
Football is the monster's ball. All-American Wentz offers
this his rallying speech, and this is how the fourth of July confounds
truth and meaning, how Frederick Douglass fine-tuned irony
and oratory by shifting from "us" to "you: "Your Fourth",
"your Independence", "your Freedom" – history confounds
our language and our hearts: the rising action and the sweet elegance
of Hamilton on Disney's screen; how much sense it makes, for there
we have hip hop black patriots playing the white heroes of America's
dream and King George is an effete white Brit on the stage,
and Jefferson, a mincing hypocrite. Who gets to be black, who gets
to be blackwashed, whose statue do we toss, whose statue do we keep,
oh poets, oh legislators of liberation? And what do we say?
"Down with George!" Let me hear you! "Down with George!"
I can't hear you! And it is the fourth, and it is the fourth;
and Wentz says, "Burn the ships down! Burn down the ships! All the ships."
Yes, all the ships tucked into the bays of the Aztec empire,
and this is the preamble before the invasion, the preamble before
the genocide, the preamble before the destruction
of an ancient history, the preamble before Bartholomew de Las Casas,
and it is Senor Hernando Cortez, hero, lord, warrior, conquistador.
How wonderful to see that Wentz knows his history, and the negroes
who follow him into battle chant, "Yes, Eagles, burn down the ships,
burn down all the ships". I am reckoning with the language of this nation,
reckoning with the president decrying the revolution of fascist liberals,
he says, the president teaches us the horror of heritage,
and he too, says, "Burn the ships down, burn the damn ships down,
here at Rushmore, here at the edge of our great catastrophes!" And Bella

our adopted dog is atremble with uncertainty, the neighbourhood
exploding with the shattering echoes of gunpowder ignited, burn,
burn, burn. It is the season of reckoning and the wrecking ball
is indiscriminate. The machinist once woke late at night
and atremble from the nightmare of that lead ball crushing
the precious things of the world caught among the despicable waste,
and so he came to the location and laboured, laboured to clear the place
of the precious things, and the wrecking ball in a time of reckoning
has tired of such care – this is the nightmare. My friend, a lovely poet,
said that poetry is not sacred, or maybe he said that poetry is not
the sacred thing, and my body felt as if it were standing in the face
of a wrecking ball in the time of reckoning, and I understood, then,
what he meant, he who stands in the swirl of history and knows he cannot
close his eyes to its terrors, and he is right, isn't he; that poetry is not sacred?
For what terrors have been secreted in the clean sepulchre of poetry,
and how many of us have not walked by the tombs and wondered
       at the stench.
Poetry is a vessel and what we pour into it is what we pour into it;
wineskins, old wine, old skins, new wine, new skins, poetry is not sacred,
though in another doctrinal dispensation, we will know that the body
is a temple, and how holy it is, and how easily it can be desecrated,
and this is the other truth of what poetry is, which is different, one imagines,
from history, which is the air, the wind, the sound of the earth
asking itself questions of what is to be remembered and what is to be
forgotten. And so, here in the season of reckoning,
so many stand atremble – this is the disquiet.
This is where we are; this is where were live today.

KD

53.

I am entangled in 'experimental' fictions of collapse, collapse of what
is called in these fictions, 'whiteworld'. It might be designated
dystopian fiction by some, but I would consider it 'utopian' in some ways,
or maybe an attempt at rewriting articles of point of view,
or maybe an attempt at justice or questioning the stories
I think I have to tell and how I can't tell even what I am part of,
or tell myself I am. I am caught up in tones of perception,
in intensities and dilutions, diversions of history — primary ± secondary —
through movement and vegetal and rock-shifts. Culpable.

Football tales are points of concentration — Australian Rules
usually, but I am familiar with many other codes, and
so are my annalists, not only from television and fiction
and social commentaries, but via living in places where
football was a version of the sacred. The Ohio State Buckeyes —
we were in Columbus when cars were being lifted and tipped over
because of an umpiring decision, a loss. I wondered then
what the relativity of loss-pain was for players, for the 'home crowd',
and/or for whiteworld business, a circumlocution for *white
     people in power*? Culpably.

But I am bothered through the voice-interphases of Berryman's
Henry and Mr Bones, and the nature of Merrill's Ouija board voices
shifting their derivations and manifestations, and who or whom is
hearing (as if there's not
*a place* but *the place we're in* that matters so ambient and yet
precise?) and how they're *hearing*,
because I listen, too, but never 'dabble', never attempt to crossover
as such — to interfere? — and it never
manifests out of me and it is not mapped onto the pains of this
life, though there is pain,
and I don't feel any ability or right to translate. Isolated here, only
partially receptive?
It seems to me that wealth and accumulation is like hardened

       arteries with regard to reception.
I pray in poems but not via fictions, and some people seem
       bothered by where my prayers go
              but not my poems? Culpability?

JK

54.

*The foreignness of our mouths*
        — Mahtem Shiferraw

1
A deep grotto, the mist softly rising, the dense mountains
above, the world on mute, a silence; the path is empty,
it trails between banana trees, mango trees,
and one coconut tree; where one expects a goat,
maybe a chicken, there is nothing; the silence is deep.
The seeing moves along the path, an open field,
the side of a mountain, a fence, then green and more riotous green.
If you cut away, then return closer to a bush,
then cut away, and return to the blank sky, and cut away,
and return to the sun glaring, and then cut away
to the sudden brash loudness of crickets at dusk,
the country is as noisy as warfare, which is merely
the sound raised, birds, the sharp cacophony of living.
Then cut away to silence, the ordinary yard, the path,
the puddle of water, and sudden unrelenting dark.
I have imagined this opening moment of a film,
perhaps the sound of water, not a river,
but a standpipe, leaking, and then nothing else,
like a place with no name, except it is Jamaica,
and it is Kingston, and nothing will happen, nothing
alarming, and yet everything happens here.
This is how I have imagined an unfinished novel.

2
So much time lost for the novelist to say, "I am a mammy's boy,
and I am a walking Oedipus cliché who will kill his father
and sip lemon leaf tea with crumbs of sweet madeleines."
How much time must pass to then say, it's a mother-thing:
Words, words, words in the boulevard, said in the French way.

3
The soul's delicate charm of the watercolour — oh to live in such
bearable lightness of truth, the filigree of a sprite's body,
not always, but in the way of a chi haloing the earthy
efforts of the flesh; or perhaps we mean the dream,
the way of dreams, even those thick as the sudden fall of night;
somehow, somewhere, perhaps on the outline of the mountain,
there is the dance of the ferns, their giggle and whisper,
the thing that makes us breathe; the indulgence of hawthorns,
the profusion of words, and more words; the soul wounded,
seeking in the open fields of spinning flowers, and their toil,
something holy, something unreachable. It is mid-summer,
and the air is heavy with heat, and I sweat without grace,
I sweat with a man's funk, the constant stench of decay on me.

4
I continue these daily walks, and the body is finding
its own kind of stasis, the kind that one associates with peace.
I test my grief by the prospect of tomorrow,
and while the thing I see before me is not a canvas,
thick with globs of muddy oils, damp, slippery and crowded
and without light — something sub-aquatic, the deepest dark
I have never seen — I remain the beneficiary of chemistry,
the peculiar conversation that continues in my blood;
how sunlight, how my dark skin, how my organs,
how the chemicals I know consume each day with barely
an understanding of what they mean to my vessels
and my heart, this is the faith of the believer. The priest says,
"This is good," and the second opinion arrives
from the monastery and I accept it, though a Nigerian
woman has been saying that she feeds her children
the ancient herbs of her village, and she knows
that they will stand before every affront
of this modern world, as aliens, as sojourners and will live.
Some of us face death this way, some of us face
the news of death this way. And we commiserate

at the news of Sue, the singer, she who would stride
the stage of the church of white singers, and bring
soul as old as mud to bear on the praises of people;
Sue, who carried in her body the disappointment of love,
the patience, the anger of love; Sue, the one who weighed
forgiveness against anger, and then said,
"I forgive for the alternative would be another death";
Sue, who when the virus stalked, her face, beautified
by the hollow of the chemo's ravage, zoomed
into our hearts with her last songs — you see it
in the eyes, I said to myself, and to no one else.
And then the news. And the march of incantations
and denials, the way death makes us inventive
so we can continue on this peculiar lottery with meaning.
Still, the light, the light, how it persists
across this prairie land, how it arrives as a defiant hope,
how it enlivens the blood, how it turns the skyline
into that Proustian delicate watercolour charm.

KD

## 55.

1.

See our way through. See history's way through.
Through history we see. See history our way, see?
Wayfinding history's legacies which are not history's
but people's and peoples'. Each word that circulates
torn down and rebuilt and torn down and rebuilt.
As we lament a 'lack of nuance' in response,
nuance will be torn down and rebuilt – but
built out of recycled materials, not rebuilt
as a case of environmental racism: the waste
in that garden, not mine, no thanks. So nuance
is desirable, is necessary, but it turns on a pivot,
its foundations those of history, of etymology,
and we know how much we can trust such things.
See history each way, see. See history's way through.
Through history we see. See our way through.

2.

And there are nuances to subtlety. Alone, I find
few things subtle, and lose track of nuance. The
kookaburras watching the yellow-rumped thornbills'
complex nest structure for the right pitch of nestlings'
plea for food, and they won't bother solving the puzzle –
work out the false chambers and hidden entries –
they'll just tear the whole thing apart and extract
the nestlings at optimal food value-point: a distracted
husbandry, a subtle nuanced sense of timing,
brutal in its process. A dictionary was the control-
mechanism of history, an obsessive countdown
of words spoken in conquest, in farming the world.
Neither 'Disease' nor 'Health' are listed in Johnson's
*A Dictionary of the English Language*, 1755, but

*Eucrasy* is: 'n.s. [ὄϵñάόβά.] An agreeable well-
proportioned mixture of qualities, whereby a body
is said to be in a good state of health. Quincy.' And
so is *Óther:* 'pron. [oðer, Sax. autre, Fr.] 1. Not
the same; not this; different.' which carries,
as a 2nd definition, an intimation of disease:
'2. Not I, or he, but some one else' – with an
example from usage: 'Physicians are some
of them so conformable to the humour
of the patient, as they press not the true cure
of the disease; and some other are so regular
in proceeding according to art, as they respect
not the condition of the patient. Bacon, Essay 31.'
*Subtle* is not listed but occurs in definitions/
explanations... *nuance* is not listed but forms parts
of the words *continuance* and *discontinuance*
in various definitions/explanations. The absence
and presence of 'nest' is tangled, maybe en passant.


3.

We intend utterances to address and redress but they
go awry because our readings are nuanced and other
people's are not? There is no nuance in *language*,
only in intent, and in a translation it is found,
which is a surprise. There is no 'translation loss',
that apologia for wanting to be the same as an original
but saying, regretfully, that you can only ever be a copy,
and a failed copy at that. But the gesture to speak
across difference can be generative – let words
escape their definitions, question our ability
to read a situation. And then we are disorientated
by the facts and figures, but the actuality, by the 'keep
my head down' until it's past self-observation and semi-
accusation. *Back to nature*, back to pollution and waste,

to desecrated waters and air, to torn skies; I know
beyond my senses that *consequence* is more
than a word under pressure, more than a word
that shifts emphasis, meaning... it is where nature
collides with de-naturing, and poems of 'history' reside.

JK

56.

1.
There is in the labour of those who have learned
the ordinary faith of a new sun, the calming balm
of a soprano holding a note so long the congregation
breaks from the holler to the deep abiding sorrow
of a moaning; of those people of service and labour,
sunrise, sunset, the long walk home, the calculation
of what one must expend to carry on again and again.
There is in those people we call the salt of the earth,
those who say, in the face of the deepest sorrows,
"God is my guiding light, God is your guiding and light",
the light of hope, the calming grace of ritual; those
who honour pain, and defeat it with familiarity,
the familiarity of the faith-filled warrior, those
who find rejoicing in the colour of a green-leaf day,
and in the tears, the antiphonal hum deep singers
bring upon them – rejoicing in feeling and beauty –
they give us the light of hope in these our sombre days.
There is a shelter to be found in those who never forget
the long litany of their failures, the haunting scent
of their fallenness, those who carry deep
in their pockets, the photos of the hearts
they have broken, the resignation of those they have
hurt. And when such a one stands in a dark suit and gloves
at the door of the church, the gleam of the hearse
glinting in their spectacles, we the mourners,
the limping wounded, the broken hearted, bewildered
by the shock of our loss, by the unfathomable
hollow of our lamentation, we find this comforting,
for it comes from one who can say with quiet truth,
"I have seen a lot of sorrow, I have seen us at our point
of deepest despair, I have seen how it will all end,
and what I have seen tells me that all flesh is grass,
and the gentle brush of nail polish on an inert hand,

or the caress of talc foundation on a face still and worn,
that sometimes these small, small graces are the mercy
the world needs; and this kerchief, raised to the cheek
is the tender act of our humanity in these dark times."
This is love in the time of pestilence, this is the art
of love in the time of the plague; this is love in this epoch
of masking. Just before dawn, in the deep silence
of respite, the hushed whispers of prayers like sighs
gather over the houses. They are the preparation
for those who will walk into the world once again,
to offer the shelter of their giving hands, once again.

2.
A camera travels through the narrow lanes of my city —
it has been years since I have been lost in that city,
years since I have walked sun-dazed roads, the stones,
the grass, brown and worn, the bodies moving with purpose,
the voices tender in the music of this island; in snippets,
the camera gives me the voice of the praying and the ill,
the voice of the gospeller speaking tongues; the voice
at the edge of bloodshed; the voice of a mind crowded
with music; a mind escaping its logic; a voice full of the mysteries
of our broken histories; the words that turn and swirl.
The girl at the corner, her voice tender as soft soil,
the words thick with a strange shyness, offers
the euphemisms: *I do not kill, I just fight, I know you look
on me and think that I couldn't mash ants, but I am nice,
and if my mind take me, I fight, and I hurt, but I don't kill,
and I stop going to church when I know that slavery
is what put us in the congregation, and when I say that,
they say I am mad, which I am not, as you can see me,
I am not mad, but the preacher tell me I am possessed,
and that was disrespectful to me, even though I get bad
dream, but he don't know that and I don't tell him that.*
The words are poems in the stone, waiting to be chiselled,
and the woman who meets us with her studification,

*those will fall on the water and fade away.* I end
this coda with the futility of one who knows he has
not heard the new language of the world – and this is
the sadness of our times. The contagion is upon us,
and the voices of the craven and the evil, the voice
of the oligarch and the white supremacist, that is the voice,
that I hear in the soft cadence of the Midwest,
of the west, of east and south, of the calm suburbs, the voice
of sheer madness offering the reasonableness of macro thinking,
of calm consideration, this is the clouding sorrow
that tires me out. I have no patience for these parasites,
I have no patience for their lies, and when I am asked
for my wisdom, I grow mute and silent, or I turn and turn,
and say after the girl in Portmore, the one sitting in the sun,
the one who says, *I am nice, I am nice despite what they say,
and I will fight, though I won't kill.* The camera arrives after
the words are spoken, the camera arrives behind the sound,
the sound goes ahead of the image, the image carries
its own madness, and the world is slipping behind the words.

3.
Dear John, these are the footnotes to the coda we have rendered
for history. I have no room for the sorrow over the earth;
these days I see the light and I am thankful; I press my hand
inside the mud in the backyard, the heavy clay, and I give thanks.
I know I carry in me the deep indulgence of thoughtlessness.
Today, I heard a man deep in his hatred, but incapable
of knowing that it is hatred in his body, and I had no language
for him. I know the gathering of witnesses were waiting
for me to offer the correction, to tell him that his long
reasoning was a mask for his deep hatred of the bodies
of black people, and they waited, and I stayed silent,
and I stepped away from the gathering, for I could not find
the will to correct, to instruct, to set him straight, to say
the words that would be his path back into the community,
the path for him to say, I did not mean this, I did not mean

hatred, what I meant is what you meant and so I belong
to the community. And I can continue to be the leader,
I can continue to be heard, and all will be well. I said
nothing. I felt the deep pain in my stomach, the pain
before my sermon, the pain before my confrontation,
the pain before I say to such a man, your wealth, your power,
your donations, those things you wear as your garment
of acceptance, mean nothing to me, Babylonian beast.
But I walked away, John, for I have lost the will to place
my hand of absolution on those like this one, who my ally
says with diplomatic care, "Oh, he means well, he just
does not know the language to speak, he knows not
what he says." She says, "Teach him, please, be patient,
with him; he is my husband, he is my uncle, he is my neighbour,
I have loved him, I know he is lovable." I walked away
from even that tenderness of my ally, I walked away
from the diplomat, I walked away from the meet-in-the-middle,
I walked away from patience, I walked away from this,
for my body could not manage it anymore. These are
the dark times, my friend. For every such gathering,
there is a footnote, the thing left unsaid, the thing set aside,
and deep into the night, my head filled with the slow
march of the hymns of the old church in Kingston;
I know I have arrived at the end of language, of words.

KD

## III: FOOTNOTES TO HISTORY

## INDEX OF FIRST LINES

1. Hiroshima Day. Vast numbers of nuclear weapons — 311
2. I watch an hour, two hours, of dull coloured film reels — 312
3. As the virus death-count rises and the age of demographics — 314
4. With each year, I am both the complainer, seeking to find — 315
5. Many peoples and people have found answers in the patterns — 317
6. And perhaps what is unsaid cannot be said in Robin Diangelo's — 318
7. I tell myself through reading, which is a list and a pile — 319
8. In my head, "what are these so withered, so withered…?" — 320
9. I was writing a story earlier this week, Kwame, — 322
10. My dear love, do forgive me, and please know — 324
11. There's no proofreading and correcting — 326
12. And sometimes we colonize the earth — 328
13. In my unreality of a disarming world of easing — 330
14. An old southern white man said to me, "I remember in 1958 — 332
15. We curtail good and bad stories to make things better — 334
16. This matters to me because in every sliver — 335
17. The give and take, oh, and take. The give of place – — 337
18. History has cursed me with the eye to search for thefootnote — 338
19. I was wondering after I woke from difficult sleep — 340
20. What persistent horror allows a thesis to take root — 342
21. I am disgraced in language I am utterly speechless — 344
22. And there is a thick morass that entangles and sucks — 345
23. And now the Proud Boys are 'standing vigil'. — 351
24. I am hoarding joys – well pleasures, anyway — 352
25. I am grass cutting over these days so don't fully occupy — 354
26. And here she is, sister Louise, who sings — 355
27. In the vastness of dexamethasone & Regn-Cov2 – — 357
28. It is October, the season of the million dollar jackpot — 358
29. The small composition — 360
30. Outside my window, the world moves — 361
31. This is the first time I've been at your home's outside — 364
32. And here is why I am ambivalent and nicely comfortable — 366
33. I believe in the efficacy of possessing *nothing* other — 368
34. Like bees caught in the wrong hive, the body is running — 369

35. This focus I lost and then remade from lenses   370
36. The footnote is the vault where I have placed these   371
37. The eastern barn owl flapping limitless slow wings   384
38. Let us then say that the news is the master's text   388
39. I am knowing different moments of communion   391
40. On the fourth day after the dentist I realize   394
41. Thanks, Kwame. Thanks. I am still in the twilight   396
42. Sometimes, on the road, as the light fades, the new city   398
43. The shifts in the days of the poem is the history of breath   400
44. There is the pillow body – painted in oils on ply-board   402

1.

Hiroshima Day. Vast numbers of nuclear weapons in stockpiles,
their controllers behind masks, protecting themselves.

Yesterday a large section of Beirut was destroyed
by the ignition of a 'stockpile' that shouldn't have existed.

The traditional owners of Uluru have tried to protect
via blockade the health of their community from tourists who want.

JK

## 2. Footnote to Hann's *Poetry in Motion*, circa 1982

2.0
I watch an hour, two hours, of dull coloured film reels
        of poets sweating – their names heavy with meaning,
and it was thirty years ago, it was forty years ago,
        many are dead, some sit before a table with a surrealist
still life of liquor bottles, the green is bottle-green the colour
        of insects, the glasses are half brown and gleaming,
and I am searching for a snippet, a word, a phrase
        to take with me, and I find nothing, as if over time
the language that was once fresh has grown stale
        with overuse, and this is humbling, and this is instructive,
why Kaufman went silent, why so many go silent,
        why I am grateful for the silencing of McNeill, and this
is all, this is all we have. Still, there is Ntozake's
        thin, girlish body, her arms making patterns, her words
round with pleasure, and this is all we have left.

2.1
The filmmaker says, "I am not chronicling poetry, I am chronicling
the picture of bodies wrenching out the last of their living
before the screen, look at the images, how I cut and edit
not for language but for the pictures. It is a comedy;
eventually, from where you are, it ends. The dead."
The filmmaker does not *say* this, but this is what the art
of the footnote is, how we sit on the margins of meaning.

2.2
1982 – A year has passed since Marley's death. Every song is a dirge.
– That year I built a space in my head – I won't be a lawyer.
– That year the cricket team I coached won the Sunlight Cup.
– That year God spoke to me about money: the prophetess knew my
  need to the decimal point.
– I was in Kingston. I walked many miles at night. My thighs chafed.
  My body reeked.

— I walked many miles at sun high-noon. My thighs chafed. My body reeked.
— I had holes in the soles of my shoes.
— I remember the year by way of elimination.
— I do not remember 1982, not really.
— That year I noticed Reagan calling our sea a Basin. The prelude to anger.
— We wash dirty underwear and dispose of domestic offal in basins.
— The basin is Timothy's vessel of common use in the Big House.
— America is the Big House who soaks its gout-fat toes in the basin.
— Two years into my father's blacklist, friends do not come to help, they fail and fall away.
— My father wears shorts made of cheap polyester — they darken at the hem with overuse.

2.3
I do not know the letters A.I.D.S, or H.I.V., not in that combination.
And the poets and the dancers in Kingston do not know what is swirling in the air in 1982 — well, not in the air, but in the blood,
and every poem written in that swirl is an elegy, though the poets do not know it. And this is a prophetic footnote to silence.
A friend tells me he is giving the Holy Ghost up for men — he does not say love, but he means desire and a certain fearful love: A pre-elegy before that other pandemic that still lingers in the blood.

KD

3.

As the virus death-count rises and the age of demographics — of crisis
        of productivity —
misfires futurity, as if economics is more purpose than life or halved
        lives, each city

a series of zones that function to make and resolve and consign
in burial demographics, and the 'opening-ups' come on

as closed, as I never revealed only opened through a strike in veins
opened to risk, as careful as I was, and whole circuits of demand like
        meteor-trains,

an astronomy eked out via short supply with a maligned grip on reality
as real as withdrawal, and so few of the addicts, my associates,
        my entirety

are alive now, though each found such purpose in stretched moments
        of narcosis
that an opening up to the possibility of love and grace

was an end to profit and loss and ownership and selfishness
and forgetting risk and consequence and sleep that was less and less.

JK

4.
Footnote to Bob Marley *Legacy,* 2020
*"... so arm in arm with arms we'll fight..."*
      — Marley, "Zimbabwe"

With each year, I am both the complainer, seeking to find
language to repeat my complaints, freshly, so as not to go unheard;
yet each year, the annals of the untruthful persist, the myths
of the hegemonic empires persist, for they carry with them
the money to hold us to repeat the lies – the conspiracy
of inclusion – like the documentaries of Marley repeating without care
the myth of his almost whiteness, the comfort of that,
the belonging in that, the balm in that against his chants
against Babylon system, the myth of peace and love, the narrative
that in the end sets the reduction of a warrior to a joyful cartoon,
and guiding this, are the inheritors of privilege, so each
documentary, each article, each calculated telling is a path
towards the disarming of the warrior – calling him a broken man,
calling him a white man caught in the brutal racism of black Jamaica,
calling him an angel, calling him a god of small things, calling him the gift
of the celebrity, calling him the roots lover, calling him the easily owned,
and this will wipe away the chant *Jump, jump, jump Nyabinghi.*
Here is the coded language of our demise, these are the rules
of the mercantilist rituals – never asked who is behind the camera,
never ask who are the crowd of bodies flooding the tenement yards
with their boom mics, their cameras, their baseball caps, their cargo
pants, their glinting shades, their designer brands, their radios,
their flasks of water, their sunscreen, their easy command of space,
their hands pointing the "locals" in this and that direction,
and ask yourself if there is any other truth that can seep through
the voices of the people, and the answer is that the world
is made by the gaze of the liberal seer, and this is the terrible
sadness of the conspiracy of lies, the conspiracy of lies.
"When they came they were nobodies, and they behaved
like stars," repeat the custos and buckra Blackwell on a loop,
the creolized Blackwell from the Jamaican brown and white

elite, the man they call the visionary, the one who persists
as the comptroller of the legacy, the language of compliance,
and he is able to say it again and again, "They were nobodies,
they were nobodies, they were nobodies, they were nobodies".
How easily we enshrine the bigotry of that privilege as if we are
telling history, speaking truth. Ask me who is behind the camera,
ask me who is asking the question, ask me who is cutting the film,
ask me who is piecing together the lies, "When they came they were
nobodies, they were nobodies, they were nobodies, they were…"

KD

5.

Many peoples and people have found answers in the patterns
of cereal crops or wild-grass plains or tufts under the influence

of winds' variations — those swirls, those uplifts and waverings,
impressions of bodies resting and rising, channels and ridgebacked
       hills,

even put-downs, flailings and flattenings, whispers, shimmerings,
a susurrustic doubt, sea-visions of travel without leaving shores,

bodies of water inland or the harsh and resistant latched-onto sand
dunes (I know desert dunes and spinifex answering in clumps);

but now, as the dead-headed buzz of crop-dusters
ping the valley, and the wheat and oat and barley fields

over the hills are swept down and strafed, parting and coming together
with chemical adhesion and displacement, the native grasses

strain to hold distant edges, to reassert their patterns, and
a harsh wind lifts which will likely drive the planes back to 'base'.

I lament the fate of grasses, the loss of voice each generation
of weather patterns endures, vexed by crop circle labels, the genetically-

modified responses to winds that are forced to question the purpose
of pollen, fed with a patent's disregard for psyche or soma.

JK

6.
*But when the young man heard this statement,*
*he went away grieving; for he was one who owned much property*
               — Mathew 19:22

And perhaps what is unsaid cannot be said in Robin Diangelo's whisper, the secret gathering we have been asked to overhear, and the surprise is not the news, is not the disclosure of things unknown, the veil-lifting of things we have known but have had soften in us by the assurance that our imagination, its capacity to trust paranoia, to find comfort in the possibility that we may have gone too far. No more what we suspected, what we have spoken, what has been said again and again, despite the denials, the blank-faced response, the hurt and outrage, the machinations of silence, the absence of vulnerability, the brilliant manoeuvering to turn us into the insane and unreasonable; all of that is gone, and the fantasy relived is the fiction of James Weldon Johnson, his secret agent colored man on a train across the Mason Dixon Line, when he revealed the things white people say in their gatherings, not bad people, just ordinary everyday people fretful of what they might lose and what they might say to betray themselves. And the weight of this, the weight of what is in this book, is a burden of terrible truth. Here is the woman arrived in her lab coat, with a promise of a vaccine against the plague, and no one dares to let her slip the needle in, the pages unopened, the brilliant deflection by silence. This is not a praise song, not a championing – I do not know the woman – and I know enough to understand that all popular things will eventually show fragility, and could collapse before us. But this is the language slipping under petticoats of the heavily dressed; this is the slippery mud rising up the legs, staining the delicate whites and the filigree; this is what sits in the margins of all elevated language – the illumination of quick scribbles in the margins, in pencil and pen, with exclamations and stretches of unreadable runes; this is the text pressing hard against the mastering text; this is how we will chant down Babylon, for it is Babylon we see painted before us.

KD

7. *code breaking*

I tell myself through reading, which is a list and a pile
and an accumulation and a revisiting and dismissal

and disorientation to the point of getting lost and then
finding a point to look out from, a niche to hide in.

I go outside to do chronological gardening, collect wood, check
everything we deny possession of, and return, in effect,

*within*, to shelter from weather, make conversation
that's different from the colloquy outside, to return

to books that are denial and affirmation, lost
and found, an imposition of order I refute,

deny, and keep myself awake by. I don't remember
learning to read by (or via) following the letters

and words with my finger, but it's likely that touch
with sound and a shaping of the face and the clutch

of unknowing pushed me towards a brink, an inherent rivalry
of expression over what happened in my 'natural' play,

that search for wordless secrets that would admit —
in the garden, digging loose or compacted sand, wariness of rust.

JK

8.
*What are these/ So withered and wild in their attire?*
           — Macbeth

In my head, "what are these so withered, so withered...?"
Have stolen words from my prison guard – they kidnapped me,

left the door wide open, but I fell asleep, afraid to try to find
my way home in the dark. Then at dawn the light through

the trees fell on my body, making patterns on my skin,
and someone – perhaps an angel or a matchmaker – said,

"Why you look lovely in this light." There were plants
all around. How curious it is that you do not see the confines

of your prison at night. Here at dawn, the quality of light,
and the scent of blooming flowers, holds me. I will not leave.

I tell myself that the matchmaker is sitting in the corner
waiting for me to say yes, and I have not said yes,

and the words keep coming, "What is new on the Rialto?"
I am stealing, and writing those words on the skin of kites,

and letting them fly out into the sky. This is how I will be free
of the monstrosity of my imprisonment; I know how my captors

can lie. This is what keeps me up at night: the fear of rupture.
I am sleeping well these days. The contagion builds walls

around me. I arrive at the commentary – a kind of note
to ground all news, in half sleep, in the dark sweetness

of half-dreaming. The President we will vote for
is an old white man, and though we know he was once young,

we can tell that he is careful in how he steps, and will not jog
up the stairs, and we imagine the voice of a black woman

singing gospel as the cliche of our salvation. The matchmaker
says, "Why did you call me here when you are already

married?" And you say, "Because I want you to reverse
engineer my love – so that I can return to my first love

as one who was told by the village and by the astrologers
that this is your destiny" – as if the language of love

is like the inevitable force of a prison, how we come to find
our cage a comfort. In my head, "What are these

so withered and wild…" My kidnappers are still asking me,
how much should we charge, how much will they be willing

to pay? The kite snaps on the wire and I cannot stop
watching it turn in the sky. "And who are these come wailing…?"

KD

9.

I was writing a story earlier this week, Kwame,
about someone being recruited into a national

spy agency and I used the descriptor 'kite' —
a different 'kite', but words get co-opted

for all sorts of different reasons, and what
serves the occasion and the next occasion

and normalises something horrific is always
going to be co-opted into the services

of control and oppression: *catchy*: the shooting
on the run, the being cut loose to fly 'free'

and drop in unannounced, and variations
on the motif… It seems not to really

constitute a theme, though hearing
certain musical phrases can trigger

responses we don't know we have in us.
There's a prism flashing nearby —

a drop on the end of a blade of grass
that is already starting to dry off

as the moisture retreats from the world
as represented here, in displaced images —

that counteracts flight which seems
to be always about the sun, ultimately,

and how long left it has to burn, as we
hear that seeds in silver foil marked

in white lettering are being sent unwanted,
unlabelled from 'secret localities' whose

purpose is undeclared, the biosecurity
parallelism of global hurt, the mail

keeping on keeping on, and a kite
as a seed that lands and germinates

and spreads its codes, and a prism
that is glorious to behold but distracts

and eventually kindles. Is this a *fait accompli*,
a recording of subjectives as *details*,

or is it a breeze that becomes a gale
where a voice lets go as pressure shifts?

JK

10.
*Dem want I fe come a dem funeral*
      — After Peter Tosh

*I ain got no time to waste on you*
*I'm a living man I've got work to do*
      — Peter Tosh, "Burial"

*"This body learns/ leaning forward on a boat"*
      — Katieann Vogel

My dear love, do forgive me, and please know
that since my sacrilege of watching again and again
the uncannily human last run of Walter Scott, my mind,
unable to untangle the strange inexplicable connection
between his name, that of some Scottish knight
whose verse was less memorable to me than his name,
a name that had as much meaning to me as Drake,
Hawkins, Penn, Venables – white bloody knights of the realm –
those who have officiated over so many wormy congresses.
But his body, dark like mine, heavy like mine,
and the familiar vegetation of an inner city, low country, empty
overgrown lot, nondescript and so-so alarmingly familiar
as a cemetery or a tomb might be, or a church's back garden,
or a grocery store – since the sacrilege of watching
him fall, in that slow clumsy way that would make any director
say, "Cut! Let's do it again, make it real, sir, realer!"
Watching him die, shot dead by a white policeman, I vowed
not to look at another black person's execution – not to stain the sacred
moment with these eyes, and yet I find myself seeking the forgiveness
of murdered men and women, black bodies, for not coming to
their place of deepest vulnerability uninvited. And they won't stop
asking me to look, asking me to stare at the absurd moment
so that my heart will fall apart, my love. And that is a poor phrase
for this unsteadiness in me – a kind of anxiety that I am
alone in this dance between paranoia and anger. If you ask,

my love, what I need, I cannot answer this question,
for it means that I will open myself to being misunderstood,
and I find the quiet turmoil of my inner conversation
a safer place than this place of language's failure. How many
times have I been told that my face is a weapon; it frightens
those looking on, that my scowl translates to terror,
and so I grow blank – do you know how the muting of my face
presses down on my fear? This is why I fear I will die young –
imprisoning in me the deep mourning of my shame;
the thing I could not say for fear of your reasoned reprimand,
as if you would rather I be stoic and strong, sturdy, kind.
You've heard me say I long for the liberations of dementia,
the man standing on the edge of the coast, on the ruins
of a castle wall, screaming to the waves whatever I have not
been able to say. So, you say to me, my love, "Tell me how
you feel," and I say, "Look, look at the sky." And someone says
"Look at this image of moving bodies, the rituals of death."
And I say, "I am not attending their funeral." Which is the first time
I have truly understood Peter Tosh's "Burial"; the funeral
is merely the gathering of those who trade and feast in death,
who ritualize the eating of the flesh of the innocents, who are
themselves, the living dead, the ghosts who walk, the Trumpians,
who gather in their castles and feed on the dead.
These are the centres where the dead bury the dead.
So, they want me to come to their funeral; they claim
they are the generals. Know ye not
that it is the season of the Festival of the Liars,
the Convocation of the Death-Speakers, the Banquet
of Decomposing Flesh, and no one can smell the stench?
Have you seen the moving images of the killing of the bodies
of the black people? And I say, "The rich man's heaven
is the poor man's hell." Now blow the "Last Post",
let it do its old colonial thing so that you and I, my love,
can tek up we foot and dance that old colonial jig.

KD

11.

There's no proofreading and correcting
that will resolve the issues of non-sequiturs,

there's no proofreading and correcting
that will allow wriggle room for apathy –

'at this stage only typographical corrections,
no changes to text'; I write elegies and laments,

celebrations of people's lives that are over
in this version of persistence, but I *avoid*

funerals – not out of disrespect, but because
I can only feel they are for the living,

not the dead, and I do not feel as one of the living
standing by corporeal remains when I am

already with the dead in their continuance.
This is something many friends and family

don't understand, feel offended by – on the
dead's behalf; but it's never that, nor

contempt for them, for I know their needs
are different from mine, and that gathering

to say 'farewell' is part of their plan
for keeping going, for addressing

their own ends. But what you say, or decipher,
Kwame, is the only time I've heard another

speak of this in this way as well. Tracy
says I shouldn't be surprised, because

there are billions of people on the planet,
and there will be many of us. But the dead

are loved by me — by us — I think,
and the living who make death will not

get to sign-off and move on, deny, forget,
ignore, delete, obfuscate, memorialise

while rewriting their parts, because
the dead are with us, with those who love

and celebrate all life, and the unwavering dead
would speak through us, and won't be silenced,

are not terrifying, cannot be proofread
out of their future, our different presences.

JK

12.

And sometimes we colonize the earth with the thing we imagine
to be beauty – how we reinvent the creatures of the sea and the birds
of the air through the splendour of metaphors in our own image.
This is not a protest, not criticism, just surrender, just a lament
for the dangers of good will. Might it be that the sun-worshippers,
and the sea acolytes, the pantheists arrived where they did
in exasperation – having finally admitted that if we outlive our births,
the rest is a peculiar kind of survival that will be marked
by contracts, covenants, treaties, compromises, compacts,
memorandums of understanding, conventions, constitutions,
negotiated deals without fears, our ignorance, our exasperation,
like a couple choosing, without signature, the territory of their love
that will never be entered – the no man's land, the mine fields,
the confabulations of silence or sham and presence, the unspoken
deal that this is how we will avoid bloodshed and rupture.
I say "we" when hungry for company – it is aspirational and the trickery
of poetic authority, as in, "we all like sheep," or "we fear death,"
as if this is a kind of ancient truth, when all it is, is me
creating the language of law to justify my vagrant ways.
"Let the dead bury the dead" says the living man on a mission;
that moment of dispassion, cold, hard single-mindedness;
follow me and you must ignore the details of humanity,
the rituals of lamentation, eulogizing and mourning; for the dead,
like the poor, will always be with us. I have no gift
for such focus; instead, selfishly and vainly, I imagine
the post-mortem pride in the weeping of those who will miss me;
and in this one can only relish the pleasure in imagination,
the suspension of necessary disbelief – all vanity. This, too,
is what one must admit is the limitation of art, and I am walking
into a cul-de-sac of meaning, so clear to me that even this,
a spark of meaning, may be jettisoned along the way, for it could
hint at pragmatism, a kind of cold rationalization of decay
and destruction. To say that the man/boy who armed himself
in Kenosha, and fired point blank into the faces of people

he knew to be black even if they did not seem black, for blackness
now, at the piedmont of the century, is an anthem, a feeling,
a negotiated deal of allies and sympathizers and woke, so the light
being what it was, low and unhelpful, these bodies in protest
were black as the nightmare that consumed the killer and his boss,
telling him through coded speech, the "dog-whistle of patriotism", to kill
and then declare the righteousness of his ways. What I have offered
above, these quaint contemplations, may merely be an apology
for murder, for brutality, for the taking of life, for the song
of one kind of Darwinian misread – or perhaps the core
despair of Darwin's regret, the thing that turned him from the bible,
how to grant God lawmaking, and rationalize the illogic of tooth
and claw, the blood and bile of uncountable time, the agnostic's
cottage at the edge of a grand un-mappable canyon – geological
impossibility; a kind of excuse, an act of exasperation, a failure of a mind,
a fine mind, a nimble mind, a ponderous mind, a willing mind.

KD

13.

In my unreality of a disarming of world of easing
all raised hands back to their activities of renewal

and persistence, in that unreality via which I know
the hand raised in anger will be a hand raised

in violence, an almost reflex action called 'cliché' – I have known
violence, I have been violence, and to renounce

the reflex and watch decades unfold their continuance
of a restive 'inner peace' twisting expressions and observances

of cruelty and distress, diminishing and response,
while my arms (bones, skin, biceps, wrists) stay by my side

though incongruously my hands wave about as I talk – it's
    remarked on,
though I don't notice at the time, scrawling the troubled air –

in all its realities, ferocity is a sensual rewriting or deleting,
the way battle hymns and pipers pipe unto death,

can kill armies and individuals with emphasis and repetition
of a tune, the way some people demanding liberty translate liberty

into a right to bigotry – *their* right to raise *their* arms, shape their hands
    into weapons.
What will de-escalate outside non-violence? – a musical pause

is likely a false phrase from an enemy looking for gain, the cops,
armed, set the trap, and the arms-merchants are the vectors for 'voters';

but in my unreality they disarm themselves and maintain
an unreality; my – our – dwelling on the edge

to be swept away by the high winds of change
while the violence to correct violence, to 'end'

violence churns over a reality that has no time
for my distractions from the immolations

preparing for the fires that will surely come down
on us soon, or, more likely, up, up from the valley below,

flames gathering pace up a hillside, a verisimilitude,
not a prophecy, and fewer people will know all that's lost.

JK

14.

*I was born before Christopher Columbus*
                —Toots Hibbert

*What happened was, on an waning gold afternoon in 2003, a flock of cardinals smashed into the amber-hued glass wall of the Welsh Humanities Building, named for old John Rushing Welsh III, whose name makes you think of how there was a first and a second, and how their blooding and naming went back into the morass of slavery-times; and the students who eulogized him in 1974, sang praise to the grandeur of the man "an anachronistic and very human man,... the last of the Southern gentlemen,... according to the values of a romanticized age,... characterized the finest qualities attainable by man." And the cardinals swooped and smashed into Welsh's hard face, though nobody witnessed it, but we all saw the brick-cobbled courtyard strewn with the twitching bodies of the broken birds — a strange and elegant horror. Now seventeen years later, on a phone call, an old Christian man and poet — a friend\** *— recalled the cardinals.*

---

\* In these times his whiteness is character and plot, and to not name it is to recolonize the authority of silence.

---

*Footnoting a footnote*

*After Ben Greer's "For the World"*
An old southern white man said to me, "I remember in 1958
going in the cinema, and it was in Columbia, yes, and I can't
say the name of the place, though I know the name of the place,
and to say the name of the place is to show how well I can recall
if I put my mind to it. And the black people had to be in the balcony;
they could not sit with normal people, and I did not think
myself privileged, and when I drank from the white fountain,
I did not think it privilege, and when I lamented for the Birmingham
girls, bombed by men who went to church, and I thought,
in my heart of hearts, that they were monsters, horrible monsters,
I did not think it was privilege. And when I visited all these years,

the Broad River Correctional Institute*, down the road from me,
off the highway with its banking gay with wisteria,
and held in my arms the long-termers, black men, Christian men,
men broken by this system, and I did not think me privileged.
But a few weeks ago, I understood, and I do not know why,
why I have been so dumb, so foolish. How did I not know
that when I was born in this society, I was born with a leg-up
that I had not earned, except where the white man's burden
is the weight of my labour, my 'cost'? Yes, I have always had a leg-up.
How come I did not know this?"

---

*The State of South Carolina execution chamber is located in Broad River.

---

                          And maybe this is how
we know that the drama of epiphanies work, why the world
loves an all-seeing metaphor, the scales dropped, the eyes
washed with spit to reveal upsidedown trees, the veil removed,
the hey-presto of salvation, the turn-around of all things
I knew, the starting over again, the hallelujah of "Amazing
Grace". Perhaps this is what we are given as a gift of change.
Still, the paranoid in me will always ask, how long before
the illogic of guilt will fade, or the overwhelming weight
of this edifice of white supremacy will leave a small old white
man helpless and so deeply silent in the fatigue of regret,
so shamed by the old values of the romanticized age?
Still, he humbles me, daily, for he visits the prisoners in prison,
writes letters, gives solace and comfort, and though they
ritualize the acts of their own destruction every time
he arrives for absolution, at least there is a body willing
to bring warmth, a face willing to see, ears to hear, and that simple
grace of human contact may be enough, maybe all.

KD

15.

We curtail good and bad stories to make things better,
to go by the letter to smash down the doors

to remake in own images which might be *better*
but so is the forest which so abruptly disappears

before us as we watch the New Holland honeyeater
whose name, as arranged, is ignored by that feeder

of nectar – cup-bearer – while a scrubwren makes a similar
but quite different argument about *locale* just as I try to hear

further into its plight, the lessening of its sector,
so what do we infer from a *donation* of a settler-

family's property where The Hills gather water,
where English oak and orchards and bauxite are *colour*

to 'local histories' over grevilleas, and censorship would offer
us a corrective, though expunction is chasmic and *deeper*

so written into where the railway was but is no longer,
as roads and arteries sit on top or alongside or near

the original overlay, the way through to a plenty of layers
that when peeled back disrupt, even fracture

the rhythms of generations of peer to peer
answers to wrongs that identify and take care

of such birds in aviaries and glass-cases and aver
to a future where there might be nil beyond such junctures.

JK

16.
*Footnote to a woman's face, a stranger familiar as ancestry*

---

1.
This matters to me because in every sliver
of meaning I encounter there is a side note of memory,
a way to locate my skin, my sorrow.
Dates ride the bassline of this island —1513
shipped from the Iberian Peninsula — Maroonage.
Bight of Biafra, Gold Coast, Congo,
ackee seeds in the belly, cowries in braids,
the deep musk of Akan at the base of the tongue,
and my grandfather found his way to Igbo land,
a body homing back home the texture of green,
the earth's welcoming, the salt of the sea.
I see history repeated in my face — the nose,
the round brown lineage, its substance, heavy
as memory, as blood, as the contours of a continent,
the repetition of history in my lips' curve.
There is beauty in the dusk's light; we are not
orphans, we are not tribeless, we are not, we are not.

2.
A city mayor promises a contract,
a compact, a promise, and handshake
of plenty, and plenty piled on
and spilling over, with the handsome
smile that politicians consider their weapon,
the tool of trust. The mayor flashed
his hope-filled mouth publicly and privately
to a gay-hearted, enterprising woman,
who ritualizes the memory of Africa
in the foods she cooks, the oils,
red and muggy with the heavy taste
of the Atlantic coast, the delicate

cloudiness of okra, the sweetness
of coconut milk, harvested and poured
into plastic bottles; those pies,
those peppers, those slimy okras,
those fingers gathering cassava,
wet and sticky, the art of texture,
the art of herbs and spices, the art
of bodies made to labour, bodies
fed to sweat and sweat. But a mayor
reneges on the deal with the woman,
and this story will fade into the dark sky
of this town licked by the Atlantic,
its heavy air of salt and the stories of trade,
the murder of black bodies still there in their salt.
And her sorrow was great, and her body
broke into deep sorrow – these betrayals
by men, by politicians, by liars. It means
something that at dawn, when the purple and gold
of first light creates patterns over the disturbed silk
of the sea, she carries a bouquet of flowers
to the rocky ocean's edge, where the tide goes
out before returning with the answers to prayers;
and she mutters her prayers to Yemanja,
her stuttering tongue repeating the mantra
of grace, and she stares at the flowers moving
like the flotsam of wrecked lives, out, out
into the horizon, the ocean humming in the way
a woman hums from deep inside her belly,
the melodies of prayers sung for centuries –
the things retained, the things the fortunate
retained in their skin, in their blood,
in their bones, in their meals.

KD

17.
*'He is splendid. With a place to stand.'*
       — Gwendolyn Brooks, 'Of Robert Frost',

The give and take, oh, and take. The give of place —
blue ribbon — that is ungiven is a gifthorse, is a farmer's

lament for a plough that furrows askew and work done
to make a poem ring changes of a certain brand

of sameness — *that* self-cut hair, that stature, that
voice of pasture in units… given a grandstand.

And so, through school, he was served up as a basis — though I took
the pain of the buzz-saw, the rural catastrophe said quietly… the
       chit-chattish

'everyday language' of his imagining speaking to our schoolroom.
Translation? Or just our capturing and reading to make familiar?

That splendid unfamiliar familiar and the leylines of manners
of farming, pastoral melancholy, a verbal cinema of entitlements.

Which ghosts are given lip-service? Whose houses meet
the building specifications of whose *national significance*?

JK

18.

History has cursed me with the eye to search for the footnote;
there is the Pocantico Hills, NY, farmer chef who says,
quickly settled in his place to stand despite the alienness
of the earth beneath his feet (how easily he colonizes,
how splendidly he enacts, without regret, his right to occupy),
"All great European cuisines come out of suffering and struggle,
but when we [sic] came here, we Americans [sic], we found abundance —
all these cows for steak, so we [sic] did not need to learn to cook
an American cuisine of invention and suffering, and the desperate
art of surviving the starvation of denuded farmlands."
And I think, "Man, who has put scales over your eyes,
you with your Beard upon Beards awards, and your organic
farm-to-table with fufu grains and asparagus
for all seasons, that you could say this with barefaced
soft-spoken pretension?" Does he not see, I think, the rice, the rice, the rice,
the hog, the chilies, the pit, the hot sweltering pit, the fat back,
the banked potatoes, the food of the poor; the kitchen,
a coal-skinned box set off from the main house, with its woodstove,
with the side garden of herbs for taste and healing,
for curses, and the poultices to suck away the poisons
of the soul and the soil, to smoke hickory through the hollows,
to drunken the mosquitoes with their proboscises of death,
to find in this laboratory of memory the last art of the ancestors,
to leave in the earth and in the heavy walls the songs of survival,
the taste of Africa in the stews, in the discarded flesh, the jazz
of turning the refuse of the wealthy into the glorious
promise of memory and hope? And yes, here is where
the sugar and starch would begin the slow muddying of blood,
the lineage of bodies battered by the capped anger
of abuse, by starvation, by the laws made to the side
of the white man's health and glory — the laws of the outside
people, the hidden people, the tools people, and in this
shrine of invention, American cuisine is made, remade.
He seems to have forgotten this, he who claims to have invented

the simple rituals of worship of the ordinary herb sprig
growing on the doorstep, its aromatic medicine, its grace.
I footnote him here, for my father-in-law's grandmother,
the barefooted centurion of Clarendon parish bush,
with her head-tie and her machete and her brain full of inventions,
the woman whose genius he seems to have forgotten,
whose hand reappears in the magic of my wife's magic hands –
the easy alchemy of want into plenty, that art inherited
in the blood and in the ritual of memory. Where is the footnote,
the disclaimer, the illumination, the confession, where the regret?
Bob Dylan says he has no regrets, and I say that his may be
their anthem – he whose songs I have lived inside for years,
yet as an interloper, as a squatter, knowing that the landlord
will return one day and say, "I have no regrets, you must leave".
I will steal from him, as I have always done, and though I have tasted
the sweet alertness of these fufu dishes, groaned with pleasure,
I know that the ingredient that is missing is the deep salt,
the seasoning of regret, the thing he envies but fails to see.
Me, all I have is a sack full of sorry, and a scrap book of those
I have hurt, a deep sadness that sits in between the near mountains,
the place where we, as boys, would look for the dark deluge over
our cricket pitch. I call that cloud regret. I am cursed with regret,
with the haunting disciplining of the footnote – the thing I know
I have forgotten; it is, John, the knife-edge blue glint at the corner
of Brooks' praise-song for Frost, the two-edged sword of lightning,
the imperviousness of iron, and the sum of "some", and "some".
She is that Clarendon barefooted woman who fills her hands
with herbs and contemplates each leaf, each twig. It is how
her poems are written, with enviable care, over time, the long,
slow, careful marinate, and then this gem of a fist, the art of survival.
Theirs is the name of the women whose faces arrive at times,
and vanish, whose eyes understand the dignity of regret,
these ghost women who greet me with, "You must not change."
And my mind searches the catalogue for the things
I should not have said – let's call those, too, regrets.

KD

19.

I was wondering after I woke from difficult sleep if sleep can
    actually be the 'easy death' many seem
to hope for when death comes – but I can't wonder, never mind
    state what is not a declaration of life. Sleep

is not death to me, it is wonder: it's necessary and affronting, and,
sometimes, even indulgent – an interior 'design' (an empty room
to be filled). But that sleep might align with a 'regret-free' wakeful-
ness, I can never even process – time and space to browse,

room for 'creativity', to be inventive. Original. No. I wake distantly
to what I slept: Britain falling to consequences of official delusion –
land/s where any classroom teaching perceived to be 'anti-capitalist'
is to be officially condemned (as 'extreme political stance'),

where 'freedom' is still sold as the liberty to spread (to 'prevent' or
not to 'prevent' stratagems) a version of 'freedom' so particular
to a weighting of history to one system, to one throne, to be an
accessory of territory and taste, to be the 'Brit expat', to others
    'migrant'.

I think back to early May and Southbank Hospital's (positive) receipt
of the Banksy 'monochrome' of a boy playing with an NHS nurse
action-figure while Batman and Spiderman are consigned to the
wastepaper basket, and the surface (at least) communalism of it –

aside from the lack of nuance in the 'signature' (demi-street artistry).
    I slept it over and woke often to its idea, its audience:
so, street art that hangs in a foyer will last longer than if painted over
    an official mural or gleaming blank wall, won't it?

If it had, say, been painted over a picture of the sovereign, which
    government official would have cancelled it… and when?
Selective disclosure. Footnotes to sleep and loss. The many tales

around every death. The different conditions of making art. Sleep on it.

JK

20.
*Vox audita perit, littera scripta manet* –

What persistent horror allows a thesis to take root and settle as proper
that the teeth of Lumumba be kept in a "safe place" in the vaults
of his torturers? What obscene logic settles in the mind of the keepers
to think that these teeth, the last things left after the dissolving
of a man's body in acid – the sheer conspiracy and macabre
efficiency of this colonial act – can simply be listed as a fact of history
while the teeth, the teeth of a man are kept in exile, imprisoned
by a logic that is as old as the rituals of colonial rule. Today,
(which means, in this epoch which may be a week or a year,
but more, it means, "now", as in whereas *before* this was so,
*now* this is so) they will return the teeth to his home earth.
And despite its ancient gravitas, in the face decomposition,
it does seem trite to say, "The spoken word perishes,
but the written word remains." Teeth. A handful of teeth.
Can a handful of teeth speak – continue to speak, bear
witness to the atrocity of murder, assassination and the brute
rituals of the colonizing agents? Teeth, this is all that's left.
The security agent keeps checking her briefcase for the velvet
forest-green sack with a cotton string to hold the mouth together,
to be sure she delivers the evidence of a nation's unmaking
to the right authorities. She is relieved, when, at the airport,
the satchel is taken. She stops at a road-side market,
buys a bottle of cool Primus, and some fish stew. She eats
as the sun falls quickly behind the forest. So, this is an invention –
the security agent, the green satchel, the beer, the fish stew –
and yet it is a kind of footnote, is it not? I find myself,
digging deeper at each strange word – the etymologies,
and where they take us. Lumumba. Now, *there* is a rabbit's hole,
that leads us to a vat of acid, and some teeth, and the meaning
of today. Or where birds find their names. In poems from
another country, I find the names of birds (scrubwrens, say)
to be a path into a certain memory. Or, Grevillas, *there* is a word.
And then digging deeper, how quickly we forget the flowering woolly

plant, gayly coloured and humble innocent in its shrubbery,
and find instead, this: Charles Francis Grevilleas,
"A website concerning the portraits of Warwick Castle,
by Adam Buziakiewicz, says that 'we know that the Grevilles
owned slaves in Tobago later in the eighteenth century'
and refers to several documents relating to a mortgage
that lists enslaved people 'owned by the 1st and 2nd Earls'
in Tobago in the Warwickshire County Record Office dated 1770-1."
It is, then, the long stain of Britannia across time and oceans;
how we know that Governor Edward Eyre the bloody,
had such a peaceful time exploring Australia, before that messy
business in Jamaica and its rebellious blacks. Which is why
my neighbours cover their ears and sing "Abide with Me"
loudly enough to block out the noise of history, its deep
inconvenience. And perhaps sitting here, in the messy
swirl of its making, one can imagine the annals of reckoning
fifty years from now, how the historians will say:
"Not so much his fault, but how he lingered over their death beds,
how they were wrested from him or died to silence him,
how they knew they were passing through the epoch of lies,
how he outlived them. This is the ultimate tyranny.
That he outlived his victims, that he outlived the teeth,
that he outlived the dead by his hand, that he outlived
the eight hundred black souls hanged on the north coast plains
of Jamaica, the earth still smoldering with the ash of rebellion,
the cane fields stretching far into the distance, beautifully
blackened, beautifully blackened – he outlived them.

KD

21. the silences

I am disgraced in language, I am utterly speechless
and yet I go on and on and try to disentangle as if it's

the best I can do, but listening is better and I will fill
with listening and relearn every mouth-shape as a word

taken away from others as a word hidden in the phonetics
and vocab testing and the reading-out-loud and the checks

and balances of blackboard rubbed down clear (but letters
and numerals still showing through from early school days,

a vague suggestion of lost lessons) *at the end of each day*.
'Introduced' flowers have closed up as a 'cold snap' has

intervened to 'buck the trend', which means hell payback
at a later date. I was startled just now by a honeyeater

snapping an insect from in front of my face, but then again
the flowers are closed and I am entirely devoid of nectar.

JK

22.
*The Art of Lies: A Tryptic*

*And if your night should dark,*
*I know you will find your way*
*to your home sweet home*
         —Burning Spear

*It's so much work being black…*

*A work that aspires, however humbly, to the condition of art should carry its justification in every line.*
     — Joseph Conrad

1
*upon the innocence of reading romantic fiction*

      — *After* Ellena Ferrante

And there is a thick morass that entangles and sucks you in,
it is called the lie, and the lies multiply. The lie is also the smoke
over an entire subcontinent's coast, the smoke from fires
rushing through the dry and brittle places – how can one see such flame,
such orange in the eerie sky and not think of end times?
And the art of lying is the art of persistence, and soon
we hold councils and conferences and study the granularity
of the lie. The coroner on BBC TV says,
while munching a sandwich over the fetid remains, "It was slow,
went on for days, these small nicks, quite ingenious, really."
I am reading the *Lies Adults Tell*, and it is a delight, isn't it?
Set in a city I care so little about, a people whose sins
I am training my ear to forgive, one wound at a time,
one benediction at a time. And yet what genius in a name –
the *lies adults tell* is a lie the teller tells and therein lies
the lie, the slap across the cheek, the enlivening of the body
to the shame of abuse, the coming of burning tears.

This is a crowded way to obscure the truth, I admit, and this is it;
there is a slippage happening all around us, and I fear
we do not know the meaning of the lie, and I fear that the forests
will be rotted to the ground, and we will stare at the melted sea,
miles and miles of it, and say, "Wow, what a view,
what a marvellous view of the sea, this is. Let's build here!"

And still I find comfort in the prose descriptions of the squalid
southern heat, humid as mould in the stinking gutters of Naples.
I have never visited that city, never thought to do so,
despite her wistful fictions. And so, I imagine it all: stewed,
sodden, damp, under the sun's oppression; and the bodies of women
heavy with sweat, and the scent of garlic and olives.
I read its landscape through the eyes of Africa –
a kind of healing that the immigrant stranger must master.
Nor have I come to adore her nonfictional manner – hardly.
Still, I am greedy for her inventive sagas, her soapy instinct,
for her way with plots, and the manner in which she bares
the duplicity of affection. There is strange comfort in this.
No one is murdered in the making of these stories,
no one starved, though her Italy is disappeared of immigrants,
the bodies of my people who wash up on their shores –
and not an Ethiopian in sight. It's as if she has mastered the art
of erasing her nightmares – the collective Italian nightmare,
the defeat on the flat grounds of Adwa and all the arrogant warriors –
from her stories. This is why I'm wary of my consumption
       of Neapolitan lies.


2

*the president is diseased; he will live, we fear; he will return to gloat*

We mark the early hours. The inventor of lies grows sluggish.
The fatigue has come over the emperor, and his body

slouches. How quickly the hint of death turns a brute
bully into a stuttering frightened baby, and the pity of the humane

becomes the ritual of good wishes. We live in an epoch
of evidence, and in tiny boxes the monstrosity is preserved.

The gloater, the abuser, the boorish buffoon with his army
of sycophantic strategists, bloody to the core, hardened to the rituals

of death, they who count not the casualties of war,
who count only the fronts gained, the dead being not even collateral

but the currency of power. You imagine asking them, Where
is your milk of human kindness? and like frat boys and the spoilt,

they say, "I am a pretty soft-spoken good person; I love babies, but war
    is war."
This is the language they speak here in "peacetime" in the time
    of plague.

3
*what is this despite the lies?*

On the day after Donald Trump declared, "Proud Boys, stand down,
stand by!" causing the dogs to growl and settle in vigil outside their
master's house praying for his healing; yes, on the eve of the news
of his succumbing to the pernicious plague he had denied for so long,
a self-proclaimed "pretty soft spoken" white college freshman
in the Midwest, USA, interrupted a zoom © class chat with the truncated
word "Nigg…", then disappeared from camera.
The Afro-Puerto Rican instructor, bewildered and blazing mad,
ended the class, and waited, the air humming with soft growls and prayers.

So, you ask, is it a palimpsest of another saying that begins "nigg"
or ends "nigg" or something interrupted lurking beneath the veneer
of decency, an old unfinished conversation, carelessly left behind,

only to rise up as a filthy pair of underpants on the corner of the room,
[we are trying]. Or, perhaps, a note heading to "...of Narcissus",
such literary ambition, perhaps, or an accidental statement,
"The Nig[erian] said this to me", or the "Nig[er] is a lovely river",
though the double "gg" is a betraying clue. A stutter maybe?
Or perhaps a rich vocabulary, reaching for "nigg[ardly]"
apropos of what? What might have been the subject of class discussion?
Not a freshman engineer's vocabulary, or the interruption
of a computer glitch, or a pernicious bomb, or a note to self, or a note
to a friend, or a note to heaven or a note to hell – you know the way;
dare I touch it? What will happen if I touch? And how we labour
to arrive at the sins of innocence, those cursed with the forgivable
conditions of their birth: dyslexia, dyslexia – a burr of racist errors
on the edge of the brain – the terrible terror of Tourette's –
there is an innocent at the doorway to this condition. But we are reaching
for a way to understand the coprolalia of this moment, afraid, I know,
to think that this soft-spoken youth of the flash smile, festooned
with scholarships and praise – the mother's *good person* – might
wilfully type first an n, then an i, then two twin g's and stop, no pause...
and then send, yes, send, yes, send it off, knowingly.
To ask why, is to seek out some shelter from the violence of it.

---

*Footnote:*
Below is the letter he wrote twenty-four hours later, and twenty-four hours before he confessed to a gathering of white administrators that it was all a lie, this tale of woes and sorrow, that no friend wrote the word, that he wrote those word, that no toilet-break drew him away, that he sat there, and wrote the word, and watched the wound break over the silence.

[*"Can't you guys take a joke – jeez, it was a joke, man, just a silly joke"*]

NOTE: This versification of horror makes it better for us to consume its violence. Emphases added, unnecessarily.

******A FOUND POEM******

**Hi**! I'm sure you're well aware that **something popped up** in chat
yesterday during our 2:30-3:30 zoom class. My room is a very open
and social room so **we have 6 or 7 people in our room at a time**.
Well, towards the end of class I needed to use the restroom
so I left my computer unattended not knowing **one of my friends**
would proceed to go on my computer and type out **such vulgar
language** and send it in chat. (I have Bluetooth headphones so
I could walk away from class and **still hear what is going on in class**.)
Well anyway, when I was walking back in my room **my friend
thought it would be funny and sent that in chat**.
**I don't know what he was** thinking but he did. **Under no circumstance**
would I **ever** use that kind of language towards anyone!
**I am pretty soft-spoken person and would never use such language**

(I hardly ever cuss to begin with **lol**.)

**[lol lol lol lol lol lol lol lol lol lol lol lol lol lol lol]**

*["Can't you guys take a joke — jeez, it was a joke, man, just a silly joke"]*

I actually **just got an email as I was writing** this saying
I have to go on a zoom call tomorrow to talk about the incident.
I hope you can be there to hear that I don't want to be disrespectful
**towards anyone and** that **I would never do anything like that**.
I'm probably **rambling** on now because I'm kind of nervous
what is going to happen next, but I hope you can understand
where I am coming from. Again I am **super sorry** for my **friends actions**
and I will take whatever responsibility there is to take.
I left my computer unattended and **that is my fault**.
Again I am so sorry and will do everything I can
to avoid what happened in class Wednesday.

*Epilogue*

This is the way of the world. And I know that around us
the dead bodies mount up, the black dead, the poor dead,
    the broken dead.

KD

23.

And now the Proud Boys are 'standing vigil'.
And now job-lots of old vinyl records mix far-left and far-right

and pop tunes and soul and swing and punk of angry love with punk
     of brute hate
all in the same batch… loss and discovery… buried away among
     the hundreds…

of old 33rpms – grab bag lucky dip roll of the dice old tech once dished up
on a DJ's platter which is chance as empires teeter on their
     collection points,

their loci of self-adoration, their vacuuming of artefacts.
What well-meaning good people poking about browsing bargain-hunting

can accidentally pick up in the opportunity shop, the second-
hand dealers, the curiosity shop, the trash and treasure, flea market.

Once, long long ago, I sold all we had down to the last left-wing protest
record at a weekend swap-meet so we could escape the city – escape

the neo-Nazis and dealers, so we could reset our co-ordinates. Start again.
And now the skinheads reconfigure vigilance – popping up in a friend's

job lot, unseen and then found amongst the 'take your luck' offering –
footnotes to a history or preludes to a history scripted and rolling?

JK

24.

*In a 2020 interview for this obituary, he said...*
            — New York Times

I am hoarding joys — well pleasures, anyway —
in the dusk light of these prairie lands.
The light crawls like memory should over the land.
It is still early enough in the autumn
for the journey into the fattening gloom
to be slow, slower than a memory,
a passing thought. Today it is a bowl,
a large porcelain bowl full of the slime-green
of okra soup, festooned with slivers
of dry kingfish, kotombre, and the delicate green
and pink rings of sliced okra, the steam rising
over the soup-washed island of banku
set in the middle of the waves.
With fingers stinging with scorch, I eat,
pulling gently, and efficient as muscle memory,
from the sticky fermented banku,
then coating it with the slime and leaf
of the soup, cupping the fluid inside the hook
of my fingers — then I lift it to my mouth,
the grit and sour sweetness of the mouthful,
the humming heat of the pepper
and green soothing forest taste,
musky and smokey — something ancient —
before the quick slide of it all down
the throat — the belly saying, ahh,
the belly saying hmmmm, the belly saying...
This is the comfort of the memory
one prolongs, holds against
the gloom, holds against the news
of a world slipping away from us.
Once, before her blindness,

when Mama the Great stood as grand witch
holding sway in the kitchen, welcomed me
with her smile, saying, "I know
you have been dreaming of this banku
for days in your exile. Here, eat it, and tell me."
It has been many years since,
long enough for this remembrance to be filed
for the sudden arrival of a death song
that will shatter me in the middle
of a brilliant sunny day of joy,
and make me think of how it is
that even when we least expect it,
the wound of loss reminds us that it is festering
beneath the veneer of normalcy and healing.
Yes, everything must pass in this world.
Still, here is the old saw of our art —
how it preserves goodness and beauty,
how language keeps the sweetness
of life secure, protected from rot.

KD

25.

I am grass cutting over these days, so don't fully occupy the words
I write. Not quite anywhere, balance never as anyone would surely
    wish it,

I stumble down the steep embankments, flailing, ankles twisting
    amongst
the rocks that make up the valley wall — pull them all out and
    something quicker

than erosion would have its way. In cut grass is a chaos of windrows
    that aren't for collecting
but breaking down and going under — or between rocks, and it is
    where I've come from against

last year's pattern of cut, *that* time. I watched Chris Marker's *San
    Soleil* last night, exhausted, and thought
it possessed by idea of memory it was forcing on its subject material
    — the very people and peoples

it cared about, and also around the animals acting as *his*
    intermediaries. But I was tired, so it's half-
reasoning, really, and a looking for more than the backwash of the
    French New Wave could offer —

that odd disrupted Marxism, so long after, really, though he was
    clearly overwhelmed by inevitabilities of loss
*and* celebration, of Pacman as metaphor, of the permeability of life
    and death. *Okra*, Kwame — I have okra

seed from the poor crop we got last summer, and when this cycle of
    cutting and tossing down is done I will prepare
the beds and plant with roughened hands. Is it sortilege to say that I
    will harvest the first pods in your honour?

JK

26.
*O, come/ in, equivocator*

And here she is, sister Louise, who sings of the ups and downs of fame –
or shall we say the stings and wings of fame, though mostly it is the eyes,
a kind of fatigue. I realize that when she says, I hate sex, she is not
bored, but drawn – and the world is framed with myths, and the privilege
of money and opportunity, and the accent shaped by upbringing.
Follow your nose, says Gogol, follow your nose to South Africa,
there is a stench there. You know, for five months I would say to people,
I am listening to the music that it takes forty people to play –
and this was a sham, a decided pretension. Music distracts me
with its wearing power. I have now realized that I never understood
the meaning of music, I was just carried by it – a body thing,
and like my ankle, aching in these later days, music sits on me
like an ill-fitting shirt, which is not enough. And here is where
I must speak in German and not translate it – or perhaps
something lovely by the Norwegians eating pink-fleshed fish –
the betrayal of olives, the bitterness of overcooked flesh, the gag
of an eye, sucked out and the swallowed. But this is not about
Sister Louise. And what of her and the night below and above
and all this nocturnal complaining? This is the last of the songs.
It is 1:00 AM. I try to remember: Did Sister Angela, the headmistress,
did she die, the tall elegant black woman, with a slightly
ironic face, and her long stride, a habitless nun, who presided
under the massive tent among the grand ficus-berry trees,
at the remembrance of my sister – did she die? Did she die?
I have been devouring stretches of absurdities – follow your nose,
is a kind of saying, though this nose has long legs, and dances
a jig. In this deep night, even this starts to enter and depart
from my mind. I have no business with Russian noses, though
the old man stood before the Kremlin in his sandals and Ghanaian
print shirt – or was it Peking? It may have been Peking. I have
inherited his nose – the fist of my belonging – we trace it back
through myths and old photographs – cricketers wearing waistcoats,
and spats, lounging under a mango tree for the photo, four black

men, one uncannily like Marcus Garvey in fit form, the Jamaican
Eleven before a match with the MCC – and there is my nose,
the fist of a nose, the clue, the culprit, the anchor of my soul.
In the White House, the President is finally snoring, and everyone
is relaxed again after his tantrum, his diatribe against all his cabinet
he betrays, his sad, sad laments about how unhappy he is with them.
And the black butler searches his email for the results of the last
test, the swab piercing into the soft tissue membrane near
his brain; just to be sure, because the sugar has been at bay, yes,
but his wife has told him to come home, to resign, they will be fine,
and he is not sure. There are no results yet. The building
is in deep slumber. Another day of chaotic death, the mansion
awaiting the collapse or a miracle. This is a cartoon of charcoal
crushed into powder, dancing over the white sheets, and soon,
there will be the President facing himself, touching the mic
asking, Can you hear me? Will you not wear a mask? Who wears
a mask these days? The tender dialogue between two men,
not alter egos, just identical creatures of bland dullness.
Knock, knock, knock. Can you hear me? Is this working?
A cyclone of dark streaks sweeps the sheet, erasing features,
Leaving us with knock, knock, knock, can you hear me?

KD

## 27. *anomalous*

In the vastness of dexamethasone & Regn-Cov2 – 'blessing
from God' – the lines compile like people they'd replace –

in this Declaration of Dependence the moment for calling
crowds to order & strife, for eternal youth paroxysms.

Literature and art of invincibility kisses play big roles
in investigative hagiographies – speculating on flowers

lost before granting of files & immunities. Military hospital
improves ratios of living to dead, but so do experimental

variations on treatment-helicopters. Trade-routed
embargoes on ordinary bodies are a lesser or non-existent

health insurance. Fridge commerce needs turning up because
outside temperature rises – routers & steroids are anterior visions

of strong rooms & wealth protection. Masts & sirens,
lashings & waves. Epics of the drowned. Re. generations.

JK

28.

It is October, the season of the million dollar jackpot
and all its ritualized disappointments and empty
pointless contemplations, plus the shame of admitting
that it seems to still matter enough that we keep
buying the lotto ticket, and hoping, even though
we know – what poor revolutionaries we are!
The shame of it. And the older I get
the more the fantasy of a phone call turns absurd,
a standard joke: "Hey, Colin, just checking if they called
you to ask for my number…" "Who?" "The Norwegians."
"Oh sugar. I thought it was one of those robocalls!"
And I am conflating the disappointment about Ngugi
with anxiety about Trump. Gluck is no Trump,
but she has always annoyed me in the knee jerk
(and perhaps unfair – blame my socialist upbringing,
blame the 1970s) that privileged American poets like Bishop,
Stevens et al, with their family allowances, and their
lands to squander, and the pleasures of cake for bread,
have annoyed me by cashing in on the consolation
of their European "inheritance" – the classics
that at least Walcott found to be "not enough",
despite their uses. And here I keep seeing her,
folded into an Amish oversized Windsor chair,
all in black – slacks and delicate blouse,
feet tucked under her, the light, the light
from the Vermont fields falling in on the scene:

"So, I take my poems to bed with me in the days,
and I live with them, and sleep with them, I do.
I suddenly woke up one day and realized
that what the poem needed was a *satz*,
a German phrase, you know, and I know
no German, [ironic giggle] so I asked a dear friend
[name drops a famous German linguist – she name-drops

a lot, by the way, but can she be blamed
when all her friends are brilliant?]. So, I said to him,
how do you render, "the petunias turned grey by twilight"
in German? [Long pause for effect] Well, [in perfectly
moderated German], *Die Petunien wurden im Zwielicht grau.*
[(c) Google Translate, *mon amis*. No language was harmed
in the making of this poem]
[Pause as she manages the amazing look of self-deprecation,
self-satisfaction, and flippant amazement
at how clever she is, and what she is sure is a gainful
coquettish look of humility, helped by a hand through her hair –
her hand is constantly in her hair, a way to be sure
her face is framed for every epic she utters –the face
she once banked on – the face she once complained
of – such sexist mentors treating her like a body,
the bob, the bobbing hair, saying *cute*: "Such
admiration, such elevation, the violence of it,
to be praised for what one does not want to be praised for;
what one deplores the humiliation of that, so punishing.
How tragic not to see the pure soul, the purest soul.
And there you have it,"
she says, waiting for the next question.]
Anyway, this is how I remember it and, obviously,
I could be misremembering the story, but not the *situation*.
Outside my house, the leaves are changing,
and the Norwegians remain dogged in their colonial souls.
The air is brittle, and it is Friday – they will announce
the Peace Prize today, and the world awaits its cataclysm.

KD

29. *pathetic infelicities*

The small composition
I am left holding, untangling,

is still shaking with grass-cutting
against the building combustions

via an irony of splendour
of a sacred kingfisher

feckless and not as
cautious as it usually is,

and maybe astounded by the gall
of quivering and swaying lyrics

in the guise of the rhapsodic,
contractions of its habitat,

its water supplies rapid-cycling along
with injustices some moral people smudge over.

JK

30.
*I Long for Silence*

*...like bees caught in the wrong hive...*
— Anne Sexton

Outside my window, the world moves
in the slow, deliberate randomness
of what I imagine to be the peace
that comes with silence. Every sorrow
I carry in me, every rupture begins
with the words spoken to me,
the noise of my deep sound coming
back into me – the voice of others,
the grand weight of their noise,
and then the weighty silence
of remorse, the silence so full
of echoes that it cannot be true silence.

The top of a squat hibiscus tree is framed
in the small squares of my window,
just above the window's border,
the lower pane, and from there
arises its untidy top; which I watch
for minutes, not long enough to be emptied
of all reason, and then, as if to shake
my growing disappearance, the peace
I long for, a crow lands, jittery
as paranoia, this delicate magic
of such dark substance held up
by the delicate leaves and twigs.
In the seconds that the moment holds,
the bird jittery and the moment
before alarm, the sky bland and reliable,
the tips of the shrub barely acknowledging
the weight of the bird, there is the silence

I long for — a kind of reversal
of chaos, and then, as if warned,
the crow lifts and vanishes, a flurry
of black blurring into bright blue —
the solitary hibiscus shrub shivering.

I am sitting inside the moment before
a new dispensation — it will always be different
after this decision. I stare at a pile of logs;
they have no meaning, all that returns
to me is the sky, and the logs. And the sound
of a machine whirring in the background
is the ominous sound of the end of one epoch
and the start of another. And though I know
my heart is held hostage to the news
that will arrive after the counting, and the suits,
I also know that these will all be new beginnings,
the end of a monster and the beginning
of the warning of the coming monster.
This is the nature of silence. It is why,
as if ordered by seasons, the poet must
grow silent, not waiting, simply emptying
of all meaning. The light of Autumn is beautiful,
I say, again and again. Autumn is beautiful.

At the credits, we will learn there was a crow-
wrangler, and the hibiscus shrub was watered
for the three days to keep it green, and the light,
the splendid autumnal light on the lawn's green,
was returned to the truck that trundled
out of the neighbourhood, leaving the world
noisy with the preparations for the evening meal.
It is October 14, 2020, at three thirty in the afternoon.
My body is slightly damp from the exertion
of the steady stroll across the back lawn
pushing the mower, its bloated bag filling

with grass and leaves, so many brilliantly
familiar leaves – stains of reds and oranges
purples; my mouth is green with the taste
of cherry tomatoes I harvest and pop
at each lap around the uneven lawn;
and then the final oversized paper bag
is filled with the evidence of my labour,
and I finally look at the paths I have taken,
across the lawn, and it is then that I see
that the light of the season is impossibly
made, such consuming amber – as if the soft
chill in the air filters everything into a clean
deliberate grace. I text: "Lorna, you should see
how beautiful this backyard looks
in the late afternoon light after a trim."
"Nice, I will," she replies. The day slips by.

KD

31.
*16-line sonnet visual heat exchange operation*

This is the first time I've seen your home's outdoors, Kwame.
I am sure Lorna liked what she saw, even as the day went by.
      Even

here I took comfort in your comfort – and I am about to plant
      summer
tomatoes, though so many trees are going going gone and it's still
      weeks

and weeks till the full burning gets its hooks in. Last night was
      Tim's
high school graduation – a strange event I watched from a vast
      distance

via streaming, while Tracy was distanced in the 'audience' down
      in The Hills.
He sang beautifully – a protest song – with his music class on
      instruments, and today

in the honey-eater vibrant afternoon, he and I went up to the old
      'arena', and gently placed
the white rose he was given last week as a farewell at the edge of
      the gravel-ant domain –

they were all over it fast, studying, working out breakdown of the
      most succulent
parts… not *swarming*, that word that has been taken away from
      ordinary

insect lives, but studying, and determined. And yes, there were
      crows – always crows –
and I consider that while Americans can no longer bet on
      elections, *some* 'joke' *someone* once 'ate crow'

as punishment for not winning a bet (backing the winning team),
    while here during the year's major sporting event,
sports gambling companies push the odds (mate!), encourage bets
    on geopolitical outcomes.

JK

32.
*Like bees caught in the wrong hive.*
— Anne Sexton

And here is why I am ambivalent and nicely comfortable with silence,
which is not comfort, really, because there are mornings I wake
and wonder why I am not heard, and what I mean then is why
nobody says me back to me, which, said this way, as it should be said,
is vanity, and to call it vanity is to accept the idea of sin, and to accept
that idea in me, and in art, is to start where the noisemakers
will say, *Do not*, and the noisemaker is not poor in spirit,
though I know how broke I am, spirit and all, but not humble, not without
vanity and anger and desire, which is the *rico*, *rico*, *rico* of orgasm,
which is beautiful, and in that purest beauty, the way in which
beauty is the clearest sky, beauty is untrammelled by the mess of earth,
in which beauty is the idea of sheer pleasure, a kind of gratitude
for what a body can do to a mind, alone, in a brightly lit room,
growing dark and shimmering out of the last dark, that is beauty,
which is what I want to own, which comes back to me every time,
which I return to as sin in a howl of delight, for sin is the frame of desire,
and the secret that I welcome, the world unjudged by my deep silence,
which sits snuggly only in the corner of the mind, the burr in the brain,
and so, when Fred Moten says that the poet is like the preacher,
like the state, like the power over the charisma of the congregation,
when he says that like a warning, when he says he has grown tired
of poetry, he means his poetry, and what I know is that he is tired
of the games he plays, and the way those games ride above the anger
he carries for the everybody and not everybody of black death,
and that is what he means, or what I imagine he means, of the teacher
who won't stop the assault on his son, and the system that comes
back to him; so, I ask, is he a holy man? and is he a righteous man,
and what has money done to him, for he wears a beard of a holy man,
heavy with locusts and the residue of honey, the last of the honey;
but I know he walks the world with Jazz in his head, and the lines
of thinkers, and the footnotes and the sic, sic, and the ibid and the cite,
and the music; mostly I will say that silence is the comfort I long for;

*I aint got no time to waste on you*,
says Tosh,
*I'm a living bee, I got work to do.*

KD

33.

I believe in the efficacy of possessing *nothing* other
than what all people are entitled to — 'bare necessities' —

I am convinced wealth only brings corruption
and that no one is entitled to any more than anyone else.

I believe that a fallen silvereye's nest looks like
an empty eye socket — woven and receptive

but easily emptied in making vision as much as
holding it. *This* nest on the ground — fallen —

is not below a branch, so was likely blown to where
it now sits, here, spent or lost. It was woven

of the finest thread of fine grasses, a swirl,
with a dangling thread of lost attachment

its optic nerve, or mine. Being a devotee, I might be vulnerable
to the influence of conferment — but, more-so, revel in re-distribution.

JK

34.

Like bees caught in the wrong hive, the body is running madly about,
the body is the container of the fluttering heart, and the mornings
are greyer now, in mid-Autumn, and the terror is what I call it,
this waiting in the discourse of black pessimism, the theory
of haunting, the theory of alertness, the theory of paranoia, the pure
protectiveness of paranoia, the wokeness of paranoia, the self-
congratulation of knowing the doom to come – the black pessimist
has seen it all before, and will see it again, and is giddy
with the knowing, is assured in the knowing, is hip in the knowing.
How often do I say, am I crazy to see what these people are doing;
the way they talk like they don't know that what they are doing
is killing us, and the way they see the monster on the screen, the bully
saying I love those who hate you, I excuse those who hate you, and what
they tell me is he is joking, can't you take a joke? And it is black
pessimism to say that where we are is where we have been; it is a theory
of the blues, it is a theory that understands darkness to be
the precursor of dawn, as the psalmist says. It is the song
I have sung, how we straighten our backs to face the future
with flame, the cross burning, the sugar cane drudgery, the terror
of that, and that is its own kind of beauty, and that is the song
of black pessimists. I have not read the book on this thing,
I am too busy dizzying around the bedlam hive, realizing that, immigrant
man, I am in the wrong hive and my mother, my mother the queen
is far, far away, so far away and I am trying to hear the hum of her call.

KD

35.

This focus I lost and then remade from lenses
gathered from old glass frames around the house —

not failed prescriptions, really, though some were ground
with dubious provenance, but the breakdown of sight

outdistancing origins. I can never bring myself
to throw them away, not because I treasure

objects, I don't, not ever, but because I know
they might act as emergency back-up, semi-restorative,

or donated, trace a focus that is in search of a corrective
that doesn't damage more that it ameliorates.

I think this walking in the humid forest — aberration
at a dry time — as detailed then merging colours

of endangered birds flicker across dead parts
of my vision, their feeding and roosting trees distorted.

JK

36.

*Executive Order*

How much can you take to feed the gap | in a people's memory, the erasure | of the language of the ancestors, | the deafness they caused you | to the whisper of the gods, the house | of bones, the valley of bones, | the deep-rift valley of bones, | covered by the weight of the Atlantic, | where the water stripped these bodies | of all their flesh, all they had | in the bowels of their undoing?"

— Kwame Dawes, from "Thieving" in *City of Bones: A Testament*

1
*Therefor [sic], it shall be the policy of the United States*
*not to promote race or sex stereotyping*
*or scapegoating in the Federal workforce*
*or in the Uniformed Services, and not to allow*
*grant funds to be used for these purposes.*
*In addition, Federal contractors will not be permitted*
*to inculcate such views in their employees.*

\*

The footnote is the vault where I have placed these incriminations,
this trail, a kind of clue for you to open, review, and to track down
the killer of a people, the killer of me – not so much an assassin,
but you know how in television shows, the unsaid prayer is that
perhaps, written on the corneas of the dead, the murdered,
is the imprint, the lasting imprimatur, the exposure, the positive
image of the killer, set there, a kind of ghostly clue – well, here it is
my note that says, "In the event of my untimely death, open
the vault of this footnote, this box of superscript numbers,
and fine print text, the tiny track marks of ants, the clues
underneath the noise of the leather boots stomping the ground.
Here is the lyric of a kind of survival, the thing I must write to you,
and dear John, do treat these with the care of an executor."

2
*The term "race or sex stereotyping"*
*means ascribing character traits, values,*
*moral and ethical codes, privileges, status,*
*or beliefs to a race or sex, or to an individual*
*because of his or her race or sex.*

*Therefor[sic] it shall be the policy of the United States:*

\*

My neighbour will ask me in that dark moment, do you love America?
It will be the test of my patriotism, and he would have learned
from Twitter and Facebook, that the meaning of patriotism is love,
and so, he will say, do you love America, not so much as a search
for the path of my heart – not a lover asking, "Do you love?",
in the giddy way of confidence – the way we say, "I know you love me,
but I want to know how, please, just tell me how the way I like to hear it."
No, this is the neighbour, and she is certain that I cannot love America,
or I may not love America, and that the answer to this is the answer
to be whispered on the emergency hotline against patriotism
in Washington DC, and she will say, "My neighbour, he does not love
America. He is not a patriot." I understand the thick molasses
of a deep insanity – the logic of affection – the husband who said
to his wife: "I am going to kill you because you have given me no choice,
because I asked you to love me, and you are now saying you won't,
and I already told you that if you can't love me, I will kill you,
so now, look at what you are making me do. Look at what you are
making me do." Walking through St. Louis, I heard this story;
a true story told by a poet about her mother, and the boulevard
in the treeful residential streets of St. Louis, felt like a storm
coming, darkness closing in, the entrapment of choicelessness,
how the policy of the tyrant, the policy of the killer, the policy
of the monster sets the terms of my affection. And my neighbour
says, as if asking, "You do not love America." And I say,
how can I love America when love of country is a foreign tongue?
Therefore, it shall be the policy of this nation, says the grandfather,

the Fuehrer, the leader the guide, the pathfinder — love is the heart
of the patriotic, how the countryman, the stark and simple notion
of a people living within the same border can become the test
of loyalty, or love. I say, forced to answer this, I stare at my neighbours,
in the autumn light, the leaves in piles around us, and I dare
not lie, and yet dare not speak what is true which is that I know
you do not love this place — what you love is the power over me;
over the ones who might turn you into occupier, and interloper.
When did this flat, unforgiving landscape turn into an object of love,
you stern Lutherans of deep devotion; when did such devotion
slip past the caution against idolatry and become this thing? The policy
of these United States stands at my doorway, waiting, watching, listening.

3

*not to promote race and sexual stereotyping.*

\*

Biden withholds his language — he has read this and will not promise
to rescind it. And this is the land in which I have planted myself.
On the throne is the author and finisher of lovelessness,
and in the wings is the cautious prevaricator, and we know
that the seasons will return, slightly tarnished for wear,
but there again, to beat us into a quiet submission.
The airwaves are crowded with caricatures — a madness
of birds filling an open Walmart parking lot — gulls,
wings grotesque with film, all in their many masks,
a comedy of absurdity; the sky is orange and pink, the backdrop
to this pantomime. This crowding of all we see
numbs us to meaning — the capacity to understand truth;
for truth is not afraid of ugliness, and soon the multiplication
of the scowling face of the caricature of ourselves,
the part of us that returns in nightmares, familiar
as a relative long exiled from our daily rituals of decency;
there is a testing of language about us — the slipperiness
of discernment. Were we to trust in the language of God,
the box of manuscripts sealed in wax, the laws, were we

to trust in a voice speaking from the broken sky, we might
somehow, sleep in peace. The faithful are eating the scrolls,
and finding them to taste of bitterness, their stomachs churning,
so they have no trust in the passed-down written words;
and when we say, "If only", they say in return, "No, no,
what is written is fickle as the heart." And this is the holy
promise of poetry, and poets come to its border blindly.
There is no sorrow more mournful and raw, more painful
and wounding than that of the faithful whose prayers
have not been answered by God – the believing one
who sitting among the smoldering ruins is met with a silence
as consuming as the wide open territory of the future.

4
*Sec. 2. Definitions. For the purposes of this order, the phrase:*
*(a) "Divisive concepts" means the concepts that*
*(1) one race or sex is inherently superior to another race or sex;*

\*
A train moves through the green dampness of Europe,
the destination, the clipped British accents of Oxbridge,
talk of the mythical cows and bulls, and excitement of upheaval;
it is 1931, and there sits a Jewish professor, a hopeless spy,
an athletic Jewish woman full of giggles and laughter,
and the train, the train, from the drone above – the camera
laconic as the dark cloudy sky, the ominous sound of the future –
is this what all narratives announce? The end of things.
And in today's novel, I imagine a family of five, in a Japanese
car of some value, black and slick with early snow melt,
moves towards the capital, and there is laughter, the sound
of roots music, and the giddiness of a black family
making its way through this country of dreams; in this novel,
what awaits is the end of things. This too is a fiction.
The executive order is to be collected and kept
in the archives; it is labelled either the object for shibboleths,
the first sign of the coming of what is to come,

candles around the sheet of paper, lit — the mantra:
we must not forget, the mantra: never again.
It is this or it is the blueprint, handed to us, of the way
that supremacy of one nation will be sustained — the first
paper of their grand plan, how we must face tomorrow,
knowing that these clues may be rescinded, but they will not
disappear. This regime is the forerunner, the tester of water,
the builder of the grand plan, and the order; here is the plot
secreted, the way that a future is to be made, step, by gentle step.

5
*The term "race or sex scapegoating"*
*means assigning fault, blame, or bias*
*to a race or sex, or to members of a race*
*or sex because of their race or sex.*

*(2) the United States is fundamentally racist or sexist;*

\*

Lil Wayne has a fetching, nervous smile. Beside the well-suited
president he grins with boyish gratitude to wave to the unmasked crowd,
standing there beside the man who has done more for black people
than anyone in the known and unknown universe.
This is how deals are made. Platinum deals — show me the money,
as American as great beats, bling bling and cash.

To prepare for battle, I must sleep. Perhaps not battle,
for what I am contemplating here is a kind of survival.
A way to offer wisdom, guidance and something like prudence,
to caution to a world of pitfalls. How can I say,
in a way that make you understand, or even see, but better,
agree, "This is not normal behaviour… This is not normal
behaviour!" I am not Obama, I have no understanding of the weight
of the world, the heaviness of waking each morning
to answer the swarming bees of demand. I confess
that it does seem plausible that the one who hungers

for power, must be fed power as a reward for the moments
of contemplation – who to bully, who to imprison, who to
send to the salt mines, who to assassinate, who to restore –
the labour of discerning the secret machinations of those
in search of power; what lie to compose, what myth
to invent – so much at stake for the world – so that each
breath of mine is a breath of history, a lasting legacy
and thing that can linger for so long. I do not admire
those who hunger and thirst after power, but I would admit
that satiation of parching hunger is the reward for such labours.
But I must sleep more, so that the dilemmas of my waking
hours may be corrected in my sleep, so that I may wake
with my heart open to the new path that such sleep brings.
Alas, I am sleeping with cavalier disregard for the wounds
my wakefulness is leaving on my body. This is a confession.

6
*Let's define fundamentally.*
*(3) an individual, by virtue of his or her race or sex,*
*is inherently racist, sexist, or oppressive,*
*whether consciously or unconsciously;*

\*

Let's define "fundamentally", let's consider fundamentally,
let's explore the generosity of saying, that someone might act
in despicable ways, but should not be cursed for this,
should be shown mercy for this, should be pitied for this,
should the offered the gift of revelation for this. One day,
the broken man returned to church angry at the congregation,
where he fell to his knees during the altar call and confessed
his broken and wounded self, and was lifted by song and by arms
and by mercy of the gift of the other broken ones, and how he
walked away unburdened, and drunk with grace, of what it was called
by the wind and the rain. It was, though, mid-winter, and his body
was replenished in the spring. His wife returned, and the children
impressed with his kindness and changed ways, returned,

and the worms, the canker worms that had feasted on his store
of grain, and his living soul, had crawled away, and were gone,
and he was fit and healthy, with a beard sparkling with vitality,
and he would wake in the morning and dance a jig, and the jig
was the jig of the healed and restored. So, the man, one day,
smelling his own strength, smelling his understanding that he had triumphed
over his brokenness, that he had conquered despair, returned
to the church with complaints, and he complained that for months
he had been watching sermons on the screens, and they were stones
being tossed at him, they were the words of the weak and sad,
they were words to batter the strugglers, the ones the world
rejected, and he remembered the day he crawled into the church
and was made to weep, by what he called "the guilt of shame"
and he came to condemn these people, came to condemn
the stained glass, came to condemn the dumb pews, and this was
his definition of the fundamental things in life. No one came
to the defence of the chapel. A grand silence settled
on the moment. Until a shuffling of footsteps, and a woman
came towards him asking, "Who are you angry with?
Nobody was talking about you, don't you know that?
You should go vote like Marvin Bell's Deadman, for Lincoln,
even though he is dead. For the dead will always be here
despite all you are saying and doing. This is fundamental.
There are tribes who have found language for your protestations –
throw stones in a pig pen, who bawl out." This is what she said.
this is how we define fundamental. It's as basic as that.

7
*(4) an individual should not be discriminated against*
*or receive adverse treatment solely or partly*
*because of his or her race or sex*

\*
"It is written, it is written, it is written, it is written!"
Who is talking? Who is talking? As yourself, who is talking?
It is written says the creature on the hill,

jump, says the creature on the hill; it is written,
scripture after scripture, it is written, and Lord,
says the preacher man, Lord, says the preacher man,
forty days and forty nights hungry is Jesus,
and he is sitting there, and getting ready to come off
the mountain, when up comes "It is Written",
and quotes the scriptures with such precision,
it is written, it is written, it is written. There is no language
for this, nothing to say but diablo, diablo, diabolical.

8
*Section 1. Purpose.*
*From the battlefield of Gettysburg*
*to the bus boycott in Montgomery*
*and the Selma-to-Montgomery marches,*
*heroic Americans have valiantly risked their lives*
*to ensure that their children would grow up*
*in a Nation living out its creed, expressed*
*in the Declaration of Independence:*
*"We hold these truths to be self-evident,*
*that all men are created equal."*

\*

So, what you mean to say is that the War of Northern Aggression
was a war about slavery, about the rights of African people,
the rights of enslaved people, the rights of those who were chattel
by law; and still you say, keep old Robert Lee's statue standing.
You say there are good people on both sides; you say those
who say the war was about states' rights are wrong, are wrong,
and still you shelter them in your midst? This is what the preacher
wants to know, old hypocrite and parasite, coming up to take a bite.

9
*This ideology is rooted in the pernicious*
*and false belief that America is an irredeemably*
*racist and sexist country; that some people,*

*simply on account of their race or sex,*
*are oppressors; and that racial and sexual identities*
*are more important than our common status*
*as human beings and Americans.*

\*

*It aint me, it ain't me*
*I ain't no millionaire's son, no, no*
         — Credence Clearwater Revival

*By the authority vested in me as President by the Constitution and the laws of the United States of America, including the Federal Property and Administrative Services Act, 40 U.S.C. 101 et seq., and in order to promote economy and efficiency in Federal contracting, to promote unity in the Federal workforce, and to combat offensive and anti-American race and sex stereotyping and scapegoating, it is hereby ordered as follows:*

10
*(g) any individual should feel discomfort,*
*guilt, anguish, or any other form of psychological distress*
*on account of his or her race or sex;*

Sometimes the classics comfort, sometimes they provoke, and sometimes,
they are the blueprint of conquerors — Césaire and Senghor thought so once,

but truth, confession can soften the warrior — and the streets of Paris,
turn into a kind of injection of love — the slippery poison that the rat-

smelling but elegantly powdered vermin gods of the sewers inject
into men drinking the best wine, eating from the glorious boards,

thinking, why not, why can I not be of this empire, of this tradition
when I speak better French than them. And soon, they admitted

their betrayal, their treason, the worst kind of treason, the treachery
of the addicted. Still, there is a blueprint of survival — the wax

melted into the air, while crossing the sea, Libya in the hazy
distance; and the blueprint is the lingua of the machinations

and devices of the war-minded — beware Greeks bearing gifts, it says;
and this is the way of scaffoldings and craft, the art of deception.


11
*(f) an individual, by virtue of his or her race or sex,*
*bears responsibility for actions committed in the past*
*by other members of the same race or sex;*

*"[f]acing your whiteness is hard and can result in feelings of guilt, sadness,*
*confusion, defensiveness, or fear."*

The edifice of this broadside, this clumsy gesture mastered by dictators,
those who have learned the playground violence as infants —
you know, hold the victim's wrist, and slap his face with his own hand,
again, and again, saying, "Why hit your own face? What you doing?
Why you want to hurt yourself? Look, you crying? Stop crying!"
Such fun, such delight, such insane hi-jinx for the lads with money
in their skins, and the silver spoons tucked in their epaulets, a fashion
statement of a sort. When the soul arrives at the broken altar,
and says in deep moans, "I have sinned, I have done so much, I have
harboured such evil in my heart," the cocky priest says, "Get up, sir,
be a man, this is unbecoming." And the fallen soul looks to the scaffolded
ceilings, and says, "I am facing my whiteness, and it is hard, and what I feel
is guilt, sadness, confusion, defensiveness, and fear." Guilt for what
I have gained unmerited, the neighbourhood, the free road before me,
the wink and nod of the keepers of the law, the lie of my ignorance,
the lie of my success. Sadness, for what else is there in me but sadness —
as joy is the dance of the triumphant one, and joy is the wanton
disregard for the bodies of the broken. A sad man has touched
his sorrow-soul and found beauty in this lamentation — it is written,
it is written it is written. And though I stand accused, my defenders stand
before me, the scowling priest, the potbellied collectors of power,

who say, How far must we go to atone for the sins of those who came
before us? It is not our sins that we lament — I never learned to tie a noose;
and my grandfather was a scoundrel, and he was tried, removed,
and so why must I weep at the guilt and sadness,
when I am a good soul at heart? This is the confusion of regret,
the confusion of thought, the beginning of wisdom.
So, I will defend my righteousness; I will say, not me, it was
not me, you have not understood me, you are cruel to call me
such and such, and it is you, it is you who accuse, it is you who are
the monster of my soul, and so I will decree this executive order against
the accusation of the withered and wild creatures, the ghoulish accusers;
it is not me; I accuse you, I curse you, I accuse you, monsters of my soul.
Fear, then, is the secreted anxiety about the ugliness of the other fear
of irrelevance, of lost privilege, the loss of something that has been called
tradition, or better still, legacy, or the truth of the tribe — and to think
one must repeat the obvious truth that the tribe was formed in a village,
but taking the bodies out to the white-clay quarry, and there to make
mud of the rainwater and the dusty gully, and to cover the full bodies
of the chosen in a clay that would dry into a stark, almost gleaming
whiteness. Without the shadow, there will not be light, and the bodies
transported here, they are the constant shadow in the the making of the tribe,
and this is what is feared — the death of the tribe, the loss of the tribe,
and vanishing of the tribe. We know it is fear, for what we have seen
of this horrendous occurrence is that it has barely begun, and all terror
is contained, not in the slaughtering of the innocents, but in the prophecy
of those who tend to prophesy the darkening of the future. It is enough.

12
*Today, however, many people are pushing*
*a different vision of America that is grounded*
*in hierarchies based on collective social*
*and political identities rather than in the inherent*
*and equal dignity of every person as an individual.*

\*

I anticipate silence to come.

It is settling on my body like a rash.
What I mean is I can sense the fever
of a long convalescence — a deep silence.
Tomorrow, I fear that words will fail me.
I will be quiet in the unsettled air
of the unspoken thing. This is the way
the eve of a new era will begin. I am alone
here, the gentle light of my new lamp
makes a circle around me, and I know
where I live; I live among those who
have cast their lot with the unspeakable.
I trust no one. I trust no one to be truthful.

13
*(h) meritocracy or traits*
*such as a hard work ethic*
*are racist or sexist and were created*
*by a particular race*
*to oppress another race.*

*Sec. 9. Effective Date. This order is effective immediately,...*

The hurry of things is the disquiet of this interim, the days of waiting,
the days in which the world awaits the answer to a question
long answered. I have asked if this document is a decree
to remind us of the ways a world can turn when left to its own deserts,
or whether it is the blueprint of a new dispensation, the opening
draft of an epoch of the dismantling of a certain truth.
What we have learned is that the tongue is a soothing organ,
how it caresses the bruised flesh, the bone's ache, how administered
rightly, the tongue seduces the naked; the tongue says
the earth will no longer be divided in lines of time, that the sun's
duplicity will be conquered by decree, that where the emperor
dwells, all time will evolve and be born, and there is a rugged
ancient logic to this, a view that defies the overtaking of time.
The travellers, walking across the continent will never notice
that the light is changing, for the light does not change;

it is, instead, the body that shifts mile after mile, until
the lungs understand their own truth – the blood is the test
of meaning; this is the continent of a body, the congress
of one, the seduction the tongue lets seep into the ear,
and this is how a nation has undone itself despite the news
that the monster is thrashing in fear, wondering whether
he will be heard, whether he will be loved. And the sycophants
are silent around, him, smiling, the gesture of those
who have been caressed by his tongue. We are waiting
to know whether the years ahead will be marked
by the edifices built on this blunt rhetoric – the language
of denial, the monstrosity that must be unleashed
and legislated by those who call themselves the winners.

14
DONALD J. TRUMP, *The White House*
*September 22, 2020*

\*

We poor fools on these his last days
have encountered that masterpiece of fraud,
the moon being our silent ally.

There's nothing Trojan about this nightmare snorting,
hoofbeats drumming on the sodden ground
where the corpse without a name is buried,
headless, with no tombstone, the amassed dead.
There is, in the end, no subterfuge here in the graveyard.

All California moans, quakes, shrouds the sky with smoke.
The prairie is tawny now awaiting the burial of snow.
The flame of our cleansing crowds the streets at the Atlantic.
The storms have not stopped their assault on the nation's soft belly.
Before us the task is given a name:
*The Index of History*

KD

37. *disjunctions*

The eastern barn owl flapping limitless slow wings
around the fragments of nightlight bursting out

from a history of poetry and a poetry of history
is a way back into superscript, into the interlinear

parsing of your words, Kwame. I wonder if my reading
Seneca's tragedies as I experience this breaking

of the fourth wall is a way of 'earthing'
through the rhetoric of horror? No. That's

an evasion through a doubtful history — the Rome
of empire, Nero's tutor and adviser

who was killed in time, in time. There's
no evidence his plays were ever performed,

and they are often described as akin to 'static'. Staged readings
of warning? Of prophecy? Or rhetorical extravaganzas?

This is the stuff of contestation among contemporary
literary historians of the period — of what the plays later

*became* — say, to the pop-up effusions of the Renaissance.
And the critic I just read, insists they were not mere

imitations of Greek models, but glorious
and unique in themselves. Blood and guts on the stage.

And *Octavia* — Seneca's 'history play' that is not by Seneca,
but imitator or imitators — might be rewritten as footnotes?

I am of no nation, Kwame, and want no nation.
I have no claims to make though realise there are claims on me.
I wander through communities and accept their hospitality and am grateful.
I respect and implore the realignments – patriots can't incorporate shifts
    into their accountancy.
I am no unified self, but hold myself accountable, culpable.
I am a trasher of ideals sold in the markets of flesh and capital.
These are just statements, but scaffolding I rely on. Mea culpa.

In depleting the poem of narrative I often take the easy path towards
    fragmentation,
the refuges of parataxis. But there are reasons for offering alternative paths –
I am not trying to hide or adapt to the conditions. I increasingly
realise that I have no *language*, and that I am also a pathetic fallacy.
I am constituted of exposures and absorptions, though my skin
is breaking down and I have been told I could drop dead
from a heart attack *just like that*. Like that. A vegan
for thirty-five years is a plus, I am told, but 'bad genes
are bad genes'. But this is not why I despise genetics – I have always
thought them irrelevant as an idea, long before discovering
my genes might be 'bad'. But is it bad to want no one else's death
and no one else to suffer and no else one to be exploited but be happy enough
to 'suffer the consequences' of *inheriting* 'bad genes'? I promise I want others
to thrive with whatever genes they've been 'blessed' or 'damned' with
    (*how unfortunate*).
I do not look on the 'good-gened' or 'strong-gened' people with envy.
In my genes is the rot instilled by British colonialism in Ireland – constant
starvation while others are drivers of colonial desiring. Grim as fuck.
A reproduction under the auspices of the church – married
on the bridge over the thin river of Barrow because the voyage
on the boat to the colony of Western Australia is a long
and dangerous one... and *and* and. Such 'big men', a line of giants
out of the ranks of mythology, and yet, they drop dead from heart attacks
for all their sparse living, their commitment to their families etcetera etcetera.
It's odd, isn't it? Genetics, heritage, inheritance, legacy... histories.
    Where survival

and profit clash. And I know that all the countries I have sheltered in,
or even passed through, are confluences of the diabolical
with the incredible, of aspiration with suppression,
of story-tellers and administrations committed
to the control of stories, of re-routing histories.

I see a zone, a massive multiplicitous zone of human habitation
being inflicted by a sickness that never should have been 'allowed'
to get *out of control*. And I see another massive zone. And another.
In the smaller spaces, the communities, people look after themselves
and each other more effectively than under the swollen vested interests
of those who govern them. The fall of a tyrant is not the fall of a system
that called out for a tyrant, that gave him the foot up he had given it.
That broke bread with him. That gave him everyone's bread
while he gave none back. The tyrant stealer of bread.
And always the machines dig and belch, background to each
and every distress – magnanimous in their largesse.
How will each 'industry be affected'? A 'breakdown' follows…

And so, Kwame, I come back to the couplets of footnotes
I have been using as a 'restraint' of a history beyond me,

but never holding back. I saturate myself in the consequences
of the collective, the 'individual' – the contradictions, the hopes
       and rebellions.

I always come back to peace, by which I don't mean quietism
or patience or caution or gently letting things 'improve' (as if), because

they won't. I mean an overwhelming active peace of non-compliance.
Beyond civil disobedience. Beyond pointing out the hypocrisies

and vigilantism and secret policing of 'citizens' who would keep
the white privilege in tune with white 'grievance' – I mean

abandoning the whole rotten edifice, walking away – distanced
until closeness is not a risk of sickness – then gathering

and saying 'racism' and 'stereotyping' are the violence
of even their softest, most placating words, and any instruction

that is deployed as rectification is a sure sign they're
not letting go. Leave them to their own directives.

Leave them but don't leave the places. Leave them disarmed
and productless, searching online stores that all say 'out of stock'.

Leave them. 'Go in peace' as the words struggle to sell a lie.
And here, as footnote to histories I am implicated in, I must

replant as trees die, I must fill in spaces excoriated by pastoral
leases dished out by the Crown in the nineteenth century,

I must grow vegetables to give to others, and to feed ourselves,
I must experience the screech of the owl as unique, which it is.

I must think of the owl as nothing to do with rhetoric.
I must maintain my records of temperature and rainfall, till the last,

I must prepare for the return of this country to Noongar people,
when they are able to enact as well as say that they are leaving the colonists…

those who do follow do so because they will share, listen, acknowledge.
I delight in that moment – and *watch*, it *will* help the entirety

of humanity to pull back from the brink, tipping points, line
in the sand, peak, point of no return… It will disrupt catastrophe.

JK

38. *On Peace*

*The fall of a tyrant is not the fall of a system*
*that called out for a tyrant, that gave him the foot up he had given it.*
*That broke bread with him. That gave him everyone's bread*
*while he gave none back. The tyrant stealer of bread.*
        — JK

Let us then say that the news is the master's text, and what we offer,
these interruptions, these are the transforming notes, dismantling

the master's text. We don't believe in the master, as some speak
of the master, but we have met him on the road, and we know

to guard against the peace that is uttered by that master's mouth —
and I am grateful for your song of peace, a peace only poetry can speak,

so far, I say, to guard against absolutes, and to honour the contradictions
of our labour for meaning. At the heart of this, then, is the unknowing.

I don't know the music I am making. I am still covered in the leaves,
the dirt of a body trying to find its living self. I have been

walking through the woods for days, and I arrive at the city,
and I am asked about my song, and I ask, Why are you asking me

about my song? and I am told, Because you are singing, you keep
singing; there is a whisper in the air saying, It is a fat bass sound

under your tongue; can't you hear it? I can't. I am describing
the aftermath of a poem — the making of a poem, the rush

and tumble of lining words, one after the other. In this aftermath,
I have no way of knowing that swirling around me is a complex

of dub and the guiding melody of song. This is the aftermath
of watching the story of Marlon Riggs in film after film, in wail

after wail, in truth after truth spoken. He is dead now. I have
left behind me a full-blown forest of terrible beauty.

Tonight, my friends said, *These white people, these white leaders
need to be trained; they need to work with consultants to have a difficult*

*discussion about race*. I try to say nothing. I try to hold
my tongue. What I want to say is: Let's not waste money on consultants,

on training, on workshops. Let us give each of them a subscription
to Criterion. Let us ask them to sit for a day and watch Marlon Riggs'

films. Let us sit with them and wait for them to talk. Then when they
stutter and we can see the plea in their eyes, rather than clear our throats,

rather than try to say: *We understand*, we should sit and let them
decide what they will say. And if they remain silent, then we will call

a retreat of silence. I believe that this is all we must do. This is all
we can do. There is no language beyond this. Look at the song.

Look at the song. It is a granddaughter's lament, there on the nation's
edge, the border city of Laredo – *el abuelo* Martin Davila is dead,

the patriarch with his fishing rod, his sip of tequila. For years he would
sit at the edge of the thick river, dusk slowly crawling across, a shifting

light, and there, in the deep silence, he thinks he is outside of nation,
that this earth is borrowed, that he has rented a few acres to pretend

belonging, but in this wide orange glow, ancient as the beginning of light,
he understands that when he goes, he will enter a kind of fiesta

of dust. Still, he admits that sometimes, when the silence
> grows stifling,
he hears a strange cacophony of voices, first whispering, and then singing,

and the language they use is filled with clicks and groans, and the soft
flat comfort of vowels spreading across the tree-line, and he knows

he understands their meaning, though their words elude him, and this,
he admits, is the comfort he longs for. He will die, and become

this sound, which is one poet's idea of belonging. We have entered
the season of convenient deaths — it was the disease, but what of it?

He was 92 — is this not the culling of the herd, the necessary cleansing
of the palate. She is weeping, a private anger at the neglect,

how they let him slip away, the home ritualizing death with the art
of disregard; never disturb the others. Their time is theirs,

what little of it is left. A woman arrived at the home for the Tuesday morning
sing-along. She plays the piano competently, her tremolo a soothing

gift. The dead are forgiven their intrusion — this epoch of the dead
will be remembered as the waning light of a full harvest moon night.

KD

39.

I am knowing different moments of communion and aloneness
in our sharings, Kwame. I have been watching *extracts*

from 'Black is... Black Aint' — what I can access in the short-term,
in the immediate, the now — but I know truths spoken about

*community*, even if it's not the community as spoken,
as speaking to and with. Not a single entity, not

discussable as fact or demographic by systems operators.
What experience gives us is more than enough, but not enough.

I listen *to listen*. I feel sure *listen* is not to inculcate or elide, not to
    claim or borrow,
not to appropriate or juxtapose, nor to compare and contrast

as we were told to do with literary texts when I was at high-
school in Geraldton where some good teachers lived in a bad system,

and colonial expeditions were re-enacted as definition,
as consolidation, as future. My non-participation is not

an asset. I did not participate in school outings if I could avoid
    them —
and *outings* of failed masculinity or gender-political compliance

was the underwriting. I knew that from earlier school camps.
    Experience
is not enough, but I'd had enough experience to know that it can
    also be too much.

I realise now, that we — whatever our family or communities —
were held bookended in a time-slip fantasy of the eternal
    colonisation,

forced into responding, to playing victor or vanquished
and that at no time ever would the word 'colonist' become 'over
    used'.

What the enactors and participants seemed not to know, or to say,
was that their sense of victory reduced community to the single
    brutal edifice,

flag-ironing their own differences into a declaration of dependence on
    other communities'
depths and complexities and beauties through simultaneously
    annexing and denying the thefts.

Community beyond the administration's comprehension was and is
    and always will be community.
The intrepid student explorers sang camp songs against darkness
    around beachfires. Flash

photos were taken. Those of us who didn't go were shown the photos
    of expeditioning
as record, as confrontation – letting the side down, even if it
    wasn't *our* side.

I listen not to offer myself contrition, but to listen as listening.
I cross the range of voice in singing with voices in my head

I had lost track of, that I can't put a name to, but the songs
are there and so many voices are singing them. It might

be difficult to forget our bodies, as our bodies are communities
and our bodies are how we know others, too, but it is too

easy to forget the entirety of other bodies and their shapes
of conversation, the hard to hear whispers of desire

and those early signs of trauma. Those exercises in bonding,
those rousing renditions I stayed out of – those false communings

that are meta data that can be dipped into across the globe where
    Republicans,
awe-struck by their Tyrant Commander and their history-saying,
    seek to invalidate a black city.

JK

40.

On the fourth day after the dentist I realise
that I have been my body's caretaker – my gut really
the guts of things. It has been years, the nightly coating
of my insides, the three seconds before the pill, delicate
as a grain of rice etched with a name or carved and implanted
with a nuclear code; in the small interim I remember the slow
anticipation of pain, the cramping, the looseness of my insides
the cold film of sweat – this since the dentist tapped on my teeth
and scratched the tenderness of my brittle molar
before the final test: "Raise your hand when the pain starts
and keep it up till it passes." The deception of the calm of ice
of healthy teeth, then the culprit touched, three seconds of ease
and the sharp bright screed of my body yelling, my hand up,
where it remains up for two minutes, while she apologizes
through her mask. It is at the root, that fissure where the nerve grows
its tendril of rooting and we know it is cracked, we can see that inside
you is a root of persistent pain. I am nauseous with pain. I think of torture
how it must always work, how simply finding a cavity of a tooth
that hurts to the touch, then the blue tip of ice, held there, just this
small hurting thing. I leave with a limp though there is only pain
in my face. The city is brilliantly lit for winter; the pundits discuss
basketball on the radio. Since then the pills, the nights of throbbing,
and this decaying of all I have protected. It is remarkable
how the body and mind assume their role after a while, and in this epoch
of plague, violence and reckoning, how much the unction of noting,
of footnoting the crowded world of history happens across
this shuddering world, where the world is recording it on phones
and cameras in deepest lamentation. And where the world
is blind to the frozen bodies of those left to fade into the earth
beside the stones, beside the shrubbery, beside the drifting leaves –
all those wide-open spaces where one person murdered another,
where someone screamed, where the echo of a body broken
by the violence of another still hangs in the air, where there is a barren
silence – my body has become that inadequate footnote writer,

that hand scribbling the expansion of the short word held there
without context; how my body says, *Let us know that what we think
we have seen is not all there is to see.* It is as if in this painful
season, awaiting the rooting deep into my brittle teeth, the scooping
out of the fleshy nerves, the dying nerves that have grown numb
after carrying so much pain, that I will know that I must keep
my too, too sullied flesh alive, tender, and open to record the pain
of this season. Language is inadequate; this much I know,
but in the absence of other songs, this is what we have, this is what
I have to offer the silencing of the master's text – the monster text.
John, when I say John, I know you know now that I mean friend,
I mean the rime of my own stuttering tongue, I mean the sheet
of embossed paper that welcomes the indelible ink, when I say
John, I mean companion in this, and so I mean you who come
to this song with an open heart. When I say John, it is a way of saying
this, this thing we are making, this thing we have been making;
it is a shorthand into a longer story, which is spoken this way;
when I say John, it travels deep into your memory where even I
have not been, and when I say John, I invoke the memories
I am seeking to reach, outside of me, outside of nation, outside
of narrative; when I say, John, the language does not matter
as much as the purposefulness of the gesture, the thing we make,
are making, have been making, will make. And when I say song, I mean hurt.
When I say John, I mean we, and this is the truth of it.
When I say John, I say the hope in community, believe me.
When I say John, I mean to quote myself inventing a space
of deep meaning: acceptance revisited, acceptance revisited.
"I can see her bandanaed there | sharp calico against the hill's grey
her wrinkled hands outstretched, trembling | her eyes glowing."
So, I mean *her*, and she has become the reason of it all, I mean.
*Then I read the monumental legend of her love*
*And grasp her wrinkled hands.*

KD

41.

Thanks, Kwame. Thanks. I am still in the twilight
of consciousness, never in those stories of nation which
I have never been part of and don't even recognise,
so I hear because it's where I dwell, and though
some might call it 'limbo', it is actually only a dispersal
of cells and notions, reaching towards each other,
maybe striving to coalesce, but remaining unsubstantial.
So, yes, yes, I know what you say and am grateful.
In such leavened spaces, I hear and see and sense,
just as the anaesthetist kept me slightly awake just
a little longer in that halfworld of halfworlds, to *keep
the conversation going*. I talked about the pronunciation
of names and counting holes in grids finite yet infinite.
She was originally from Mauritius, and I have been via
that island to Reunion, so we had stuff to talk about,
even if I don't remember talking about it as such,
just as the words of body critique stated an end
of talk on my part, and I said, I will remember
the pronunciation. I found this out later,
but I was asked a name and I uttered it,
and was told, Well, it does start with that
letter and is three syllables, so that's
something, at least. And that's how I loop
beginnings to ends, ends to beginnings,
and keep my body going as blood pressure
drops and they all work extra hard to normalise
the fleshly bits between the birth time and date
and time and date of *the procedure*. But I was thinking,
below the thoughts of going and coming back...
I was thinking about the strangeness of hospitals
in pandemic times, Kwame, and all the protocols
strictly observed by some and less strictly by others.
And one nurse told me, Kwame, that she'd just
come out of quarantine after urgent travel,

and that she'd been tested five times
and almost gagged thinking about it,
and I gently wiped the spittle away from near
my mouth that had landed with the enthusiasm
of talking over environmental issues while taking
my blood pressure, pulse rate, and other vitals.
And I thought about those who strictly
adhered to the 'two only in a lift at a time',
and those who didn't – four in the steel box
talking as they emerge as if their breath
was naturally one, flowing through their talk.
In theatre, tracing likelihoods as I was wheeled
into place – into the slot – I said to the team,
I said to them, Kwame, that I will see you
all again soon, and then fought the drugs
so hard that I woke up fast, hyper awake,
in the ward, pinching time together,
eager to finish stories begun that I only
slowly realised and kept going while
I was under their care, in the strict setting
of story-tellings. In the space on the admittance
sheet that followed 'What is your religion', I said,
'none'... and the receptionist asked, *What
does that mean?* And I said, *It means
that I believe in ALL religions, that I have faith
but that faith has no denomination*. She stared at me,
and said, *That's just like me, but I've never heard
anyone say it before*. I remember that, Kwame,
and that was before the conversations
got intense, before they were wired
    into the monitors.

JK

42.

*For Ntosake Shange*

Sometimes, on the road, as the light fades, the new city
of arrival rising out of the plains, the shimmering buildings,
the slowing of traffic, I can tell my body is hungry
for the ease, the release of tension, the concentration
of driving the repetition of the highway, staying alert
to the extraordinary ordinariness of a careless straying
mind. In this falling place, I rehearse the route we have
taken – by rehearse, I mean I re-picture the bridges,
the service stations, the farm barns, the uneven stretch
of pavement, the long delays around fleeting tragedies,
the lights, the gleaming broken upturned vehicles,
the bewildered bodies looking out of place on the grassy
banking of the meridian. I am filled with gratitude
for a safe journey and for the lessons learned. It is
this satisfaction of safe arrival that settles on me now,
as if we have come through a storm, a loud, tumultuous
storm, and broken through the deep purple gloom.
I have said after much thought, and by said, I mean,
I have thought before not writing this down, or saying it,
or having the answer in my pocket ready for the interviewer,
the NPR voice with that over-joy of the "poetry segment",
the spot of light, the spot of hope, something different,
as they say, the tender exaggerated, like tender
is exaggerated when adults bend to children; the way
the voice slows, and then asks, "So does poetry change
anything, poet?" The answer I have kept in my side pocket,
shaped to an assured mixture of questioning, probing,
flippant irony, and the studied gravitas I will let hang over
the airwaves, before the soft chuckle, the ease of a man
of unimportant importance – "Does poetry change
anything?" I would have said, "No", I would have said,
"Poetry lives in the world it belongs to, and it never leaps

into the world when things must change." A lie – a lie
I would not know then to be a lie, a lie I have shaped into a lie,
and smoothed into a lie, and marinated with time into a lie
of great substance. Today, I arrived at the truth that my body
of deep questioning, my whole fear of my body, of my manhood,
of my spirit's meaning, of my darkness, of my youth,
was changed utterly, was altered fully, was shifted in ways
I could not understand, for I could not know
the way my world changed forty years ago; I could not have
known it was turned in on itself, for what settles in the body
is poetry – the way the words handled right, turned right,
guided right, settled in me, a kind of seed, a kind of herb
letting its spice alter the blood of me. The women
in their many-coloured frocks, saying words, praying words,
flooding me with words, opening up the free masonry
of their mystery to me; somebody always took away my stuff,
somebody, Toussaint, the samba, the babies falling,
the impossibility of pain – a woman who loves on purpose,
who loves on purpose. Ntosake Shange, I will say this again,
and again; now, I will say, you walked into my body,
sat there, and kept growing something in me; and Willie
letting go of Kwame and Naomi, he dropped me, he dropped me;
it broke me then, it broke me again, and again, I found god
in myself. This is my addendum to words, this crowding
of words, this reckoning with words, and I must return
always to the gender of language, to the why of it, the point
of it, the honesty of saying that sometimes the hanging sound
over the held word brings tears, and then I return to the seed
of this business, the she of God, the shattering of God,
the shattering of language, the sound beneath my art;
as if to say, to my children, "Yes, we have made it,
we are in your city, and we came through the storm,
and though a little shaky, say amen, we have arrived."

KD

43.

The shifts in the days of the poem is the history of breath
as if there are no longer winds or air currents but storms

still form. If in *medias res* is always a state we will lose
and attain the too rapid heartbeat pounding the chest-cage

before stopping — that final run home, lunge for the finishing
tape in a competition you never wanted to participate in,

never believed had any worth. Whatever competitiveness
was fabricated through schooling and extra curricular

activities and just being full of childhood zest has been
exuviated under the pressure of the brutal-get-ahead-

sell of competition. Winning is nothing and there's nothing
to win. Reassured by a generous onlooker as you come last in the race,

you smile — breathless — knowing 'Winning *is* everything' will be
kicked into you by those in the team — *the faction* (with explorers'

and early colonial prominents' names) who very much
think otherwise. Storms in eyes of beholders. The shifts in these days,

the transitions of loss, the blank tablet of life carved
or engraved, signatures in life's guest book. But the currents

still circulate and all the dead entwine and love each
other in ways that competitiveness in fleshly lives

might have prevented. And, as I know in my own
in-between state, that meditative space between pulse-beats

like a star crushed by its own weight, a timeline
without high or low points, without 'success' or 'failure',

is the arterial weather system in which body flows with soul,
and the solar winds are reminiscence and prognosis.

JK

44.

There is the pillow body – painted in oils on ply-board, the white
paint is streaked, the shadows around the curves suggest
decay, a kind of humanity, and it is not strange to think
of an old billboard, rusted by time, overlooking the record
store in Cross Roads, the concrete walkway strewn with empty
juice boxes, banana peel, and the plastic of our demise,
piles and piles of it, waiting for the torrent of cleansing rain
to drag them down the river of brown to the sea, and to the other
sea, and to the other coast, the miles, and miles and miles
of the planet – smoke travels, detritus travels, the slow March
of our demise – that word again. The body stands over
a severed limb – it is a white limb, there on the hardwood floor,
and the blood is black, a kind of suggestion, and we think
that the earth is continuing, but I will admit that the news
around us, around me, is unsettling. When the assistant pastor
arrives at dusk with gifts, he does not wear a mask,
and we stand back, and he won't stoptalking, as if what
he wants to ask is if we are coming back; but a white Christian
finds it hard to beg a black Christian for mercy – or maybe
not mercy, but the tithe, the tithe of blessing, because he knows
that they both know this is a man trying to make a wage,
but he does not wear a mask, and he won't stop talking,
and we stand back, and we don't tell him our daughter
in Jersey is recovering from the plague, that my dear friend
the poet in Macedonia is lying in a hospital bed in Skopje
in the COVID hospital, with an oxygen mask, and vials of infusions,
and his body longing for the calm that poets desire;
or that our friend the doctor in Tennessee is praying for breath,
and he keeps on talking, and won't stop talking, till we grow
so silent the dog settles on the floor, and we have not said
come in, we have not said this house is not welcoming you.
And the light fades fully now, and he smiles, and he leaves,
and no one says that there is a weight of anger over all of this.
The year will end soon. It began simply enough – the promise

of more of the narcissist's absurdities, a campaign of errors,
and perhaps the beginning of an era – the epoch of Trump,
the horror of it. The tribes, even then, had built their fences;
it's been so long since the dream of unity, the swirl of lies,
the cabals of the white supremacists gathering in the small
houses, the ordinariness of this strange moment. I wrote
then, as a prophet would: Is this the beginning of an epoch
or the flailing end of an era? My poems grew tentacles deep
as the wet underearth, and there was comfort in the elegies –
a kind of ordering of the universe by the patterns of death.
It was Kamau, it was the soft light of his passing, the stone
of it, that fed me. A year begins, and then the year truly began.
The neighbours' Trump yard signs have been put away,
and the wreaths, pepper-lights, and garish snow-sleds
gleam on the lawn. The war is over, the air is heavy with loss,
and winter is upon us, John, the snow is spinning about,
and on my walk, it is a startling music of living – a kind of song
that comforts me strangely, for the soft silence of its blanketing
makes me think of Marvin Bell, who went a few weeks back,
the notes of Chet Baker about him; or Barry Lopez, now in hospice,
listening to the sound of rain sticks, his family gathered,
the McKenzie River making its music from beyond the gathered tree line,
and him saying he sees powerful forces around him, in that slow
cadence I connect with a man who has seen so many trees
from deep inside their sheltered place, and man who has written
words that have shaped how we understand pain and love.
This winter comes upon us with its slow assured sorrows,
the way poems arrive, softly handing to us a kind of peace.
At night, I wake testing my body's vulnerability, to see
if the scratching in my throat is the start of more rituals
of dying. We are never ready for this, and yet, we know
we are always ready for this: and to die is gain.

KD

# IV: INDEX TO HISTORY

# INDEX OF FIRST LINES

1. My pulse runs fast and has lost its timing.     411
2. Throbbing hunger is my belly's elegy,     412
3. At a time of accelerated death,     413
4. It is the colonial quandary, the human (stain)     414
5. The prosody of the colonial     415
6. And we, the Jonahs of the gospel of peace,     416
7. Questioning motives behind the telling     417
8. I'm grateful for schoolboy learning, shadows     418
9. I am distressed when language is controlled,     419
10. And on a night of sleeplessness, Scratch opens     420
11. Broken English from Ngukurr, southern     421
12. My obit writer arrives in a dark suit,     422
13. My body moves fast though time moves slowly     423
14. We are living in the House of Greedy     424
15. The broad strong easterlies continue     425
16. I am rummaging through the midden     426
17. As more and more fires erupt around     427
18. On the sloping end of Stevens Ridge Road,     428
19. To distract myself from what I don't want     429
20. They stormed the Capitol in January.     430
21. Historical figurism, triumphs,     431
22. "It is a theocracy they want."     432
23. *So…* if Surrealism was a response     433
24. I know it is too early to declare     434
25. I am drafting a work entitled 'Dis- (arming)     435
26. Now that what is numbing me is fear     436
27. The meaning of these words we use will change     437
28. Kwame, I say, go walking in the cold     438
29. Tent cities have been established in Perth     439
30. My desiccated soul just will not breathe;     440
31. The good governance of all our spirits     441
32. Think wind. Think pipe. Think music. Think song stopped.     442
33. This life bookended by unemployment     443
34. In truth these neat boxes are the index     444

35. Apart from the appalling ethical                         445
36. Due preparations for a suburban walk.                    446
37. Here, as humidity mocks the terrain                      447
38. There's much in a name and naming is all,                448
39. I have no heritage worth speaking of —                   449
40. It has snowed, again, and the street is white;           450
41. So much we recognise but then undo                       451
42. And to think that this has all been fashioned            452
43. Where the blood is thinned and thin blood loosens        453
44. And the flag is down – a blue counterfeit                454
45. It's hard to cope with the incredible                    455
46. So, all joy is a prelude to history,                     456
47. I thought that this stanza should have no more           457
48. The research is in my body, sweet                        458
49. The loss of wildlife is the loss of all                  459
50. Grief, I imagine, fills the open lands                   460
51. Just where and how will we meet up across                461
52. To write the chronicle of this season                    462
53. If trees grew on the sun, this seems what they'd         463
54. Montserrat tells of her mother's contract                464
55. In the hesitations marked as pauses                      465
56. Today the sun spreads over Pioneer Park                  466
57. Really… maybe, what's being said is that                 467
58. When the Butter Bay becomes the Fort of Slaughter,       468
59. How far away from act and consequence                    469
60. My shadow dances across the open                         470
61. I am pursuing a path of error                            471
62. "Let's get *Gone with the Wind* back, please," Trump whines  472
63. I have an intense feeling that something                 473
64. Can a black body live in a white space?                  474
65. This.is.how.i.find.my.way.through.my.own                 475
66. I apologize on behalf of my staff, if…                   476
67. Preparing for *Seroja* – such a rare                     477
68. There is a hiatus – a cool day of fresh light;           478
69. I have been thinking about the nature                    479
70. For new altars we strive to rebuild                      480

| | |
|---|---|
| 71. Though it is likely a tautology | 481 |
| 72. Across the burnished land, light balms the heart. | 482 |
| 73. And late last night for me, Kwame, it was | 483 |
| 74. I have now become a curator of | 484 |
| 75. I have no interlocutor, no flow'r | 485 |
| 76. We've arrived at the season of twin dusks | 486 |
| 77. Things always start and end near the middle | 487 |
| 78. They rehearse lamentations of penitence | 488 |
| 79. I have been wondering if poetry | 489 |
| 80. We have circled back to the elegies | 490 |
| 81. It's easier to think flowers outside | 491 |
| 82. We end at the banquet of remembrance. | 492 |
| 83. It is still silent here after the roo | 493 |
| 84. In these suburbs, I read your song of roos | 494 |
| 85. Thanks, dear Kwame, but you take the bathos | 495 |
| 86. And what of those who've seen so much? Outside | 496 |
| 87. How many storms have passed over since we | 497 |
| 88. The elders squat, and one says, *Bend down low*. | 498 |
| 89. Biography denies its own failure. | 499 |
| 90. Not nationalism. Instead, I make poetry | 500 |
| 91. Birth is embedded as exile re-routes | 501 |
| 92. The Gulf of Mexico is on fire. | 502 |
| 93. And those billionaire space adventurers | 503 |
| 94. In the end, the truth matter is now set | 504 |
| 95. What I see and what I can write about | 505 |
| 96. Before his passing, the man-poet carves out | 506 |

1.

My pulse runs fast and has lost its timing.
How do we decolonise the stanza,
how do we write against its collating?
Deep in the Munster Plantation, Spenser
set tones for a poet's extravaganza
while feeding on the endocrine
system of the Irish – a composer
who lavished language with dispossession,
and dished up allegory to his sovereign.

JK

2.
*Cruell death vanquishing so noble beautie*
*Oft makes me waile so harde a destinie*
    —Edmund Spenser

Throbbing hunger is my belly's elegy,
and history is the persistence of tyrants
while the poets die. Today's lament: Barry
Lopez, the McKenzie's bubbling sound
the first notes of mourning. Morrison
it was then, though the tyrant remains,
licking his wounds in the Florida sun.
Deerskin, beaver sticks, river water, the stain
of our lives. And in the end, that is what remains.

KD

3.

At a time of accelerated death,
executions are stepped up just to show
that the out-of-control with their great wealth
still have control over those on death row,
and as killers who worked to overthrow
innocents in foreign zones are pardoned,
other killers are killed off quid pro quo.
As if there isn't enough death to hold
the interest of the vengeful, satisfy their dread.

JK

4.

It is the colonial quandary, the human
stain. Spenser executes the commands
of his liege and tribe, breaks bones and hangs
a blood-soaked fortress of rebels, their demands
snuffed out by duty. At dawn, his hands
tremble to make poems. We who live inside
history go blind to its machinations;
and this is the use of poetry. I've tried
to break this curse, my friend, I've tried, I've truly tried.

KD

5.

The prosody of the colonial
shapes its conquests into transportable
components to feed its industrial
complex from expanding 'sustainable'
'versions of the pastoral' – reliable
primary sources for embellishment
of profit and godly callings to recall
holy words in effete word-vessels – lent
on serviceable terms if not quite heaven sent.

JK

6.

And we, the Jonahs of the gospel of peace,
carry that secret envy – no, resentment –
for Nahum. This red hunger will increase
in us, here inside history. We lament
while greedily consuming the firmament's
destruction. Mark each mention of Jonah,
not the great fish tale, but the depressive
wallowing with the worms; the poet's horror
of sight, and the callous seduction of terror.

KD

7. *omnium gatherum*

Questioning motives behind the telling
of history – scope of entertainment,
the lessons to be learned, the templating
to suit a cause – or tracing what is meant
by exclusion, occlusion, annulment –
we isolate when such isolation
is a version of our presentiment –
the premonition that's underwritten –
science bodies know beyond investigation.

JK

8.
*I pray thee, / Why do the heathens rage?*
         — Big Youth, 1974

I'm grateful for schoolboy learning, shadows
of meaning, histories of the coloniser's
way, and the healing lament and sorrow
of the enslaved liberated. Liars
are exposed in the holy fires
of dubwise – I pray thee, listen to Scratch
deconstructing Versailles and Waterloo.
Rituals of Africa flame my blood, fetched-
up, released, and efficiently dispatched.

KD

9.

I am distressed when language is controlled,
that assumptions will be made over why
words cannot grow and decay aside
from their 'origins', shift, especially
against instances of rapacity's
utterance – planter speech seeks erasure
to pronounce a primacy: I say,
undo those words to reclaim words, utter
as mouth shapes, or listen, say, to Irish speakers.

J K

10.

And on a night of sleeplessness, Scratch opens
the sound system and lets the tape roll.
The dubwise locks and the mouth begin to run.
His roots autobiography chants, "Fire in the hole".
These snow-blind mornings, sorrow takes a toll
on the body; my belly is darkly heavy
with foreboding, the roll call of the gone
on the radio. This year of ghastly
acts of tyrants, "Chant fire!" toasts Lee Scratch Perry.

KD

11.

Broken English from Ngukurr, southern
Arnhemland, were a legendary band
up in the Top End who only laid down
one studio album, which I take heed
of now – that is, a listening beyond
comfort, listening into communal
journeys, ears burning… lament that delayed
justice. *Replaying* isn't time – I fall
deep awake with 'Greenhouse Effect'… instrumental.

JK

12.
*My family tells me I must write happy poems — every poem
I write is a failure, I know this now, and I wonder if my excuse
is the decay of all history.* ["History # 12"]

My obit writer arrives in a dark suit,
carries a worn notebook, sits cross-legged
and probes. "Please sir, tell us of the fruit
of your labours," he says. But he just begs,
instead, for the secrets, the hidden dregs
of my life. He says, "This will be the last
account of you, and know we will fact check
everything you say, meaning what has passed
must be provable, and we will lose what is dross."

KD

13.

My body moves fast though time moves slowly
and this perhaps means I will catch an end
before an ending catches up with me –
can I be part of the story ahead
of its plot… will meaning catch up and send
the blood back into a quick heart's vortex?
I say this as heat drives an old blue-tongued
skink to the Great Tank to lap at moist cracks,
to adjust flesh to the desiccated codex.

I speak as heat is driven by raging
winds – *severe winds* – winds that eviscerate,
snap branches, turn sap, get under roofs, bring
fear and undo great conjunctions. It's late
in the day as we inspect the event
horizon and explore the emergency
site as a grim bearing of the present.
See 'prescribed burns' listed for forestry…?
Thirty ks away a fire has cut the highway.

JK

14.
*For griefe it thaw'd into a teare,*
*Thence falling on her garment's hem,*
*For griefe it freez'd into a gem.*
    —— William Strode "On a Gentlewoman walking the Snowe"

We are living in the House of Greedy,
I say "greedy" as a hopeful moralist,
but have no space for an index of greedy,
there is no time for the feeding of disgust
that comes with the making of such dark lists;
instead, I walk the wintery roads listening
for the bark of the faithful geese arrowing
through the Nebraska sky. I am flying
with them, across the stark blue, a poet's healing.

We began in mid-winter, this reckoning,
though for you the summer's hot pace
fermented your poems. This right confluence
of language and feeling, is how we faced
the year – as if we knew the storms would raze
our calm world, dissidents in the rotting
House of Greedy. We stammer in this haze
to thaw all tears of grief that have frozen,
and record what's surely been a cruel season.

KD

15.

The broad strong easterlies continue
and the fires spark across containment
lines in a hurry to consume what flew
from the furnace, a disturbed agreement
between place and plight, language and event,
as Wundowie, now under threat, was built
as a 'garden town' to accommodate
foundry workers to work fire and iron, tilt
trees into distillation – town planned without guilt.

JK

16.

I am rummaging through the midden
of poems written quickly and put aside,
(what we've called "History") in search of hidden
things unsaid, and at times I see I've lied
to art. Mine is a poetry of asides,
rarely the main thing. Is it enough,
all this chattering? Such hubris, such pride.
Of course, it is normal to be so rough
on one's own art, and even more normal to laugh.

KD

17.

As more and more fires erupt around
the state, as more and more people escape
to 'evacuation centres', we sound
the blown note of the easterlies — that pipe
that will never hold a tune, that sharp leap
into *shrill!* We are ready to go — leave
at earliest sign which is still late — steep
hillside carrying fire fast — to move
quicker than words on a memory stick, or love.

JK

18.

On the sloping end of Stevens Ridge Road,
the Trump flag flutters, still, beneath the stars
and stripes, while he whines and tantrums and goads
the Georgian Secretary of State. Bar
obscene miracles, this horribly marred
season will be over, and he'll be stood
down before the melting of the last dark-
stained snow. I will not gloat, but instead brood
and put to rest for good this Epoch of the Crude.

KD

19.

To distract myself from what I don't want
to be distracted from – keeping an ear
out for what's coming, hoping it doesn't,
like history catching itself, layer
bunching up fast on another layer –
I start reading historical fiction,
not wanting 'the facts' but some kind of 'seer'
event about present situations –
but there's no escape from the past's impositions.

JK

20.

They stormed the Capitol in January.
Pause and review. This is our history.
They marched on the Capitol; the Greedy
House grows fat, the King of Greedy
grows skittish, the petulant monstrosity
works his mealy mouth. Still all that spews
from him is filth, and lies, and ugly
that God don't like. They stormed. Pause and review.
Pause. Review. The chickens come home to roost

KD

21.
*against the MAGAists*

Historical figurism, triumphs,
'public works', cenotaphs, statuary,
monuments, battlefields, paintings with sheaves
of wheat showing eleemosynary
underpinnings to the great industry
of declaring just who will fly the flag
dressed for the occasion. *Heredity*
will be evoked to glorify, lollygag
a past that disrupts the present, speaks to sleazebags.

JK

22.
*I swear by the mud below my feet*
*You can't raise a Kane back up*
*When he's dead in defeat.*
— The Band "The Night they Drove Old Dixie Down"

"It is a theocracy they want," barks
the reformed evangelical. His regret
reeks of panic, but there is a stark
truth in this. Of course, I can't fret
over these matters of faith, I'm set
in hope. My Marxist compost, still fed
by revolution, bubbles in the great
campaigner in me. I've always fled
those damned theocrats: the defeated and the dead.

KD

23.

*So…* if Surrealism was a response
to trauma, an utterance out of sleep
of people edgy with war and collapse
into grand narratives… with little leaps
across inflamed synaptic gaps, those neap
tides of ambition a form of social
retrieval from the hero's antisleep
(the routing of art 'treasures'), was the fall
of beauty from fixed stars a grotesque rationale?

JK

24.

I know it is too early to declare
the death of the marching monstrosity;
after all, the dried skeletons stripped bare,
smooth as alabaster, rejoin quickly
only to march again — this is history,
this is white supremacy. Still I'm digging
the graves, chiselling the stone elegies
in this ritual act of more than hoping.
I stand sentry at the gate to kill the dying.

KD

25.

I am drafting a work entitled 'Dis-
arming the World' — a missive of total
life, of undoing the language of dis-
missal, of removing battle symbols
from maps, of defused weapons as landfill,
though terrain doesn't deserve such returns.
And the contents page is a refusal
to 'bear arms', a flagless declaration
of returns, refusals and renunciations.

JK

26.

Now the thing that's numbing me is fear,
but a fear whose balm is the deep low
voice of Aba, chuckling comfort. I fear
the recurring sorrow, the terrible sorrow
of the shock – how a world can grow
untethered. Yes, it is the season of dark
decay, and each morning I feel hollow
in my stomach, the tension in me stark
as helplessness: this nation, this fear, this beast's mark.

KD

27.
*variational methods*

The meaning of these words we use will change
and yet we write sure of why we use them –
what choice do we have? But spirit ranges
across eras and varies with quantum
frequency – analogous with the hum
of interactions, with parcels of light,
a physics of art and memorandum
where equations don't take momentum quite
in the same way, where symbols are *words* for 'insight'.

JK

28.
*The history of this moment, lengthens in shadow.* \*

Kwame, I say, go walking in the cold,
with each footfall take a deep breath, and slow
breathe away the stringent scrutiny you hold
your body under, then look at the wide bold
mid-western sky; let it be your healing lie.
I think of Will Brown, his charred body sold
in daguerreotypes, beneath that same sky;
September twenty-eighth, nineteen nineteen; how time flies!

\*From Marvin Bell, "Ars Poetica at the Window"

KD

29.

Tent cities have been established in Perth
and now in Fremantle on the park grass
kept green even in summer – those home berths
in the port 'under palms' with the sea breeze
coming in to give comfort to homeless
dwellers, to acknowledge traditional
owners, while the Premier accuses
anarchists of contriving to instal
folk with 'complex problems' to suit *their* demurral.

JK

30.

My desiccated soul just will not breathe;
holds itself alert. The flag's still waving
on Steven's Ridge despite the wreath
of peace laid in the Capitol, praying
president and the promise-words spoken
from the stage. My body says, "Alert!
Keep your eyes open for the battle goes on
in insidious silence." Outside, the sunburst
bathes the avenue. Body, may that quench your thirst.

KD

31.

The good governance of all our spirits
is a commitment to others? When I
was homeless, I experienced distaste
and loathing from the 'enough to get by
and work hard for it' crew, but sanctuary
from others who had less than enough to
see the week through. It is far too easy
to say 'no fixed abode' and step into
the good life we've deserved – our reward, our motto?

JK

32.
*haul an' pull-up, operator*

Think wind. Think pipe. Think music. Think song stopped.
Think emptiness; ghost of wind, air forced, pushed
through the steel carved in heat's delicate cups
of sound. Pipes. The brassy whistling burnt brush.
Think wood-wind song – wind. Think pipe hushed.
Crushed muscle, fleshy tendons stretched, popped
at the breaking point. Think breathlessness.
Think absence of air. This is how language stops.
I am not shocked. Think wind, think pipe: then think, "Pull up!"

KD

33.

This life bookended by unemployment
slots itself into a demographic
but only up to a point – those skills learnt
to live outside the 'mainstream' are graphic
examples of licence that are basic
to an obscure exceptionalism
which tunes in enough to be synchronic
but not take the full burden – a schism
that first off would have been viewed with cynicism.

JK

34.

In truth these neat boxes are the index
to our histories, the middens where fleshed bones
grow soft, from which heat fills the convex
of the sky, fogging the earth. These tombstones,
these stanzas are our leavings, the milestones
along the road, our stain left on the tracks
of our witnessed worlds – the lower echelons
of our seething memories. They are the stark
measure of how we got here and how we get back.

KD

35.

Apart from the appalling ethical
failure of the rich countries of the world
buying up and stockpiling nigh on all
prospective vaccine supplies for Covid-
19 their avidity will soon end
their best laid plans as newer variants
will outrun the life of profit – no 'herd
immunity' across the continents,
not forgetting the poor of elsewhere, their infants.

JK

36.

Due preparations for a suburban walk.
Gloves, red gloves, or brighter still, a yellow
pair for open-handed waves, for kindly talks
through a mask to make you an unmarked fellow,
your scowl, well-concealed. But the beard below
the mask must be grey, makes you safely old,
(more uncle, less boy), and add the slight limp,
of a retired coach. A dog sans growl,
Caucasian, yes; and as you pass the Trump
flag, lower your gaze, pick up pace and mute your skin.

KD

37.
*mixed messages?*

Here, as humidity mocks the terrain
which crackles with dryness, politicians
of the right-of-the-right warn *citizens*
to call themselves 'libertarians' —
this covers a multitude of functions:
confederate flag as marker of 'loss'
*and* 'resilience', masks as an action
of The Left!, virus as *hoax extremis*
(via 5G), and their spectre called 'George Soros'.

JK

38.
*Mine already is an African name –*
    — Lucille Clifton

There's much in a name and naming is all,
though how we're named is imagination
and self-indulgence, the clairvoyant's call
to the future – a way to shape every mention
of this name: all it contains, all it retains
inside vowels and consonants. Already
an African name, and this is our poetry.
*Nation* is not enough, it's an invention,
but blood persists, and casts us back into our skins.

KD

39.

I have no heritage worth speaking of —
I have no speaking of worth heritage —
I'm of town but more so the country — of
the bush *and* the streets, and that 'old adage'
of *this or that*, one or t'other, won't merge
genealogy with chronology,
in my case at least. You know, friend, the age-
old remonstrance of *needs must* as edgy
lives pushed heritage into realms of elegy.

JK

40.

It has snowed, again, and the street is white;
such light, such startling glaring light,
bounces off the fresh covering. I can't write
my poems without this framing. It is bright
winter here, and even my secret diet
of morose distraction must now succumb
to this snow-sparked day. It's not my birthright,
this landscape, where breathless cold consumes
and shapes all, but I've learned the art of adoption.

KD

41.

So much we recognise but then undo
so much we might love but undo — stories
of lives connected to our own but too
unalike to draw into new stories,
though these might actually be the stories
of our origins, these might be a form
of personal history — families,
those inherited traits, mannerisms
that almost catch us out in our solipsism.

JK

42.

And to think that this has all been fashioned
on ancient transgressions: a son staring
at the dick of his father reposed and drunk;
then comes the curse, its convenience of rank,
a stretching of greed's laws, and we now stink
with the residue of bad-mindedness –
convenient to make us hewers of wood,
carriers of water by our dark and blessed
skins – such a skein of lies, such a sordid mess.

KD

43.
*prayer stanza* ('blood makes noise' – Suzanne Vega)

Where the blood is thinned and thin blood loosens
please keep the blood flowing through the body,
please let it flow though arteries thicken,
please let it make its way through as steady
as it might go, not as a threnody
sung in fits and starts, not a dribbling
into the thoughts of a lifetime, ready
to transmute matter to energy, to sing
silently – no, not yet, let the blood keep moving.

JK

44.

And the flag is down – a blue counterfeit
with an illegible coat of arms in place,
and here I think of the safety of streets
in this sun-blanched neighbourhood; the grace
of kind neighbours ploughing the wide spaces
of snow, the sidewalks, gutted streets, the driveway.
Someone asks me, again, "Where will you die?"
I say, bury me where voices will say,
"Hello cousin, blood, bone-friend, welcome home to stay."

KD

## 45. 'we'

It's hard to cope with the incredible
weight of history… especially when
people denied unscroll indelible
stories of loss and leave us to question
things taken for granted – perhaps spoken
in the classroom, historical method
with a minor flaw, or a mistaken
interpretation or oversight. Did
'the record' lack, or did we just lack the record?

JK

46.
*But I am tired today of history*
*its patina'd clichés*
*of endless evil.*
    — Robert Hayden, "Islands"

So, all joy is a prelude to history,
a prelude to the skein of consequence.
This does not appear in our history,
this is not indexed in the blood-madness
of our memories. I begin with dance,
cricket, the belly of stone, nostalgia,
no pretence, just the haunting consequence
of illusive joy. Ernie Smith sings, *Pitter*
*patter, coming down and*...: A prelude to terror.

KD

47.

I thought that this stanza should have no more
in it than 'everything is fire' and that
the word 'fire' should consume the space that fire
takes as its own because fire is all that
we have to hand, driven by winds so hot
they take fire for granted and want fresh fuel
even where there's no fuel, pushing a point
of view that's as unholy as the cruel
conditions demand, while 'fire' impels its own tale.

JK

48.
*I've been down on the rock for so long,*
*I seem to wear a permanent screw*
       — Bob Marley

The research is in my body, sweet
as death, the chemical processes
that thicken to a curdle hurts and beat
the blood in me, into the creamy mess
of decay. *Talking blues*. This press
of tenderness in me. They know, they do,
they know how we have been made to repress
hope, to plan for early death, the stark blue
of the irrevocable. Yes, *blues, talking blues*…

KD

49.

The loss of wildlife is the loss of all
measures of life – the loss of animals
the loss of birds, insects, frogs and reptiles,
the loss of whole families… and mammals –
marsupials burnt in hollows, to boil
in their own skins, or hopping into voids
filled with swirls of flame rolling without fuel,
and the domestic and 'feral' and wild
animals lost without funerals, without odes.

JK

50.

Grief, I imagine, fills the open lands
of your territory. The fires swarm
in waves and waves. You make the last stand
against decimation, your house storm-
tested by persistent faith against harm
to all creatures, the tiny and the gross.
It's winter here. We've not heard on the news
the conflagration you face. Still the loss
of our elders continues; no remorse, no fuss.

KD

51. *for Kwame*

Just where and how will we meet up across
the distances, blurs, and divides, across
the chasms, rivers, and trenches, across
the 'good people' and 'bad people', across
the indifference, flatness, caution… across
the misplaced intensities and across
different versions of history, across
the lines of time and migration, across
the damage and loss, while others need to reach across?

JK

52.
*Given the choice of democracy or white privilege what will they choose?*
    — Taylor Branch

To write the chronicle of this season:
the pestilence, the riots, lies and great
truths unsettled; to keep record of goons
wielding brutality, the reprobates
petulantly wrecking their own states;
spoilt, mean-spirited children, breaking the ribs
of their own temples – these acts of cancerous hate.
To write this is my pressing art, to be the gib
wedging right things and truth, to protect beauty's crib.

KD

53.

If trees grew on the sun, this seems what they'd
look like, or intimate – flares that retract
as if they never were, though on some tired
heliograph that lost life-moment was tracked
and recorded, a retractable fact
as suits industry and its glib captains;
the sun rising towards the sun, intact
as technology that enhances with scorn,
as Tracy breaks down into tears after the burn.

JK

54.
*the deals we make with God*

*"name the dead, name the dead, name the dead": Tigray, November 2020*

Montserrat tells of her mother's contract
with God and the deal she made to survive
the tumour; growing, sitting back-to-back,
her foetal twin, fighting to stay alive.
Despite the bruja's prayer, how she strived
to outlive the child. "Name her for the saint,
the saint of the mountain Island." Well, five
days later her twin died, and she remained,
to become this woman with magic in her name.

Today I have in me the hymn of saints
dying at the hands of killers, blood flow
in the sacred places, Emanuel stained
for another century, shattering tomorrows;
where was God? No shelter, there was no
shelter in those walls. November, the stone walls
of Maryam Dengelat echo
with gunfire, the blood, the blood; bodies fall.
Sandals, cell phones, pencils and a child's bloody shawl.

I say, "Deals we make with God", though I mean
the deals we make with history, and how history
betrays us, how history betrays with clean
precision whole nations, tribes, families.
We return to the ground to ask for the reveal
of memory – what the poets must mean;
the lineage of suffering. Not to seal
it off, but to disrupt the steady stream
of lies, a way to unfurl truth, a way to dream.

KD

55.
*'He hated all good workes and vertuous deeds,*
*And him no lesse, that any like did use,*
*And who with gracious bread the hungry feeds,*
— The Faerie Queene

In the hesitations marked as pauses
we might sequester ourselves, letting lines
move on as instructed, reading with less
concern for trouble, just hoping the signs
will be enough. But an exclamation
mark is the spark that might realign faith,
might allow the foul documentation
to be read as the primary source – wraith
of heroics that conjures the stolen 'so saith'.

In working through this I might be thinking
of Churchill College, or at least some members
of the college, confronting, undoing,
and speaking out about the racist slurs
and racist attitudes of its saviour,
of its namesake, of its central pillar,
who is really *nothing* to do with our
sense of community, or that 'thirst for
knowledge', or the best aspects of human nature.

Now, I am sad to hear of the passing
of Bunny Wailer, and am thinking of
how you, Kwame, who knows, must be feeling
the loss of a visionary, loss of
a percussionist who lifted the roof.
And I am thinking over the nature
of faith in *The Faerie Queene* and the proof
of conflict in the spirit, of Peter
Tosh and truths of racism parsed without censure.

JK

56.

Today the sun spreads over Pioneer Park —
every inch of this prairie is an afront;
the cult of pioneers persists, forgetting dark
rituals of slaughter, the way to blunt
the wound with "nice", as if the brunt
of the wounding can grow soft with forgetting.
We walk — sun, golfers, children; easy
to mask the blood history percolating
under the wild grass. It's spring, pioneer season.

KD

57.
*lulling*

Really… maybe, what's being said is that
there's no lull, no reset, no redress or
counterpoint, no way through the idea that
'landscape' is a pinned reality for
those who don't want take a long detour
or backstep out of the nation-building
exercise, with those cut and dried flowers
of history so essential to well-being
in choice photos that prove less and less wrong-doing?

JK

58.
*Second Desmond Rebellion, Ireland, 1580*
*Moneague Camp, Jamaica, 1977*

When the Butter Bay becomes the Fort of Slaughter,
what is a beautiful sun-glazed coastal
picture, reddens into history: the murders
of surrendered soldiers, the bestial
remains, the air thick with death, faecal
stench – the dying lose all their decorum.
You should know that I am regurgitating
the memory of a half-dead cadet strung
up by a barking captain, call him Kurtz-strong.

KD

59.

*percentages in history and colonial notions of 'tautology'*

How far away from act and consequence
am I on a hot day along the rail-
way line at the once fecund and rich place
of plenty where no words I can entail
as descriptive will do, though *is* and will
always be a meeting place, a sacred
place for its people with their complete skills,
their science and their arts not divided
into two cultures but always fully engaged

with cosmology, whereas I usurp
with every step in withering, exposed
heat as I walk into the follow-up
appointment with the specialist who feeds
my life into a holistic, measured,
and matter-of-fact aporia of
vital statistics and readings of blood,
into a widget that deals at removes
from history… type 'white' to boost chances of life?

JK

60.

1
My shadow dances across the open
path. My shadow is a god who is tender
to the bruises I get from my stumbling.
He gently says to me, "I remember,
I remember all the ways you clambered
over my dark, even when I walked ahead,
even when I dropped behind." My tender
shadow says, "I am your god. I'm not dead.
I'm your history returned from where the shadows led.

2.
If the bush in the front yard catches fire,
let me know. The bush in the front yard
never catches fire. Instead, the spire's
soft shadow falls on it twice a day, turns hard,
and this is another way of saying the word
of god is a shadow that moves softly
over my skin; it is the whispering herd
of regrets and doubts. I ask you, "History,
will you now rearrange the cells in my body?"

KD

61.

*'Enforst to seeke some covert nigh at hand,*
 *A shadie grove not far away they spide,*
 *That promist ayde the tempest to withstand:*
 *Whose loftie trees yclad with sommers pride*
 *Did spred so broad, that heavens light did hide,*
 *Not perceable with power of any starre:*
 *And all within were pathes and alleies wide,*
 *With footing worne, and leading inward farre:*
*Faire harbour that them seemes; so in they entred arre.'*

— Spenser, *The Faerie Queen*, Canto 1

I am pursuing a path of error
that is no loss of star or leaf, no threat
to direction, that doesn't own the here
and where of mirages and forests.
The gnarled, agèd York gum at the topmost
place of the block — safe harbour for many
birds, marsupials, reptiles, and insects —
lost its mast to termites, humidity
and endless summer. Will shade regrow harmony?

JK

62.

"Let's get *Gone with the Wind* back, please," Trump whines.
"Can we get *Gone with the Wind* back, please?"
Already the great whitewash — take down the signs,
pretend we have been dead asleep for four years;
and don't bring it up again; no one cares —
except the trail of sorrow is sealed in memes,
the callousness of the monster's ways.
And while his followers grin as they scheme
his return, I sleep with one eye open, no dreams.

KD

63.
*'O sacred hunger of ambitious mindes,*
   *And impotent desire of men to raine'*
      —The Faerie Queen (Book 5, Canto 12)

I have an intense feeling that something
is amiss, which sounds absurd when so much
is clearly amiss wherever we bring
focus to bear as 'Faults Escaped', to lurch
from world to allegory and, as such,
from allegory to world and *mischance*
upon loss of light, loss of song – that clutch
of ontology we allot to chance,
to find a way past those who corrupt utterance.

JK

64.
*For Kekeli*

Can a black body live in a white space?
Syllogism fails and so does syntax.
Can a white body live in a black space?
And if we should live up in the hills: ask,
why far over and way, way over? We wear masks.
And Burning Spear says it's a big disgrace
to forget the almost dead. Remember,
do you remember old slavery days?
When history recalls, we will all find our place.

KD

65.

This.is.how.i.find.my.way.through.my.own
disappointment in myself, how I take
the portion of works and days and disown
them. Thus: every opinion I uptake
or discard, each pink salt in the dry lake
that sparkles off the spectrum, catching sun
in its own way for *just there*, the earthquake
in aesthetics (which I never had trust in)
as sold through the mart; a 'for whom' emoticon.

JK

66.
*the kindness of nebraskans*

I apologize on behalf of my staff, if…
I am sorry, deeply, deeply sorry, if…
On behalf of all here, I am sorry if…
I truly regret, truly regret if…
So, here it is, then: I am sorry if…
Please, please accept my apologies if…
I hope you know how sorry I am if…
There is a bomb blast inside of the "if".
There is a bloody wounding that comes with the "if".

KD

67.
*'Like as a Ship with dreadful Storm long toss'd,*
  *Having spent all her Masts, and her Ground-hold;'*

— Spenser, *The Faerie Queen*, Book VI, Canto v

Preparing for *Seroja* — such a rare
event this reach of ocean-brewed cyclone
into the heart of the wheatbelt — I clear
the gutters and secure 'outdoors' as tone
of atmosphere hushes birds, trees and stones
alike, a stillness of anticipation
or my channelling of threat as koan
of house-as-ship tubed by hillside wave — on
and on to capsizing or making port, station

by station, landfall inside landfall, call
to distant neighbours in thrall of the storm-
surge of trees and buildings, the fall, the fall,
the giddy notions of inland stripped form
by form. Yes, preparation as it looms
over interactions — meditation
with heart murmur... and sawing a phantom
limb from a jam tree catch its fragrance on
a soft breeze, letting it go as premonition.

JK

68.

There is a hiatus – a cool day of fresh light;
the neighbourhood, a bland suburban dream
when it seems that all that matters is the bright
green of spring lawns; and from my window the stream
of families – white locals that all seem
like a truce; a break from hostilities.
I ask the silence, "Is it all redeemed?"
But the dark void says, "Men have been great fools
and put words in the mouth of spirits. Be careful."

KD

69. *amenity?*

I have been thinking about the nature
of machinery and the corruption
of 'historical records' to favour
invention of devices – those machines
of warfare sold as remediation
of labour, as answer to unfairness
re class, culture, the classification
of 'owners' per 'workers', of looms and dress
codes, of the Tsar wanting steam to drive his fountains.

JK

70.

a)
For new altars we strive to rebuild
the emaciated face — I hadn't known
that such weariness, such brokenness dwelled
in the sorrow of my voice like a stone,
an inexplicable guilt, a fractured bone
under skin. She came and they killed her.
I was there, and yet it seems I had gone
in this year of stillness and secret groans.
Home is guilt. Home is lament. I must leave this home.

KD

71.
'the drums of war beat'
— Australian secretary of the Home Affairs department

Though it is likely a tautology
to say that the Defence portfolio
is now occupied by a 'hawk', really,
the contents of such a portfolio
would insinuate that the ratio
of doves and hawks are likely to favour...
well, you know, as a gun is to aggro
and the secretary of Home Affairs
is to peace and well-being. No, it's not satire.

JK

72.

b)
Across the burnished land, light balms the heart.
How much we leave behind, how much we keep.
I hold in abeyance sorrow's retorts,
and when the flight lifts, the green dark seeps
under my skin, the mourning in me spreads deep,
the dis-ease of loss, the broken lamenting.
We avoid with laughter. Death sows, we reap.
I meet my mourning self at each landing,
and there I hear the house wren's noisy alighting.

KD

73.

And late last night for me, Kwame, it was
an owlet nightjar tapping at my soul,
picking insects from the light-soaked fringes –
not 'messenger of death, the ghastly Owle'
but still, in stormy weather, 'death'… a call
disconnected from my search for a 'chere-
full' bird whose 'sweet musick'… is a moth's fall.
And as I <u>read</u> *The Faerie Queene* to clear
away the tense before I dream(t,) more birds appear(ed).

JK

74.

I have now become a curator of
white regret, the doorkeeper and linguist.
Papa Legba is teaching me the stuff
of Babylon, a way to resist
with the conjurer's art, by weaving mists
of their silvery tears, their machinations.
At the edge of the village of Smerwick,
did Spenser not consult spirits and ghouls
to bless the slaughter? These are the struggle's new rules.

KD

75.

I have no interlocutor, no flow'r
of the afterlife, no mediator
to guide me speechless through to ancestors
who would likely be curious, but far
enough away to say *Dia dhuit*, store
an after-memory and draw closer
to the scene of disaster, massacre,
as the poet speaks, records the Butter
Bay dossier, so many overlaps, trauma.

JK

76.

We've arrived at the season of twin dusks.
These walks have slowed to a stately gait
and the faces reappear, now, their masks
put away. They smile as if to say, the wait
is over, and all is settled – the great
chaos of the year of unrest and mistrust
is behind us. Smile, they say, celebrate
the end of hostilities. I've lost my trust
in smiles, this humid season of repeating dusks.

KD

## 77. extremities

Things always start and end near the middle
around here — at least I think it's the case
that wilting greenery is neither full
of life nor giving way to death, a race
to make a spirit-level existence.
No, no… the poisoners propel the green
down to confront its roots; the hunters brace
eye to eye to keep seeing for their own.
From between I radicalise peace… its refrain.

JK

78.

They rehearse lamentations of penitence
as acts of oblivion – and with tears
all is named, all confessed. Jah in heaven
and peace on earth. They've become caretakers
of white reform. In the sierras the scars
are being cut into the faces of women
who squat in a circle, chewing peppers,
waiting there for Mother Nanny to grant
them power. They march now, in the deep morning gloom.

KD

79.

I have been wondering if poetry
can be anything but historical –
dated as it is written and entry
into a future that is arguable.
I look back over earlier scribble –
poems roughed out when I was just eighteen –
and realise they are distillations, all
moments extracted from a lost timeline
though I was a student of history back then.

JK

80.

We have circled back to the elegies
that we have been writing for this epoch
of the almost dead who have been buried
before their time, and the etched rocks
of those who died in their time. We took stock
of the states where we bivouac and pitch tents,
their slow dying, the things lost, the broken earth
the brutish ways of the imperialists.
We return, we circle back, history's elegists.

KD

81.

>         *... when Una her did marke*
> *Clymbe to her charet, all with flowers spred;*
> *From heaven high to chase the chearelesse darke,*
> *With merry note her loud salutes the mounting larke.*

    — Canto XI, *The Faerie Queen*

It's easier to think flowers outside
a location where they are sourced by roots.
In the dream, they flower without sap, hide
machinery and explain a brilliance.
I wanted to replay seeing the first
York gum blossom open in situ, on
a short but not the shortest day – its fruit
brewing under the display, rotation
and revolution: sun in earth and earth in sun.

JK

82.

We end at the banquet of remembrance.
We carry the trace of what was carried.
Oh, the way we survived. The backward glance
shifts the tense and number – how we tarried
at the crossroads to be one. We ferried
across that sea with seeds in our bellies,
we who now feast on the slime and sustenance
of okra, greens, slivers of dried fish,
and the holy rice of our sorrow. Say, Ashe.

KD

83. *holding my breath too long I become giddy*

It is still silent here after the roo
shooters cut a late Saturday night swathe
through the area, and searching hard, though
doubting I'll find a roo alive, I breathe
in prayer-breath which I usually unbreathe —
an exhalation of relief or loss;
but now it's bottled up and now I strive
to keep my breath held inside till roos rise
from those exits where thrill-killed they fell to bathos.

JK

84.

In these suburbs, I read your song of roos
slaughtered. We are worlds apart; the swathe
of cruelty still haunts. On my walks, though,
the scent of farms carries for miles; I breathe
manure, the industry of it. I un-breathe
the complex of it all. I think of your loss;
the kangaroos, the way the shooters strive
to build empires of violence. I rise
knowing my small quarrels are at best mere bathos.

KD

85. A double (I wrote a poem called 'Indexing' last week because I
literally had to make indexes)

Thanks, dear Kwame, but you take the bathos
out of situations through honesty
in all our exchanges. And as we close
in on an ending to this History
I take your solace and speak it freely
to the night air and all it enlivens.
These Saturday night shoot-outs travesty
life in all its forms and each death weakens
all destinies and earth's journey around the sun.

And I have been working at a tangent
to our timeline as I've had to index
a critical book when indexes are sent
to try me! And to make things more complex
I've constructed a conceptual index
to a colonial 'Land Selector's Guide' –
finding my way through Hell, I placed red ticks
alongside each word of destruction sold
as *opportunity!* – each 'property' indexed.

JK

86.

"...they wrote so well because they saw so little..."
    —C.L.R. James, *Black Jacobins*

And what of those who've seen so much? Outside
of elegies, epitaphs, and the tree roots
soaked with libations, they who've seen must hide
their hearts, and build small arks of brilliance:
the songs of Simone, Marley, Fela, first
light at dawn, the proverbs of our truth on
the bodies of the generations, these fruit
of our hope. I write to chart the rotation
of our history: sun in earth and earth in sun.

KD

87. '*Best musicke breeds delight in loathing eare:*'
    —*The Faerie Queene*, Canto 8, XLIV

How many storms have passed over since we
started keeping records, Kwame? It's less
a case of silence between notes than 'free
access' to a distressing background noise
that accrues and builds and intensifies —
an anti-music that we must listen
through to understand a grammar's splendours:
that essentially musical colon:
that place of waiting where we hope proof will be shown.

JK

88.
*As with old-time people, the*
  *word their one rescue, words*
*would be our rescue we'd been*
  *told. Believing so braced us,*

                              book

*of the book's advantage, book of*
  *the word's leverage, lift...*

                    Nate Mackey *Blue Fasa*


The elders squat, and one says, *Bend down low*.
I enter the circle. She says, *This was*
*the meeting place. I'll tell you what I know*
*like the ancients should.* So, it will come to pass
that all history will be lament and alas.
It's the ritual we practice in our cells,
illuminating the crass trespasses
of this epoch. The elder says, *I'll tell*
*You everything you need. Now, go and mix and mell*.

KD

89.
*the failure is in me as I read the new Clark biography of Sylvia Plath*

Biography denies its own failure.
Biography feeds and is fed *failure*?
Biography relies on the allure
of failure, of life set in another
*success*: time, place, those tangents of Culture.
Building a portrait from within pictures.
Laid out before us as if the matter
is decided, subject caught: to render.
I fail to believe for all the data. *Never*.

JK

90.
*"there is no history of this world that is not written in black"*
    — Brenda Marie Osbey

Not nationalism. Instead, I make poetry
of epochs — etchings of the historical
account of a hemisphere, each entry
written in black ink, in the arguable
discourses of freedom, all this scribbled
in the pidgin of skin. When I was eighteen
I made a pact: *Allow me, Spirit, all*
*the rights of outrage against the timeline*
*of colonizers.* Now is now and now is then.

KD

91.

*I don't want to be deprived of what I was born into. For example, when I was in exile, I always had to pretend to myself that I wasn't in exile. I used to use expressions like 'I'm just on political sabbatical'. I carried Nigeria with me everywhere.*
— Wole Soyinka, "Nobel Prize Winner Wole Soyinka Discusses Brexit, His Time in Exile and Nigeria at SOAS" (2016)

Birth is embedded as exile re-routes
where the touch of rich air laid down its maps.
As I follow word-lines of the poet
I think over loss and who profits. Graphs
of commodities and boardrooms, backslaps
between office towers where wealth accrues:
operating to instil the deathtraps
old and new imperialism issues
as dividends. Poet, calling out histories.

JK

92.

The Gulf of Mexico is on fire.
The geese can see the smoke miles and miles off,
as feeding grounds burn. They will soon tire
from their search for the comforts of soft
landings. We all see *le grand catastrophe*
of our runaway world. We know the way
a tragedy begins — a pot's slow boil,
the seduction of heat's tender embrace.
How soothingly and greenly is this house disgraced.

KD

## 93. 'overview effect' of the rich

And those billionaire space adventurers
who would own and commercialise those 'last
frontiers' in their own image – those allures
of 'Space' as franchise, as the ultimate
enterprise, the zone of wealthy elites
who can share in the glory of gazing
down on the earth from whence they… *that aspect*,
that Blue Marble phantasm, aspiring
with the thrill of zero gravity while voiding.

JK

94.
> *The guilefull great Enchaunter parts*
> *The Redcrosse Knight from Truth:*
> *Into whose stead faire falsehood steps,*
> *And workes him wofull ruth.*
> — Edmund Spenser

In the end, the truth matter is now set
before us – Trump still roams. He's again star
of his grand inventions, and the world's wet
with the slime of rot. This, friend, is how far
we've come, which is really where we always are,
and where we've been and will be. Hear the shrill
complaints – they will never stop. We will drag cart-
loads of index cards up the eastern hill,
broadcast them wide like seeds until the sky is filled.

KD

95.

What I see and what I can write about
are very different things – the seeing might
be intense with expression and call out,
in my configuring, to be made out
of its form into another form, but
a lack of awareness about layers
of 'history' leaves nature's 'nature' short
on tones and trapped by modes of exposure –
think wetlands and Caspian tern over samphire.

JK

96.

*A poet's autobiography is his poetry. Anything else is just a footnote.*
  —Yevgeny Yevtshenko

1
Before his passing, the man-poet carves out
on a palm-sized stamp of wood, the words
he will seal in red ink, the remnants of lost
folders, the files he has bound in cords,
in sisal and placed in the darkest world
of his cottage: the secret recipes,
the letters, the notices, the photos
of the clandestine dreams and memories,
*Footnotes*, he writes. *And all that matters is poetry.*

2
There are other words, I know, but *bathos*
is the secret shadow that honesty
clings to me – the muted doubt so close
I can mask it with the noise of history,
the duty, the steel of my brain freely
tamping feeling. My ancestry wept – this enlivens
me – and this, too, is a myth. The travesty
is the way I avoid mirrors. They weaken
me, like poems, like language sheltering me from the sun.

3
I do not know their value. Tangents;
they are my tearless distractions, index
to my hidden self. I stopped the man, sent
him the way of old journals, the complex
self of the much-examined life burnt. Perplexed,
eventually I forget the man. These poems guide
me back to the love of self, of ticks
and quirks, the man-poet waiting to be sold
the future, the promise, but left simply indexed.

*I consider these poems of parts,*
*as bits and pieces of the truth,*
*of us, of mansions of stacked steps,*
*of your eyes and their artful ruth;*
*of our eyes and their lust for truth.*

## ABOUT THE AUTHORS

Kwame Dawes is the author of over thirty books, and is widely recognised as one of the Caribbean's leading authors. He is the Glenna Luschei Editor of *Prairie Schooner* and a Chancellor's Professor of English at the University of Nebraska. His latest book with Northwestern University Press and Peepal Tree is *City of Bones: A Testament*. His third book of poetry, *Prophets* (1995), is republished this year with a *Reader's Guide*. He was born in Ghana, grew up in Jamaica and has lived most of his adult life in the USA.

John Kinsella's many books of poetry include *Jam Tree Gully* (WW Norton, 2012), *Drowning in Wheat: Selected Poems* (Picador, 2016) and *Insomnia* (Picador, 2019). His newest collection, from Arc Publications, is *Brimstone: a book of villanelles*. He has published work in all genres and across a few of them as well, and collaborated with many artists, composers, writers and poets. He is a fellow of Churchill College, Cambridge University, and Emeritus Professor of Literature and Environment at Curtin University in Western Australia.